Essential Economics

David Sapsford and James Ladd

Essential Economics

Hart-Davis Educational

Granada Publishing Limited
First published in Great Britain 1978 by
Hart-Davis Educational Limited
Frogmore, St Albans, Hertfordshire

Copyright © D Sapsford and J D Ladd 1978
Illustrations © Hart-Davis Educational 1978

ISBN 0 247 12719 1

Printed in Great Britain by
Fletcher & Son Ltd, Norwich

Contents

Acknowledgements

The authors would like to thank the many individuals and organisations who have contributed material to this book and helped in other ways to make the undertaking possible:

The Bank of England; BP Educational Services; Barclays Bank Ltd; Cadbury Schweppes Ltd; City of Glasgow Planning Department; Commission of the European Communities and in particular for the information on which Figures 16.13 and 17.4 are based; Co-operative Union; Equity Capital for Industry Ltd; Finance for Industry Ltd; Ford Motor Company Ltd; Greater Nottingham Co-operative Society; H J Heinz Co Ltd; Her Majesty's Treasury; Imperial Group Ltd; Leicester Polytechnic – David Sapsford's colleagues and in particular Mr G M Adams BA for his helpful comments on several sections, and Mr D Greenaway BSc(Econ) M Comm for his comments and suggestions on the draft text; Midland Shire Farmers Ltd; Marks & Spencer Ltd; Ministry of Agriculture, Fisheries and Food; National Giro; National Enterprise Board; Mrs Jean R Nielsen for typing and secretarial services; Nottinghamshire County Library; Office of Population Censuses and Surveys; Rank Hovis McDougall Ltd; Retail Consortium; Mrs Mary Sapsford for her encouragement and patience while we were writing the book; the Stock Exchange; the Association of Investment Trust Companies; the Unit Trust Association and Waddington House of Games for permission to mention their game *Monopoly*.

We would also like to thank examining boards for allowing us to reproduce questions from their examination papers: Associated Examining Board (AEB), Chartered Accountants Foundation Course (CAFC), Institute of Works Managers' Certificate (IWMC), Institute of Chartered Secretaries and Administrators (ICSA), Joint Matriculation Board (JMB), University of London (L).

Introduction

Economics and economics as part of other social study courses are set out in this book for students of O-level or equivalent courses. Since the themes of each chapter develop from concrete facts within most readers' experience, we hope that you will find the theories easier to follow than you might expect as the book builds up into a comprehensive study.

Chapters are subdivided into topics so that these may be matched to one- or two-year courses. After each topic or group of topics is a set of Assignments, including typical examination questions. A short bibliography for reference is given at the end of each chapter.

The Assignments are a mixture of individual, group and class work, and include a number designed for discussion. The early Assignments in each block cover the main points of a topic, while those marked with an asterisk (*) contain more detailed work suitable for those on a two-year course.

We hope that you will find the Assignments useful as the basis for your notes.

Many of the Assignments are also devised to provide project work suitable for local and other studies. They include elements of learning by enquiry as this we consider one of the surest ways to understand applications of economic theory.

We have used metric units where possible throughout this book. But you will find when doing the research for some of the Assignments that the data (in some government statistics, for example) is given in Imperial units. Conversion factors for all the units you will need are given in Appendix 1 on page 281.

There are a set of multi-choice questions at the back of the book to test your knowledge either as you progress through the topics or in revision.

The diagrams link physical events to the information shown in numerical form and given in the text, making economic principles easier to understand and providing useful memory aids. This is equally true of many examples given in the text. The page references for key definitions are set out in Index of Definition on page 282 to help you in the course of your studies and as an aid to revision.

This book was researched in 1976.

D Sapsford
J D Ladd
Loughborough

Chapter 1
What is Economics ?

Economics *is the science which studies human behaviour as a relationship between ends and scarce means which have alternative uses* – L Robbins
  In *The Nature and Significance of Economic Science* (London, 1934)

The Problem

A definition
The definition given above of *Economics* may seem complicated at first sight, but you will find this subject is all about possible solutions to the 'economic problem'. In a simple form this problem is faced by all of us for no one has a limitless income. Our ability to buy things (our purchasing power) is therefore limited. Yet nearly everyone wants more than their limited income enables them to buy. So taking everybody's wants together, these are endless, leading economists to speak of individuals or groups having 'unlimited wants'.

Economic terms
In economic studies words have precise meanings that do not always follow their use in general speech. The Index of Definition references on page 282 lists the terms you are likely to meet in O-level and similar courses; they are explained as you meet them in the text. Let's look at two examples – goods and services. Economists use the word *goods* to refer to things you can touch; a single product is 'a good'. *Services* are those intangible things you pay for like haircuts or a cinema visit.

The problem of choice
For the school student, £5 a week from pocket money and a Saturday job may represent all of his or her limited purchasing power. Yet there are many things he or she would like to buy – new clothes, perhaps, and some records, or a haircut. But with only £5, a choice must be made. Maybe this week buying a shirt leaves only £1 or £2 to put by for the moped.

Everyone faces this 'economic problem' all the time. Even the philanthropist would like more to give away. We all have to keep making choices as to how we use our scarce resources to meet unlimited wants. *Economics* may therefore be described as the subject concerned with such choices (see Figure 1.1). Just in the same way as individuals face these problems of choice, so also do countries. In some way the people or their representatives must decide the best (*optimum*) way to use or allocate the community's resources.

In later chapters we will see exactly what these scarce resources are, but in simple terms they include labour and materials needed to produce any good or service.

The economic problems faced by two very different people

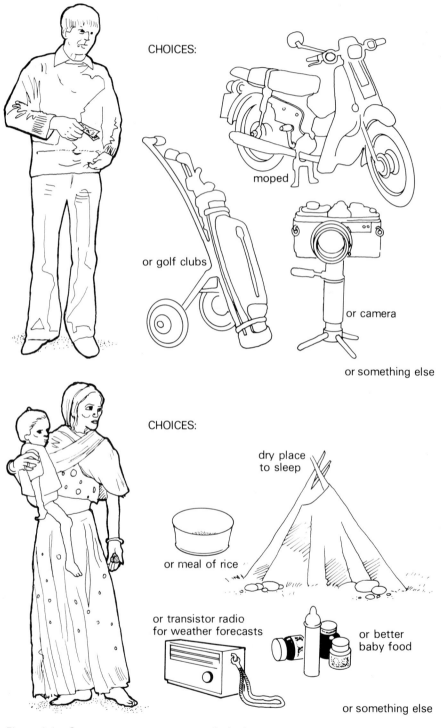

CHOICES:

moped

or golf clubs

or camera

or something else

CHOICES:

dry place to sleep

or meal of rice

or transistor radio for weather forecasts

or better baby food

or something else

Figure 1.1   Scarce resources to meet unlimited wants.

Economists therefore refer to these resources as *factors of production*. Some goods and services produced with these factors may be consumed by private individuals (*consumers*) in one 'go' like food, and are called *non-durables*. Other goods can be used by consumers many times, such as washing machines, and are called *durables*.

Besides consumer goods, there are goods which themselves are used to produce other goods. These are known as *producer goods* and can also be subdivided into durables (machine tools, for example) and non-durables (such as raw materials).

Goods may also be classified in another way: public or *social goods* – parks, roads, sewers, health services and so on, are those 'consumed' collectively by the public in general. In this classification all other goods are *private goods*.

The choices facing the community in Britain as an economy or economic system are more complicated than those facing individuals, but the problems are similar. At any moment in time there are limited resources – insufficient factors of production – in the country. For instance, only so many men and women are available for the work force. There are only so many machines, and so many hectares of land. Yet there are unlimited wants for both public and private goods and services – more schools, more roads, more colour TVs, more hospitals, more washing machines and so on. Decisions must be made on the best or optimum way to allocate the scarce resources, just as the student had to make a choice on how to use that £5.

Production

The factors of production – a piece of land, an hour's labour, are examples – can be regarded as inputs, which a producer must bring together to produce a good or provide a service. You will see in chapter 3 how the factors of production are classified into four groups including land and labour. But for the moment let us look at production using only these two inputs – land and labour. They may come together because an enterprising settler finds a piece of uncleared land, clears it and farms it. Maybe in another case a farmer buys the land and makes what he can from raising crops. Or the farmer may be given the land to farm for himself or the community. Perhaps the land could be used for some other purpose than farming; certainly in most cases it may be used for growing different crops. Deciding on how land is used is one of many decisions that must be made in finding the solution to the economic problem.

Assignments

1.1 Start your own set of definitions with: the definition of a good and of a service including two examples of each. As your study progresses add new definitions to this list, always including examples that will make clear to you on revision what the definition *means in your own words*.

1.2 List four typical choices of unlimited wants you have faced or face. When making such lists always leave a couple of lines between the items for later additions and comment.

Choosing a Solution

The production possibility curve

There are several tools or concepts of economics to be mastered, before considering the ways different communities set out to solve their economic problems. The first of

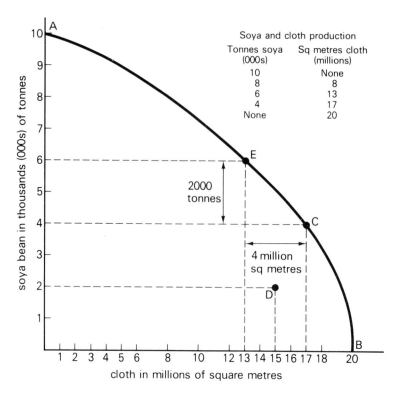

Figure 1.2　Production possibility curve for a soya and cloth economy.

these concepts is the *Production Possibility Curve* (PPC). In its simplest form (see Figure 1.2) this is a way of showing the choices faced by an economy where only two goods are produced. All the available resources (men, machinery and other inputs or factors of production) might be used to produce soya beans, or they might all be used to manufacture cloth. Take a look at Figure 1.2: when all the available resources are used to produce soya (at point A), this economy might produce 10 000 tonnes annually. Alternatively, with all the resources used to produce cloth (at point B), this economy could produce 20 million square metres of cloth.

In practice this community will probably use part of its available resources to produce one good, and part to produce another. They might use three-quarters of their resources to grow soya and a quarter to produce cloth. In short: they try to reach a satisfactory solution to their economic problem. Each choice gives a different combination of soya and cloth production from this economy's use of its scarce resources.

The Production Possibility Curve in Figure 1.2 shows all the combinations of soya and cloth this community can produce. Points A and B are the extremes, all soya or all cloth. At point C, however, resources are allocated at an intermediate point between extremes, for the production of 4000 tonnes of soya and 17 million square metres of cloth.

The curve or boundary of the graph represents the use of all available resources in the production of soya and/or cloth. What might a point inside this boundary represent? At point D 2000 tonnes of soya and 15 million square metres of cloth are produced. But these quantities are both less than those produced at point C – 2000 tonnes less soya and 2 million square metres less of cloth. This shows that at point D not all of the resources are being used or possibly that some are being used inefficiently. Part of the land may be derelict after flooding and/or some cloth weavers may not be using the best available methods. This illustrates two aspects of the economic problem in the full and the efficient use of scarce resources. In terms of the Production Possibility Curve this means 'being *on* the curve of the graph not inside it' in the first place. Second, the choice should give the optimum combination of goods produced – the optimum point on the PPC.

Opportunity cost
We have seen that for an individual or an economy, the economic problem requires a choice to be made. The student chooses between clothes and records, the community in our simple example choose between soya or cloth.

Economists see these choices between buying extra clothes or records, producing extra soya or cloth, social services or consumer goods for the home, in terms of *opportunities lost* once a choice has been made to consume or produce a particular good or service. The choices for an individual may be an LP record or a new book or a visit to the cinema because they have only the money for one of them. For a community the choices must be made not only between different public goods – roads, hospitals and so on – but between all goods and services whether consumer or producer or public goods. Whatever the choice the cost of the student's extra clothes or the community's new road are seen in terms of the opportunities given up.

This idea of *Opportunity Cost* is an important concept in economics. Look again at Figure 1.2. A change in the allocation of resources from producing 4000 tonnes of soya and 17 million square metres of cloth at point C to a new allocation at E alters the output of soya and cloth. At point E 2000 extra tonnes of soya are produced and the community has foregone the production of 4 million square metres of cloth. So the production of 2000 tonnes of extra soya was made by giving up the opportunity to produce 4 million square metres of cloth. In other words: *the Opportunity Cost of 2000 tonnes of extra soya is '4 million square metres of cloth'.*

You will come across many examples of opportunity cost throughout this study. They often include several choices – roads or rail or aircraft, perhaps; records or books or cinema visits – but in economics the Opportunity Cost of any one choice is usually seen in terms of foregoing the next most desired alternative. For example, for an individual an extra shirt may have an Opportunity Cost of an LP, the record being this individual's next most desired alternative. In community decisions alternative choices may be set out, but people's views may differ on what is the next-most-desirable choice to building the school extension in Figure 1.3. Some may see the ambulance as the opportunity cost of the school extension, others may see it as the extra home comforts foregone.

Alternatives in a national economy may be compared in terms of Opportunity Cost. An extra stretch of motorway may have an Opportunity Cost of so many TV sets not now produced, perhaps because scarce resources devoted to the motorway cannot now be used to extend a TV factory. But such decisions among many others are made by individuals, families, other groups and governments as participants in a national economy. Their various activities then contribute towards the solution of the economic problem.

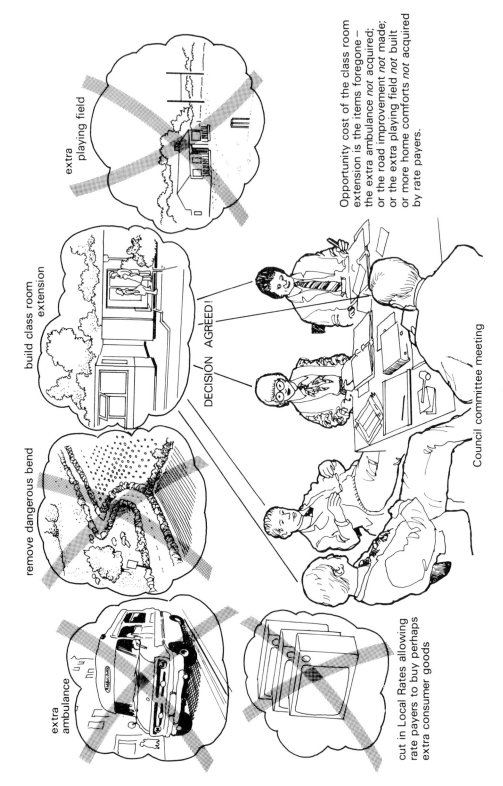

Figure 1.3   Typical opportunity costs for a school room extension.

Economic systems

As a consumer you take into account several considerations before choosing one or other opportunity. We will look at these considerations in chapter 9 but they include your preference for one commodity over another, fashion or taste, and prices. Producers in a similar way must also decide what they will produce and offer for sale.

We have seen that the economic problem boils down to the optimum allocation of resources. But in thinking about an economy made up of consumers and producers, not to mention savers and spenders, a solution to the economic problem is difficult to find. Most consumers are also producers, as workers help to produce goods for sale to others and buy products others make. Nevertheless, the basic economic problem comes down to: what to produce?

In our soya-or-cloth economy, the solution lies in picking a point on the curve in Figure 1.2. Does the economy produce 4000 tonnes of soya and 17 million square metres of cloth as at point C? Should the choice be point E or some other point? In real life there are many different goods and services produced and a wide range of wants, leading to an almost endless variety of possible choices complicating the problem. Although economists can provide many useful ideas in analysing this – the concepts of the Production Possibility Curve and of Opportunity Cost are but two. A look at two sharply contrasting ways of solving the economic problem can help to show how a community may decide what to produce. We can then bear these in mind when studying possible solutions to the economic problem in different situations.

At one extreme is the *free-enterprise*, laissez-faire or capitalist system. At the opposite extreme is the *command*, collectivist or socialist system. Both are theoretical extremes as real-life economies include elements of both systems. Let us create two imaginary states to sharply contrast these extremes: *Maxforus*, an imaginary free-market economy; and *Doforall*, a command economy. These models (as theoretical examples are sometimes called) – see Figure 1.4 – show starkly the claims often made for the merits and drawbacks of each system.

There are essential differences between them. The *Maxforus* capitalist society stresses the economic freedom of the individual. Their consumers' wants are reflected in the price of goods in the market, attracting or discouraging producers, as we shall see in chapter 10. The government of *Doforall*, the socialist state, believes it should estimate what people want and then organise production accordingly. This government controls all *Doforall* resources and directs how these are used to meet the wants of the people.

Which system?

Many considerations come into the pros and cons of the alternative extreme systems, including political and social considerations. From the economic viewpoint, there is no clear-cut answer to which of these systems is preferable in solving the basic economic problem. Each system has advantages and disadvantages, and the economies of various countries reflect to some extent government attempts to lessen the disadvantages of their chosen system.

The USSR, China and Cuba are countries with systems nearly approaching the command economy. Yet these societies allow some privately owned property and use some elements of a *price mechanism*, a characteristic of free-enterprise economies. The USA and Japan are examples of national economies near the opposite extreme.

	MAXFORUS people's claims for their FREE-ENTERPRISE economic system
Estimating Consumer wants	Nobody can estimate everybody's wants, but the price mechanism expresses these wants and production is adjusted accordingly.
How many officials?	Free-enterprise does not need officials nor filling-in-forms, we therefore do not have bureaucracy and 'red tape'.
Profit incentive	This ensures that producers make what people want. Producers change plans quickly to meet new consumer wants. Because people use their initiative in 'enlightened self-interest', more goods are produced that people require. People working for profit operate efficiently because it is in their own interests to do so.
Environment	The benefits of free-enterprise outweigh possible discomforts from pollution and social nuisance.
Competition	Competition encourages efficiency and innovation of new processes and products. Monopolies – see chapter 11 – cannot operate to the disadvantage of consumers because high profits attract new producers into any section of production.
Scale of production	Producers aiming for profits will organise production on a scale that minimises production costs.

Figure 1.4   A comparison of systems.

However, their governments command resources necessary for their defence, the administration of laws, and provision of some social security benefits, among other fundamental needs of their populations.

A mixed economy
A *mixed economy* uses some elements of the free-enterprise and of the command system. The British economy is an example. Individuals are essentially free to decide what they consume and produce, but the British government also enters into economic life, for reasons discussed later, in nationalised industries, and in matters of health and education among others.

What economists do
As your study of economics develops, you will build up a full picture of how these

DOFORALL people's claims for their COMMAND economic system

The Command System ensures production of important and necessary commodities for all the people.
Essential services receive the correct priorities, with *all* production organised 'for the common good'.

Many of our officials only do jobs that have anyway to be done under any system.
More than this: officials can direct the economy so this avoids the imperfections which occur in practice with the price mechanism.

Because people are working for the community this commitment is itself an incentive to work efficiently. Those motivated by profit alone take account only of the £:p and not social costs like pollution of the environment.
The Command system produces less profitable necessities which free-enterprise producers may ignore in making more profitable luxuries. We get our priorities right between production of luxuries and necessities.
Planned production leads to planned distribution and a fairer sharing of output than by the luck of good fortune in a free-enterprise system.

Command society planners take account of social or public costs, which free-enterprise producers may ignore in the pursuit of profit causing pollution through untreated factory fumes and effluent (waste).

Competition can lead to wasteful duplication of resources such as having two railways running in competition from 'A' to 'B'.
Free-enterprise producers may band together in monopolies and other restrictive practices to the disadvantage of workers and consumers.
Industries in private hands may be run down for short term profits, Command economies' planners aim to keep industries well equipped to take advantage of long term benefits. Planners can avoid periods when resources are unemployed.

Industries like the electricity supply and railway services are more efficiently run as large scale concerns. Organising an industry as a monopoly avoids needless duplication, but to avoid abuses must be controlled by the State.

free-enterprise, command and mixed economies operate. But to round off this introduction to the subject you need to understand the role of economists.

You have seen the problem and a little of the way economists approach it. As the study unfolds you will find many other ways economists analyse problems. They often advise governments, organisations or individuals on the likely outcome of different actions. This advice is based on the economists' analyses of the problem. The economists' advice as to the optimum economic solution, however, is only one consideration in making many such decisions, as social and political considerations must also be taken into account.

This is not to say that economists are unaware of the way their suggestions relate to people. For economists know – or should know – that their work involves *people*, and reflect this as far as possible in their analyses.

Assignments

1.3 Select a point on the Production Possibility Curve in Figure 1.2 which provides just sufficient soya bean for home consumption in that economy, when its 2 million population require each year 400 tonnes per 100 000 people. What is the maximum cloth output at this point?

1.4 Select sections (or sectors) of the UK economy which resemble: (a) the command system and (b) the free-enterprise system. For what reasons do these sectors take these forms?

1.5* A 45 minute discussion should bring out most of the points on topics in these studies. You can also explore them in informal chats with friends, or if there is no opportunity for discussion you may think over the problem yourself. Whatever form the discussion takes, make a page of 'conclusions reached' for your notes.

Discuss the statement of a *Maxforus* citizen: if talented people can keep the rewards for their efforts, there will be greater use of their initiative and so more commodities for everyone. *Doforall* man's reply: people who need bribing to give of their best are anti-social.

1.6* Read and study the minutes of a local council, a Parent Teachers' Association, or any club minutes of past meetings. Find and note examples of Opportunity Cost facing or faced by these bodies in choices they have made or are considering. By working in groups of four or so, you can pool your research effort, each group taking a different project. Exchange notes made on this and later topic with other groups.

Suggested further reading

P Donaldson, *Economics of the Real World* (Penguin, 1973), Chapters 1–3

R T Gill, *Economics: A text with included readings* (2nd edition, Prentice Hall, 1974), Part 1

J Harvey, *Elementary Economics* (4th edition, Macmillan, 1976), Chapters 1 and 2

Chapter 2
Questions of population

The connection between people as a population and men and women as consumers and producers in any economy is perhaps too obvious to mention. But any study of economics requires an elementary understanding of *demography*, the study of populations and their influence on the demands for scarce resources.

Population and the economy

Size and structure

The size of a school class may be measured as its total number, while its structure can be stated in many ways including by sex, age and income. If its total size were 16 students, then the structure by sex might be 8 men and 8 women. The structure by age group might be 10 sixteen year olds, 3 of seventeen and 3 of eighteen; by income groups there might be 8 with an income under £2 a week, 3 with £2 or more but less than £5 per week, and 5 with £5 or more. From these figures we know the class size is too great for a 14-seater mini-bus. At the same time the structure suggests that we need as many male as female lavatories for the class, and that the shop at the college entrance can expect half the class to spend under £2 each week in term time.

In the same way the total population in a region or area or economy gives a measure of the likely demand on its scarce resources. At the same time the structure of its population – by age, by sex, by type of job and so on – shows one measure of the likely demand for different goods and services, and also gives some indications of the potential number of workers.

Reports and studies on various aspects of the population are needed by governments not only to know present needs but also to forecast future demands. How many children will be of school age in five or ten years? How many people will need homes? Without population forecasts both in terms of size and structure, a government or other groups cannot plan in the broadest terms. For instance, several years are needed to build new schools and to train an appropriate number of teachers. Building and equipping a hospital can take ten years from the time a decision is taken to start it. In providing homes, time is needed to divert scarce resources to a programme of house and other building. This may involve building a new sewage system, a long and expensive job. Possibly more plumbers and other skilled building workers have to be trained before any additional allocation of resources to home buildings can be sustained.

An economist allows for these consequences, as we will see in studying forecasts of the likely demands on an economy's scarce resources. Once a decision is made, say, to build more homes there are often great problems in organising and coordinating the factors of production needed. On a world scale, the economic complexities are immense – never mind the political and social problems in deciding what to produce and where and how to produce it.

World populations
The most significant fact about the world population is the rate of its increase (see Figure 2.1). This shows that the world population took 150 years from 1750 to double in size, but only 65 years to double again between 1900 and 1965. Some demographers believe it will double again to 7000 million by the year 2000. Such forecasts are made by estimating the expected birth and death rates, that is: the number of births and deaths per 1000 of the population, a calculation we will come back to. The difference between the birth and death rates is defined as the *natural increase* in population. In terms of world population, the death rate has fallen dramatically during the 20th century, a trend the World Health Organisation expects to continue although at a slower rate. The improvements have been mainly due to advances in agriculture and medical science. In particular there has been a fall in the numbers of small children dying before they are a year old. In Russia, for example, the infant mortality rate dropped from 260 per 1000 live births in 1900 to 81 per 1000 by 1950 and 27 per 1000 by 1965. In the same country during the period 1900 to 1965 the life expectancy at birth rose from 32 years to 70 years.

The rapid increase in world population poses some obvious economic questions which have been of concern to economists and others for at least two centuries. The most important is the possible imbalance between population and scarce resources.

Malthus's theory
In 1798 the Reverend T Malthus wrote a now famous essay on population. He explained his belief that populations tend to expand faster than food supplies can be

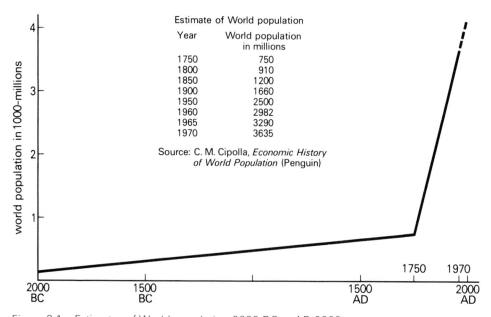

Estimate of World population

Year	World population in millions
1750	750
1800	910
1850	1200
1900	1660
1950	2500
1960	2982
1965	3290
1970	3635

Source: C. M. Cipolla, *Economic History of World Population* (Penguin)

Figure 2.1   Estimates of World population 2000 BC to AD 2000.

increased. According to Malthus in this pessimistic theory, an expanding population soon reaches the limit of food production available to support it. Then any further increase is not matched by increased food supplies with inevitable 'misery for the masses'. By this Malthus meant, famine, infanticide, and living standards that stick on a subsistence level at which people can do no more than just keep alive.

Malthus's theory has been frighteningly accurate in some regions, but so far it has not come about on a world wide scale. For Malthus did not foresee the great increases in food production from modern farming with mechanisation, fertilisers and new breeds of plants. Nor did he realise that the New World would become a major exporter of food. With North America shipping 36 674 562 tonnes of wheat to other countries in 1974, the New World has become one of the world's most important granaries.

Nobody today can be certain what improvements will take place by the year 2000. Although Malthus wrote about population and *food production*, today his theory is applied to *all* resources and their possible imbalance with population. The logic of his theory warns us of possible dangers ahead. Aware of these, economists take into account as far as possible all expected developments – good and bad. In particular they take notice of likely changes in the patterns of demand, the way people's wants change, the availability of resources and advances in technology.

Pessimists are convinced that alternatives cannot be found to increase food output and replace known energy sources quickly enough to avoid Malthus's calamity. Yet solar or nuclear power may replace coal and oil as a source of energy. New varieties of food crops may replace existing plants, and so on.

On the other hand, long-term population forecasts are extremely difficult to make accurately with many influences affecting birth and death rates. Demographers, however, forecast likely population changes; economists interpret their probable effect in terms of demands balanced against scarce resources.

Assignments

2.1 Newspaper cuttings can supplement your written notes. On questions of world population, watch out for reported comments from the World Health Organisation. For topics related to the next section of this chapter – UK population – look out for items reporting on population census details.

2.2 Discuss: has history proved Malthus wrong? Will future events inevitably prove him correct?

The United Kingdom Population

UK Census
The British first examined their population with a census in 1801. Since then regular censuses have been taken every ten years, although in World War II no census was made for 1941 (Figure 2.2). Supplementing the complete census, a sample of 10% of the population completed a census form in 1966 midway between the full censuses of 1961 and 1971. This was taken because changes during the decade made a mid-period census necessary for a more accurate picture.

In working through the Assignments at the end of this section, you will find some

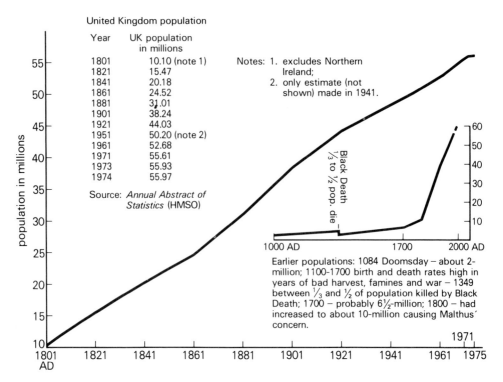

Figure 2.2   UK population AD 1800 to 1975.

examples of census questions and resulting figures. Each census is carried out by circulating all heads of households and making them responsible for recording the required facts on people living in their homes. Special forms are used for hotels and other institutions. The completed forms are collected and analysed by the *Office of Population Censuses and Surveys*. This Office's staff are legally bound to keep confidential the personal details of individuals.

The 1971 census included detailed questions on employment, qualifications and changes in residence, previously only asked of 10% of people in the 1961 full census. From these censuses a picture can be built up of the size and structure of the UK population at particular dates.

The forecasts of future populations are quite sophisticated, taking into account expected developments in birth control, medicine, food production and so on. Like any assumptions, these are always clearly stated with the forecast.

Total population in the United Kingdom
In mid-1974 the total UK population was estimated to be 56 million, making this the twelfth most populous country in the world. The density of population – the average number of people per square mile – was one of the highest in the world at 602 per square mile. This compared with 996 people per square mile in the Netherlands in 1973, 829 in Belgium, 419 in Italy and 248 in France. These densities by country indicate how concentrated its population may be, although this must be further related to habitable and unhabitable land areas. The distribution between rural and

Year (a)	birth rate (per 1000) (b)	death rate (per 1000) (c)	net migration	
			emigrants (per 1000) (d)	immigrants (per 1000) (e)
1750	35·0	30·0		
1850	33·9	22·7		
1880	34·2	19·7		
1900	28·6	17·4		
1920	23·1	12·7		
1930	16·3	12·2		
1940	15·0	13·9		
1960	17·5	11·5		
1965	18·4	11·6	5·1	3·7
1970	16·3	11·7	5·3	4·1
1974	12·2	11·9	4·8	3·3

For these decades examples of the net annual migration: 1901–11 net outflow 82 000; 1921–31 net outflow 67 000; 1931–51 net inflow 22 000; 1951–61 net outflow 7000.

Sources: Cipolla – *Economic History of World Population* (Pelican);
Annual Abstract of Statistics (HMSO)

Figure 2.3   Influences affecting UK population.

urban areas is often even more significant as a pointer to economic and social conditions and is explained later.

Changes in total UK population

UK birth rate
We have seen that populations and their structures are affected by changes in birth and death rates. But in considering the total for a country or a region a third element must be brought in: *migration*. (See Figure 2.3.)

The calculation of birth and death rates is made for this purpose by dividing the number of births or deaths by the number of thousands in the total population:

$$\text{Birth rate in the UK } 1974 = \frac{682\,834}{55\,970} = 12.2 \text{ births per } 1000$$

'Births' means live births, and the total population, given as 55 970 000, was a mid-year estimate of people in the UK in 1974.

Changes in the birth rate are brought about by many social influences. For instance, from 1880 until the mid-1930s most people married later than they do in the 1970s. This was due in part at least to their wish to avoid large families which were inevitable before birth-control methods were widely available and understood. But there are what might be called 'hang the expense' upsurges in a birth rate owing to parents making up for lost time as they did after World War II with a UK baby boom in 1947.

Influences on the birth rate can be summarised as follows:

Increase the birth rate	*Decrease the birth rate*
More marriages.	Fewer marriages.
Times of financial security, with earlier marriages, prospects for wives working part-time and better family incomes.	Prolonged financial insecurity (often through unemployment).
Increases in government allowances contributing to family budgets.	Increase in the financial burden of raising children, as occurred on raising the school-leaving age, so that parents cannot afford to bring up as many children in the way the parents wish or indeed any children at all.
More children to help support parents in their old age – see below.	Smaller families more fashionable and parents prefer alternatives (consumer durables?) or wives pursue full-time career.

Outside the UK, the economic considerations can be quite different, as a primitive farmer needs a modest family to work his land. Nor, for that matter, are present-day economic influences similar to those of earlier times when in 19th-century Britain parents could benefit from the wages of their children.

UK death rate
The death rate in the UK changed most remarkably between the early 19th and early 20th centuries with the greater appreciation of the need for hygiene, increased numbers of hospitals and other medical improvements. These considerably reduced infant mortality and deaths from smallpox and other infectious diseases, while improved food supplies from better agriculture led to general improvements in health.

During the 20th century the fall in the death rate continues but at a slower rate. The major killer diseases have been conquered, so further medical advances which will have a dramatic effect on the death rate are less likely. Nevertheless medical improvements, and improved social care for expectant mothers and babies, have brought about substantial reductions in child mortality. In 1900 142 babies under a year old died for every 1000 live births. By 1930, this had dropped to only 67 and by 1970 to 16 per 1000.

Medical improvements have also contributed to a better chance of survival for all age groups, and the elderly have also benefited from a better diet throughout their lives. Social legislation has had an impact too, with unemployment benefit, better housing, the National Health Service and improved working conditions increasing life expectancy in Britain.

What is not always realised is the effect a change of custom can make. Primitive people died sometimes because in grinding corn, chips from the grinding stone became mixed with the flour and were eaten in bread. Court beauties of the 18th century used mercury-based face powder which caused skin diseases. In the 20th century few if any Britons die from these causes, but other killer diseases have arisen from 20th-century habits of life, with heart disease perhaps from stress and eating excessive amounts of animal fats, and cancer from smoking, among them.

Migration
The difference between birth and death rates causes the natural change in population. The third element of change in any population is *migration*. This has two
components: *emigration* – the number of people leaving the country and *immigration*
– the number entering the country. Although migration is usually related to those
leaving and those entering a country, and shown here in relation to the UK, such
movements of people can occur between regions within a country. These movements
are aspects of geographical mobility described in chapter 3.

Migration is summarised in Figure 2.3, with examples for net annual migration
(the difference between the numbers of emigrants and immigrants) given for the first
six decades to 1961 of the 20th century, and for subsequent years.

People emigrate for many reasons. The most important are: to search for employment or better employment opportunities, to avoid political and religious persecu-
tion, and to search for adventure. The movements of people *to* some countries has
made immigration a major element in increasing their populations. The USA,
Australia and New Zealand, for example, have all received large numbers of immigrants. On the other hand, countries like Eire have had a consistent outflow of
people, emigrating in the case of Eire mainly to find employment in the USA and the
UK.

In the UK from the 1860s to the 1930s there was a net outflow of migrants. But
the total numbers were small, as shown in Figure 2.3, and had little effect on the
population. Since World War II (when there was a net wartime inflow) there has also
been a net outflow of people. Many Britons emigrated to 'old' Commonwealth
countries, including Australia and New Zealand where both countries' governments
provided subsidised passages for their immigrants. These in the main were seeking
better opportunities. In the same post-war period there was increased immigration
from Commonwealth countries, mainly by people seeking work in the UK.

Principal changes in UK total population
The principles explained above are related to the historical aspects of these changes
in total UK population. Looking again at Figure 2.2 showing the population changes
from 1801 to 1974, the changes during these years can be conveniently grouped into
three periods:

1. 1801 to 1900. The UK population increased nearly fourfold during this century.
Birth rate remained high throughout the period and the main reason for the increase
was a fall in the death rate which was almost halved between 1750 and 1900 (see
Figure 2.3) due to: (*a*) improved hygiene, (*b*) medical advances, especially with their
resulting reduction in infant mortality, and (*c*) better food supplies available from
improved methods of agriculture.

2. 1900 to 1940. The population continued to increase, but at a slower rate. This was
mainly because the death rate continued to fall, but less rapidly than in the previous
century. The outstanding feature of this period was the halving of the birth rate
between 1900 and 1940 (see Figure 2.3). This fall in the birth rate was due to: (*a*)
people getting married slightly later in life, and (*b*) a reduction in the size of families.
This practice of having smaller families was the most important feature and occurred
through the increased use of contraception, a fashion for smaller families, increased
opportunities for wives to take jobs, and the increased cost of parenthood when
children had to stay longer at school.

3. 1941 to 1976. The population continued to rise slowly, from 48 million in 1941 to 55.97 million in 1974. Immediately after the war the birth rate rose but fell back slightly to remain roughly constant throughout the 1950s and 1960s. After the war people tended to marry earlier due to the post-war promise of prosperity. There was also a slight increase in family size perhaps because of family allowances paid by the government and having children became fashionable. The death rate continued to fall slowly with a marked improvement in the reduction of infant mortality due to improved health and welfare benefits, and services. However there is evidence in 1976 that the birth rate is falling again, perhaps due to the expense of having children who stay at school even longer, rising unemployment and another change in fashion over family size. As a result the UK population fell by over 80 000 in 1976.

Distribution by sex
In this first of our tables of population structure in the UK (Figure 2.4) there are shown to be about 106 women to every 100 men – actually 1.056 women to each man. Yet this total figure cloaks several facts – men outnumber women in all age groups up to 44 years of age, offset by a greater number of women than men in the older age groups. The reason for these differences within the total is that women live longer than men – of the 85 year olds in 1974, there were 299 women for every 100 men.

Yet at birth there are generally 106 male babies born for every 100 girls. This is a biological fact. This excess of males over females at birth changes during a life-time as more men die than women in each age group. Wars accelerate this swing as men's life expectancy is shortened, while more men than women emigrate making a further preponderance of women in the UK's total population.

Distribution by age
The numbers of the population in the different age groups – its distribution by age – is influenced like total populations by past and present birth and death rates. We have seen how medical and other improvements lead to changes in life expectancy which rose from about 47 years at birth in 1900 to 68.9 years for men and 75.1 for women in 1970. But for people living in West Africa in 1970 the life expectancy was

Year (a)	Population in 1000s (b)	Males ('000s) (c)	Females ('000s) (d)	Proportion of females to males (see note) (e)
1961	52 807	25 528	27 279	1·068
1965	54 218	26 300	27 918	1·061
1970	55 421	26 880	28 542	1·062
1974	55 974	27 219	28 755	1·056

Note: Column 'e' is calculated by dividing column 'd' females by column 'c' males

Source: *Annual Abstract of Statistics* (HMSO)

Figure 2.4   Distribution by sex of UK population.

Year	Aged under 15				Aged 15 to 64				Aged 65 +			
	population (millions)			% of total	population (millions)			% of total	population (millions)			% of total
	male	female	total		male	female	total		male	female	total	
(a)	(b)	(c)	(d)	(e)	(f)	(g)	(h)	(i)	(j)	(k)	(l)	(m)
1901	6·214	6·206	12·420	32·4	11·494	12·514	24·008	62·8	0·784	1·025	1·809	4·8
1931	5·643	5·531	11·174	24·3	14·945	16·500	31·445	68·3	1·472	1·947	3·419	7·4
1951	5·781	5·544	11·325	22·5	16·089	17·344	33·433	66·6	2·284	3·219	5·467	10·9
1965	6·512	6·175	12·687	23·4	17·280	17·666	34·946	64·5	2·508	4·077	6·585	12·1
1974	6·800	6·490	13·390	23·7	17·430	17·570	35·000	62·5	2·990	4·730	7·720	13·8

Source: *Annual Abstract of Statistics* (HMSO)

Figure 2.5   Distribution by age of UK population.

only 39 years. As the death rate falls in the UK (or anywhere else) there tends to be an increase in the proportion of those of pensionable age – over 60 for women and 65 for men under National Insurance Acts in 1976. In the UK in 1900 this group represented 5% of the total population, but by 1974 this had risen to 13.79%. Since pensioners generally make no current full-time contribution to the work force who must provide for their needs, and who also provide for those of school age, both school children and pensioners are termed '*dependents*'. A fall in the death rate may – as we have seen – also result from lower infant mortality and therefore may tend to increase the younger age groups of these dependents.

Three interesting years for comparison of the dependents are 1901, 1931 and 1974, for the increase in pensioners was offset by a decrease in those under 15 (32 + 5 = 37% and 24 + 14 = 38%) in 1901 and 1974 (Figure 2.5). In 1901 the school-leaving age was 13, so perhaps a quarter of these children would at that time be in the work force and not regarded as dependents, while in 1974 dependents included 15 year olds as well as those of 15 and under.

UK's ageing population

Figure 2.5 shows how the UK population has aged over the 20th century with the proportion over 65 rising from 5% in 1901 to 14% in 1974. This ageing is the result of *past* and present birth and death rates. As you have seen there has been a steady fall in the death rates; and the survivors of those born in the first two decades of the century (when the birth rates were comparatively high) are in the 65 and over age group or will soon join it in the 1970s and 1980s.

The effects of this ageing of population is important. The resulting change in the pattern of consumption means fewer schools are needed but more homes and pensions for pensioners, more walking-sticks and fewer babies' feed bottles, and so on.

The increased numbers of retired people also mean there is an increase in those dependent on the *current* working population's efforts, an aspect of the supply of labour we will come back to in chapter 3. There is also an argument for saying that ageing populations tend to be less dynamic, for older people are often less enterprising: they tend to be less willing to change their job or where they live.

Geographical distribution

Figure 2.6 compares the distribution of the UK population in different regions at various dates. This comparison is explained in more detail in chapter 6, but arises in the main from the changes in industry's distribution with fewer people working in industries based on coal and iron ore deposits. Industries like steel making, textile manufacturing and ship building had to be near sources of power and raw materials in the 19th century. As the location of industries shifted, so too did the distribution of population, particularly towards the south-east and Midlands of England.

By 1974 we have seen that the density of the UK population as a whole was 602 people to the square mile. This breaks down into 928 a square mile in England, 342 in Wales, 175 in Scotland and 298 in Northern Ireland. These figures themselves can be broken down further. In 1975 the density in Glasgow was 11 270 people per square mile, with a higher concentration still in its Camphill district, with 24 019 people to the square mile. There are, therefore, several facts to weigh up in any comparison of population distribution. How habitable are the land areas being compared? Are there any points of high concentration in these areas?

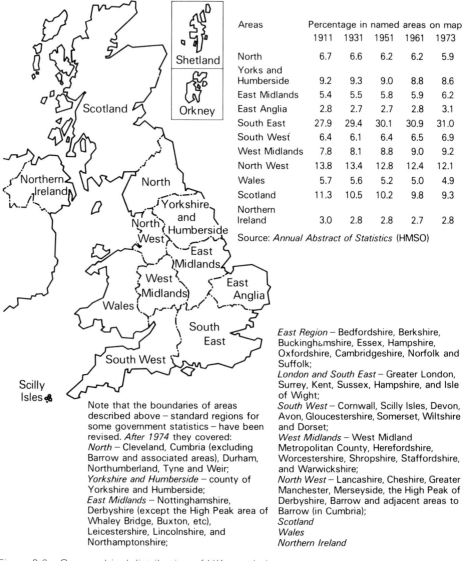

Areas	Percentage in named areas on map				
	1911	1931	1951	1961	1973
North	6.7	6.6	6.2	6.2	5.9
Yorks and Humberside	9.2	9.3	9.0	8.8	8.6
East Midlands	5.4	5.5	5.8	5.9	6.2
East Anglia	2.8	2.7	2.7	2.8	3.1
South East	27.9	29.4	30.1	30.9	31.0
South West	6.4	6.1	6.4	6.5	6.9
West Midlands	7.8	8.1	8.8	9.0	9.2
North West	13.8	13.4	12.8	12.4	12.1
Wales	5.7	5.6	5.2	5.0	4.9
Scotland	11.3	10.5	10.2	9.8	9.3
Northern Ireland	3.0	2.8	2.8	2.7	2.8

Source: *Annual Abstract of Statistics* (HMSO)

Note that the boundaries of areas described above – standard regions for some government statistics – have been revised. *After 1974* they covered:
North – Cleveland, Cumbria (excluding Barrow and associated areas), Durham, Northumberland, Tyne and Weir;
Yorkshire and Humberside – county of Yorkshire and Humberside;
East Midlands – Nottinghamshire, Derbyshire (except the High Peak area of Whaley Bridge, Buxton, etc), Leicestershire, Lincolnshire, and Northamptonshire;

East Region – Bedfordshire, Berkshire, Buckinghamshire, Essex, Hampshire, Oxfordshire, Cambridgeshire, Norfolk and Suffolk;
London and South East – Greater London, Surrey, Kent, Sussex, Hampshire, and Isle of Wight;
South West – Cornwall, Scilly Isles, Devon, Avon, Gloucestershire, Somerset, Wiltshire and Dorset;
West Midlands – West Midland Metropolitan County, Herefordshire, Worcestershire, Shropshire, Staffordshire, and Warwickshire;
North West – Lancashire, Cheshire, Greater Manchester, Merseyside, the High Peak of Derbyshire, Barrow and adjacent areas to Barrow (in Cumbria);
Scotland
Wales
Northern Ireland

Figure 2.6   Geographical distribution of UK population.

Distribution by occupation

Less than half the UK 55.9 million population were in the work force in 1974, although there were 32.5 million (16.99 million men and 15.46 million women) between the ages of 16 and 65 for men and 60 for women. However in 1974 (mid-June) the total *working population* was 25 655 000 made up of: 22 790 000 employees in employment (see Figure 3.3, page 42); employers and self-employed 1 977 000; Her Majesty's forces 345 000 and registered unemployed 543 000. The difference of 6.9 million between the 32.5 million above and the actual working population (25.6m) is mainly accounted for by women who stay at home while their children are young, or those who keep house, and students over sixteen but still in full-time education.

A significant feature of Figure 2.7 is the change in numbers employed in various occupations. As the century passes fewer people are needed in the primary industries like farming and mining where mechanisation has taken an increasing part. Between 1901 and 1973 the number of workers employed in coal mining fell by 66% in Great Britain but the output of coal fell by only 41%. However, the percentages of the total work force employed in manufacturing have changed little. There have been impor-tant changes *between* industries as employers of labour in manufacturing, for over this period the rise in numbers employed in motor-car and other consumer durable manufacture has tended to offset the fall in mining and heavy engineering. However there are signs that the numbers employed in manufacturing may now be falling, to the benefit of service industries. Over a longer time, the changes in service industries are shown in Figure 2.7. There are fewer domestic servants, for example, shown under the heading 'Catering, hotels and domestic service'. Almost 18% of the work force in 1841 were domestic servants but only about 1% in 1974. The numbers in professional and scientific services were a much greater proportion of those em-ployed – 14.9% against 2.4% in 1841. There have also been substantial increases in the proportions employed in distributive trades and government services.

Population and economic forecasts

We have seen something of the importance of population statistics in economic studies. Knowledge of present facts here are important but the demographer's fore-casts of population are even more significant in many economic studies. The 1973 estimate by the *Office of Population and Census Surveys* gives the estimated total UK population in the year 2001 as 59.4 million including 30.2 million women. Therefore the pattern of demand in that year is likely to show – all other things being equal – a change over 1974, since by the year 2001 on this estimate there will be 1.035 women for every man against the 1974 ratio of 1.056.

Population forecasts, however, are constantly reviewed in the light of changing circumstances. The government statistics published every April or May in the *Monthly Digest of Statistics* (HMSO) include these population forecasts. This and other sources of population information are shown in the Assignments below. While working through these therefore you will become familiar with the principal sources for information on UK population. Later in this book, as economists' techniques are studied, we will see how frequently population statistics enter into the analysis of situations.

	1841		1968		1974	
	('000s)	%	('000s)	%	('000s)	%
Agriculture, forestry and fishing	1 639	22·30	423	1·80	417	1·80
Mining and quarrying	225	3·20	489	2·10	349	1·50
Manufacturing industry	2 452	35·50	8 790	38·10	7 877	34·60
Construction	377	5·50	1 554	6·70	1 321	5·80
Gas, electricity and water	2	0·03	421	1·80	347	1·50
Transport and communication	200	2·90	1 610	7·00	1 506	6·60
Distributive trades	426	6·17	2 832	12·20	2 761	12·10
Insurance, banking and finance	95	1·40	675	2·90	1 116	4·90
Professional and scientific services	162	2·40	2 753	11·90	3 374	14·90
Catering, hotels and domestic services*	1 244	18·00	580	2·50	806	3·50
Miscellaneous services	142†	2·00	1 558	6·70	1 320	5·80
Public administration	43	0·60				
National government services			606	2·70	610	2·70
Local government services			834	3·60	986	4·30
Total in civil employment	6 907	100·00	23 125	100·00	22·790	100·00

* Includes domestic servants
† Estimate based on data from Historical Abstract of Labour Statistics

Sources: 1841 – *Historical abstract of labour statistics* (Dept of Employment, HMSO)
1968, 1974 – *Annual abstract of statistics* (HMSO)

Figure 2.7   Distribution by occupation of UK employees in employment.

Assignments

2.3 Define: (*a*) the birth rate, and (*b*) the death rate. List the major influences (past, present and future) on both of these.

2.4 The population of Scotland in mid-1974 was 5.226 million and there were 64 740 deaths that year. Calculate the death rate.

2.5 Comment on the changes which have taken place in the UK during the past century in (*a*) birth rate, (*b*) death rate and (*c*) size of population. (L 1971)

2.6 Describe and account for the existing geographical distribution of Britain's working population. (AEB 1972)

2.7* The recent (1971) Census of Population showed that between 1961 and 1971 the population of the UK rose by nearly 3 million. What were the causes of this increase? What are some of the likely consequences? (AEB 1974)

2.8* What would be the likely social and economic effects over the next 15 to 20 years if there were to be a decrease in the UK birth rate? (AEB 1975 – adapted)

2.9* (*a*) Indicate clearly how the occupational distribution of the British population has changed over the 20th century.

(*b*) Estimate the probable changes in this distribution in the next 25 years giving the basis of your opinions.

2.10* The following typical census questions gave the results shown below:

Census question
A1   How do you and your household occupy your accommodation?

A5   Has your household the use of the following amenities on these premises? [includes: a flush toilet (WC) with entrance inside the building.]

Information from answers to A1 and A5 for England and Wales:

Tenure [rented, owner occupied, etc.]	Total households	Shared use of inside WC		No inside WC	
		number	%	number	%
All tenures	16 509 905	539 170	3.3	1 994 845	12.1
Owner occupier	8 290 010	68 370	0.8	744 460	9.0
Rented from a council or new town	4 629 085	23 900	0.5	292 625	6.3

B2   Write date of birth of the person (present on census night 25/26 April 1971)

B3   Sex of person

Information from answers to B2 and B3 for England and Wales:

	Males	%	Females	%	Total	%
All persons of pensionable age	2 491 770	100	5 514 605	100	8 006 375	100
One-person households	317 850	12.8	1 611 280	29.2	1 929 130	24.1

A4   How many cars and vans are normally available for use by you (as head of household filling in the form) or members of your household?

B21   What means of transport does the person normally use, for the longest part by distance, of the daily journey to work? (Note ... give means ... used most often ... do not use terms such as 'public transport' ...)

Information from answers to A4 and B21 for a 10% sample *for England and Wales:*

	Total	In households with no car
Total persons in employment	2 109 797	754 391
Train	138 879	61 931
Bus	502 328	315 289

Study the above figures and list the following for England and Wales:

(*a*) The percentage of owner occupiers without an inside WC.
(*b*) The number of one-person households occupied by women over pensionable age.

(c) What is significantly different about the figures for transport to work and those for outside toilets and pensioners in one-person households?

(d) Discuss: what are the likely effects on grocery shops' trade when nearly 2 million households are each occupied by one person of pensionable age?

The extracts from the 1971 Census have been reproduced by permission of the Controller of HMSO

Suggested further reading

C M Cipolla, *The Economic History of World Population* (6th edition, Penguin, 1974)

Harvey, Chapter 3

F W Paish and A J Culyer, *Benham's Economics* (9th edition, Pitman, 1973), Chapter 9

J Powicke, D Iles and B Davies, *Applied Economics* (Edward Arnold, 1972), Chapter 16

Chapter 3

Factors of Production

You will remember from chapter 1 the economic fact of life that there are only scarce resources to meet our unlimited wants. These scarce resources which economists call the *factories of production* used to produce commodities are grouped into several distinct categories (see Figure 3.1).

Quality and definitions

The quality of resources

Factors of production, the scarce resources, are classified as land, labour, capital and the activities of the entrepreneur. Each has a special meaning in economics. In broad terms land covers not only '*space*' but also minerals; labour is by hand and brain; capital includes machinery, tools and other buildings used to make commodities; while the entrepreneur among other things organises the first three factors.

Clearly not all factors of production are of the same quality, for barren hillsides will not normally grow good crops nor a clumsy person produce the exquisite detail in fine jewellery. The capital tools may be new or worn. The entrepreneur may be a genius in having ideas and ability or he may make a hash of the project he undertakes. There are, therefore, different qualities within each factor classification. Differences in quality and degrees of scarcity can be as important as the fact that the total available quantity of a resource is limited.

For example only 80% of the total land area of England and Wales can be used for some form of agriculture. Of the remainder: 9% is mainly urban and 11% has other uses. The 80% agricultural land was further divided in a government survey (1974), according to the land's limitations for agriculture: 2% had virtually none; 12% had only minor restrictions; 38% had moderate restrictions due to rainfall, soil and so on; 16% was severely restricted, including land over the 600-foot contour with a high rainfall and 12% was even more restricted through poor drainage, 1:3 slopes and/or being over 1000 ft. On some agricultural land, however, it may often be possible to build towns and factories.

Factors as inputs

The scarce resources employed in producing goods and services constitute *inputs to the production process* – those physical materials and equipment, the labour of hand and brain, and the enterprise (know-how and organisation) which all go into production.

Landowners (people or states), the workers, owners of capital – as explained below – and entrepreneurs, all these supply or sell factors for which they receive rewards.

Land and natural resources
1. factory site
2. housing site
3. water in well
4. agricultural fields
5. barren hillside – poor quality land

Labour
6. by hand – factory and farm workers
7. by brain
   but note each type of worker does some brain and some manual work

Capital – private
8. fixed – buildings, machinery, and tractor
9. working – stocks

Capital – social (or public)
10. fixed – roads, sewers, and telephone lines

Entrepreneur
11. the miller who organises his mill (capital) and the millers (labour) while taking the risks of production, eg: no farmer sending him corn to grind

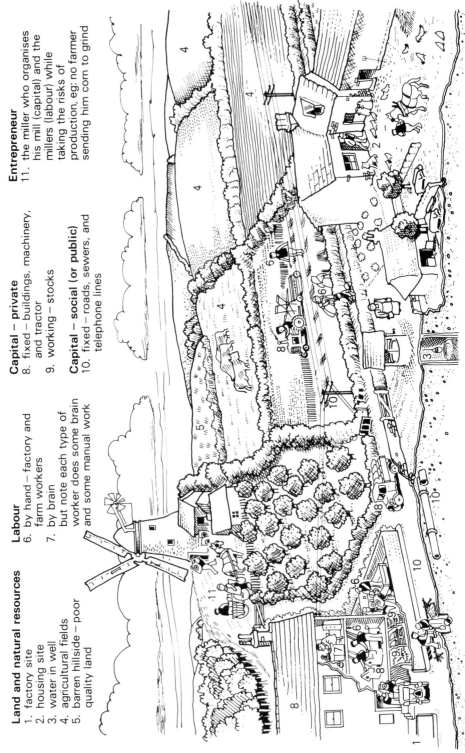

Figure 3.1   Examples of factors of production.

These rewards are called *factor payments*. A worker, for example, has his or her pay and perhaps pension rights.

With these concepts in mind – factors of production of various types and qualities used as inputs-to-production – we can look more closely at the definitions of the four different factors of production.

Land as a factor of production

Land and natural resources

Land as a factor of production includes natural resources, those bounties of nature like mineral deposits which are not man-made. This is a wider definition than the usual meaning of 'land' but nevertheless includes conventional land space for agriculture, housing, factory and other sites.

The available total quantity of land is virtually fixed since the natural changes in land area are infinitesimal, and natural resources are non-renewable in the foreseeable future. This in short means that the total available supply of the factor of production, land, is fixed. Not only is the total supply fixed but the available areas of different qualities are also fixed at any time. However, the quality may be improved by adding something – fertilisers, perhaps – to poor land, or the use of some other factor of production. For example, the irrigation of a desert requires wells, pumps and irrigation ditches. Marshes may be drained or hillsides cleared of bracken and fertilised, all improving the land for agriculture. Yet these changes also involve the use of other factors of production as well as the land itself. Even wild strawberries need the factor of labour – the picker – to gather them for eating.

Geographical location of land

An important characteristic of any piece of land is its location. A coal mine in a remote Pacific island, for example, is less conveniently situated, other things being equal, than a pit near an established centre of production, since coal is generally expensive to ship.

The choice sites for retail shops are generally in city centres where many potential customers pass them on most days, so a shop owner looks for choice (prime) sites where he can expect the most consumers to come to shop for his type of goods. The considerations vary a little with the types of commodities sold but the main ones are summarised in Figure 3.2.

The number of choice sites meeting all a retailer's needs is limited by the size of the town and its frequently used shopping streets. So if the demand for these prime sites increases, owners can ask higher prices for shop rents for these properties than for other premises in the town. For no matter how high the demand, the supply of prime sites in the focus area does not increase in that city centre; not that is until there is some long-term development, involving the use of other factors of production. Even then the number of shop sites in any one precinct cannot be increased in normal circumstances.

Factor reward to land

The factor reward or payment to landowners is *rent* for supplying this factor for use in the production process. But in economics there is a distinction between rent in the everyday sense as payments for hiring a flat, a car or whatever, and *'economic rent'*.

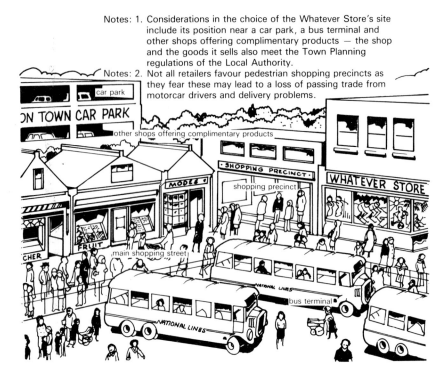

Figure 3.2   Considerations in choosing a prime site for a store.

Economic rent is a concept developed principally by David Ricardo (1772–1823) through his analysis of differences in land prices and their relationship to the price of corn. These findings have been broadened to cover all factors. So economists see economic rent as a surplus or amount over and above the minimum payment necessary to keep any factor in its present use.

Labour as a factor of production

Labour – brains and muscle
Labour in this sense includes physical and mental effort and a mixture of both. Indeed all types of work involve some mental and physical effort albeit in different proportions. A semi-skilled hod carrier uses mainly muscle but must organise the flow of bricks to keep the bricklayer going steadily. The surgeon has skilled hands coordinated with his or her knowledge of the human body.

The total supply of labour at any time is made up of many different kinds of worker – unskilled, semi-skilled and skilled. The total population sets an upper limit on this supply, just as the global area of land sets a limit on the supply of land as a factor of production. Other influences set limits not only on the total supply but also on the supply of unskilled, semi-skilled and skilled. For just as everyone cannot run a mile in under 4 minutes, so people have differing potentials at work through their natural abilities and/or training.

The scarcity in the supply of those with *particular* skills is often as important as the scarcity in the total supply of workers – the total numbers available for work. The shortage of supply may even be in those willing to do unpleasant or mundane jobs. For this reason, during the boom years of the 1960s, Germany recruited immigrant Turkish, Italian and other workers to sweep the streets and empty dustbins.

A shortage of workers with particular skills or training may be met by training more of these specialists. However such training – like the reclamation of land – involves the use of other factors of production. Training hospitals, colleges, instruction workshops and instructors must be employed – inputs to the production process on these occasions 'producing' skilled workers. This is a form of investment in 'human capital'.

There are some obvious natural – untaught – skills which cannot be acquired, however, by increasing the resources employed in training facilities. Artists, musicians, great actors and craftsmen, for example, have some abilities that cannot be taught. What is less often understood are the limited numbers of people with abilities that training can develop for more common skills. Not everyone can be trained to inspect goods made in a factory, for inspection needs powers of concentration if faulty goods are not to slip by and reach customers. Not everyone has nimble enough fingers or the coordination of hand and brain to sew a fine seam. Nor does everyone have the courage needed to work in a mine or the patience to nurse the mentally sick.

There are also people with potential skills that remain unrealised through lack of opportunity or encouragement or facilities.

Factor reward to labour

Those who supply or sell their labour – people who work with hands or brains – receive 'wages' as their payment or reward. Although some may be paid by the hour, some by the week, others monthly as annual salary – these are all factor rewards or payments to labour. The American term 'compensation' is perhaps more appropriate for these payments which may include pension rights, free living accommodation and other benefits an individual can receive for doing his or her job. The way these rewards are determined can be quite complicated. The following comments on trade unions illustrate some of the realities as they have developed over the last two centuries or longer.

Trade Unions

From the 12th century, if not earlier, craft guilds have endeavoured to make the most of the scarcity value of their members' skills. But in the late 18th century when the first craft unions of skilled workers were formed to improve their members' wages and working conditions, unions met with hostility. This was not only from their employers but also from Parliament. The Combination Acts of 1799 and 1800 made any union of workers illegal. In 1834 some agricultural workers from the village of Tolpuddle, suspected of union activity, were transported to Australia for 'administering an unlawful oath,' and are remembered as the Tolpuddle martyrs. Nevertheless in the following century trade unions developed.

Four broad types of union have grown from these early beginnings:

1. Craft unions of skilled men.
2. General unions of industrial workers such as the Transport and General

Workers' Union (TGWU) and the National Union of General and Municipal Workers (NUGM), both with origins in the 19th century.

3. Unions of administrative (white collar) workers such as the National and Local Government Officer's Association (NALGO).

4. Industrial unions trying to organise all workers in a particular industry, regardless of their individual work or status. The Union of Post Office Workers (UPW) and the National Union of Mineworkers (NUM) are examples that tend towards this form.

However the organisation of unions for single industries has not become a generally accepted practice in the UK although it is more widely adopted on the mainland of Europe and in the USA. In Britain most industries are served by more than one union. The railways in the early 1970s had three main unions (approximate membership shown in brackets); the Associated Society of Locomotive Engineers and Firemen (29 000) with a membership drawn from drivers and firemen; the National Union of Railwaymen (198 000) whose members are porters, ticket collectors and in similar work; and the Transport Salaried Staffs' Association (75 000) with a membership drawn from clerical workers.

In addition to acting for their members as a whole, unions also help individual members. A member may have a grievance over the apparent allocation of difficult and not so difficult work, believing others are favoured with easily earned bonuses. After an accident at work, union lawyers help the injured member claim from his or her employer. Convalescent homes and pension schemes are run by some unions for the members' welfare.

All services and the administration of unions are financed from members' subscriptions and the income many unions have from investments.

Trade unions also have a national body known as the Trades Union Congress (TUC), which since it was founded in 1868 has been the body speaking for its affiliated unions at national level. The TUC can influence unions in their actions but has no powers to direct what they do. Its own policies are determined at an annual conference attended by representatives from these unions.

Not all associations of workers may include union in the title of their society. In 1969 a Royal Commission, the Donovan Commission, defined a trade union as 'any combination of employees, the principal activity of which is the regulation of relations between employees and employers'. In 1973 there were 495 unions within this definition and their 11 507 000 members were 45% of the working population.

The objectives of those trade unions affiliated to the TUC were spelt out in the TUC's evidence to the Donovan Commission. These aims are:

1. Improved terms of employment
2. Improved physical environment at work
3. Full employment and national prosperity
4. Security of employment and income
5. Improved social security schemes
6. Fair shares of national income and wealth
7. Industrial democracy with workers involved in running the businesses they work for
8. A voice in government
9. Improved public and social services

10. Public control and planning of industry.

These ten objectives include political and social as well as economic objectives.

Collective bargaining
With the general aim of improving the living standards – including wages and conditions of work – for their members, one of the principal activities of a union is conducting negotiations with its members' employers or employers' associations, a process known as *collective bargaining*.

These negotiations can take place at several levels. At the top level it may mean the TUC formulating policies with the Confederation of British Industry and Government, when account is taken of wide-ranging economic issues. Alternatively, the negotiations may be at industry, company or factory level.

Many considerations come into negotiations between unions and employers. The number of hours in the basic working week, overtime premiums, allowances perhaps for dangerous and for dirty conditions, and so on, all entail complicated bargaining. There are many different methods of payment. Some people are paid by the month, the week or hour. There may be piece rates to be considered – that is so much per item produced, special allowances for shift work and for working unsocial hours. There may be special schemes like some form of measured-day-work when the rate of pay is related in part to a factory's output.

Over and above these are the differences in pay and conditions between workers – *the differentials* – including those for skilled as opposed to unskilled work, often requiring delicate negotiations with different unions representing each body of workers.

The supply of labour
The supply of labour is defined as the amount of work, measured in hours, provided by a country or region's population. The two elements of this supply are the number of people in the work force including those seeking work, and the number of hours each is willing to work (see Figure 3.3).

There are many influences affecting the size of a work force. In the UK, for example, there are institutional influences like the school-leaving age and the official retiring age – 60 for women, 65 for men in the 1970s. Yet often individuals retire later or earlier than the official ages. In June 1974 there was a total working population in the UK of 25.65 million out of a total population of 55.9 million – note the details in Figure 3.3. Participation was by about half the total population. This and similar 'labour force participation' rates are calculated for various regions, sex and age groups as a preliminary to analysing the influences affecting each group's willingness to supply their labour – why they do or do not seek or have employment.

The population structure – by age groups, sex and so on – also has an important bearing on the size of a work force. Examples of these effects of population structure (studied in chapter 2) are shown in Figure 3.4.

The number of hours people work is also influenced by institutional forces. In the UK 40 hours is the basic working week for most workers in the 1970s, but the Factory Acts and other legislation limit working hours of 'juniors'. However, workers often put in overtime and exceed their basic hours. Figures of the average hours actually worked in the UK in 1968 by manual workers were 44.5 hours per week

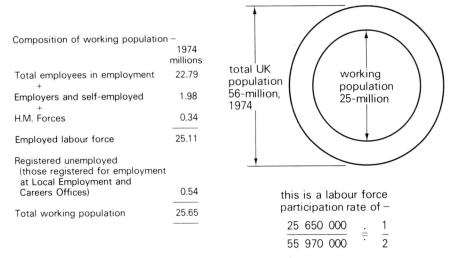

Figure 3.3   Labour force participation in the UK 1974.

Example of two individual's working lives – labour force participation

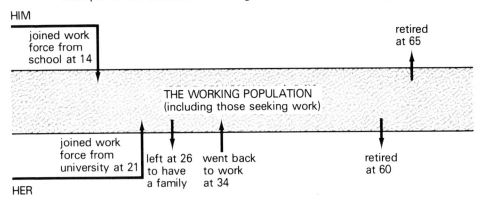

Figure 3.4   Working lives.

(46.3 hours for men and 38.4 for women). The hours people are willing to work can also be measured by the year, so holidays affect the hours worked in any year. More holidays giving longer leisure time lessen the hours available for work (see Figure 3.5).

Do high wages reduce the labour supply?
There is some evidence to suggest that under some conditions a rise in wage rates leads to a fall in hours worked, for some people are unwilling to work longer than is necessary to meet their needs. These workers doing 40 hours a week at £1.50 an hour for £60 may prefer if possible to work only 30 hours if the rate rises to £2, since 30 hours at £2 gives them £60, the sum they consider adequate for their needs. The wage rise has then reduced their working week and given them 10 hours more leisure. They have chosen to take their increased reward as leisure, that is, they chose to consume more of the 'good' leisure.

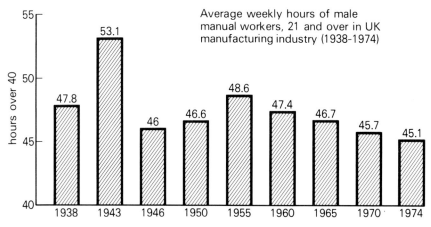

Figure 3.5   Example of hours worked 1938 to 1974.

This approach is hard for some executives and others to understand. They would expect increased wages to motivate workers to work more to improve their living standards, for an increase in the rate to £2 raises the opportunity cost of an hour's leisure, since before the rise only £1.50 was foregone by not working for an hour.

Assignments

3.1 Linking with your study of geography or through research in the local library, list areas of the UK particularly suited to the following: (*a*) growing wheat; (*b*) fruit farming; (*c*) dairy farming; (*d*) siting of office blocks; and (*e*) siting of shops.

3.2 List and describe two examples of each of the following:
    (*a*) a job where an increase in wages is likely to lead to a decrease in hours worked;
    (*b*) jobs with different methods of payment;
    (*c*) conditions which are likely to encourage housewives to join the work force.

3.3 Distinguish between a craft union and a general trade union. What benefits can a worker expect from joining a trade union? (AEB 1975)

3.4 Describe the functions of a trade union. What part does the Trades Union Congress play in the trade union movement? (AEB 1974 – adapted)

3.5 Group research: each group selects a different type of shop and chooses a suitable site for it in the nearest town. List reasons important in the choice.

3.6 Discuss: why are such shops as Woolworths, Marks and Spencer, and Littlewoods usually situated close to one another in a town?

Capital as a factor of production

Capital – fixed and working
In simple terms, capital means all those buildings, machines and other equipment – *producer goods* – used in making things we consume. A machine tool lathe is a producer good making components perhaps for cars or other goods. The milking

machine on a dairy farm is a producer good used in milk production. These are two examples of producer or capital goods which are all used not for their own sake but in the production of other goods. In manufacturing motor scooters there are a wide range of producer goods needed; these include equipment for casting engine parts, machine tools for shaping them, metal presses to shape the mudguards and engine covers. All these and more machines must be housed in a factory building where the parts are assembled into scooters. All these inputs are capital as a factor of production, and taken together can be seen as the manufacturer's 'stock' of capital used to make scooters. These producer goods are called *fixed capital goods* because – unlike raw materials – fixed capital goods can be used several or more times in the production of a good or goods.

The Assignments at the end of this section show several other examples of capital as a factor of production. But note how this 'stock' of capital (Figure 3.6) also includes a basic stock of raw materials, for production is impossible without them. These raw materials, however, change their form during production and are known as '*working*' or 'circulating' capital.

To increase the 'stock' of capital in scooter manufacture takes more machines which have themselves to be produced. Adding these to the 'stock' of capital is called investment. Warning: you will later see that the word 'capital' can also mean funds used for investment.

Since increasing capital involves the use of other factors of production in its manufacture, the increase presents an opportunity cost. You can either forego the use of scarce resources in the production of goods for consumption, to get increased capital 'stock'; or you can go on using the scarce resources to produce goods for consumption. The machines used to build the extra tools needed for increased scooter production and the men's time – the labour – in doing this might alternatively be used in making scooters. But the same men and machines – the same factors – cannot do both at the same time; they either make new tools or make scooters (see Figure 3.6). So when scarce resources are allocated to increasing the capital 'stock', then some current production of consumer goods must be sacrificed.

This idea has a general implication, for to add to capital 'stock' a society must forego current output of goods and services for consumption. The addition to or accumulation of capital has, however, a general objective in increasing future production. With his increased capital 'stock' the manufacturer will make, say, 10 000 *more* scooters a year, than could previously be built. In wider terms, the society accumulating capital accepts a lower production of consumer goods now, in the expectation of higher production of these later. For later, when the capital stock has been increased, there will be the potential to produce a greater quantity and maybe quality of consumer goods and services.

Figure 3.6 makes clear the distinction between fixed and working (or circulating) capital. To sum up: capital is all those man-made aids to further production such as tools, machinery, plant and equipment – including everything man-made which is not consumed for its own sake but is used in the process of making other goods.

Capital therefore includes raw material stocks, goods in the process of manufacture and finished (completely manufactured) but undelivered stocks. The materials, goods in process and finished stocks are constantly changing their form. As raw material is used in a process it is replaced by fresh material, and the goods in process become finished goods and so on. These are therefore circulating or working capital.

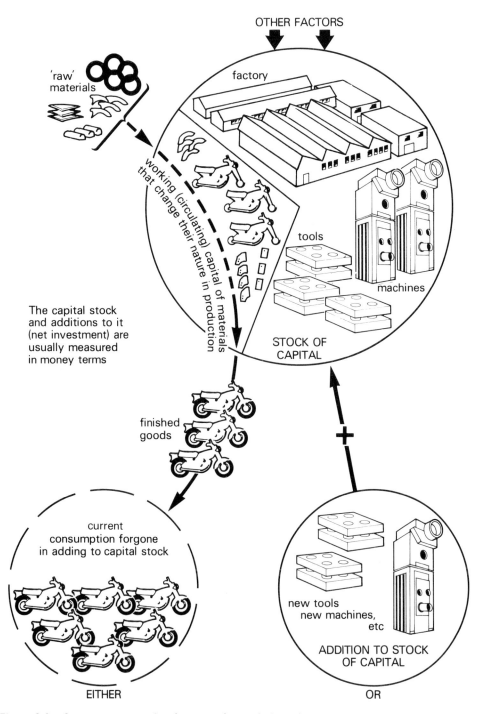

OTHER FACTORS

'raw' materials

factory

working (circulating) capital of materials that change their nature in production

tools

machines

STOCK OF CAPITAL

The capital stock and additions to it (net investment) are usually measured in money terms

finished goods

current consumption forgone in adding to capital stock

new tools new machines, etc

ADDITION TO STOCK OF CAPITAL

EITHER

OR

Figure 3.6   Current consumption foregone for capital stock.

Factor reward to capital

To build up a 'stock' of capital or investment usually involves raising finance (as you will see in chapter 8), with a reward paid to those who supply this finance as owners of capital. The reward is *interest* or a sum regarded as the price for the funds required to purchase the capital goods, and therefore income to its owners. For example: a producer borrows £100 from you to buy a sewing machine, and may pay you £10 a year in interest for the use of your savings as financial capital. This £10 is your reward as the supplier of financial capital.

Depreciation and obsolescence

The machines, tools and other equipment in our scooter factory inevitably wear out. As each press tool stamps down in making a mudguard, part of the tool wears. So there are a limited number of mudguards it can make even when kept in good repair. In this way most if not all producer goods are said to *depreciate*. A school building depreciates over the years, until perhaps it cannot be repaired. Your record player depreciates until it no longer plays records without distortion, unless expensive repairs are made. Then you would probably find a new one a better bet.

Producer goods may also become out of date in design or method of operation. Then, no matter how mechanically sound they may be, they are said to be obsolete. This obsolescence is not related only to the condition of say our press tools making a scooter mudguard, but also to their efficiency relative to new machines. A new machine may stamp out twice as many mudguards each day. Capital goods therefore may still be capable of producing goods, yet be taken out of use because they are obsolete and more efficient equipment can replace them. For this reason the British Steel Corporation closed some steel-making furnaces in the mid-1970s in their programme of modernisation.

There are some special cases of capital items which do not depreciate or become obsolete. These oddities need not concern us but obviously the whisky maturing in a Scottish warehouse or wine in a French cellar is appreciating as working capital. Neither hopefully will become obsolete, although you can never tell when somebody may come up with a simpler way of achieving the taste of mature whiskies and wines without the high cost of prolonged storage in maturing them.

Net investment

We have seen that capital 'stock' is eroded by depreciation and obsolescence, so that these producer goods become less efficient if not completely useless. Depreciation and obsolescence therefore can be regarded (Figure 3.7) as consumption of capital. This consumption has to be made good to maintain society's stock of capital. It must be topped up, in other words, to keep the capital stock intact. Otherwise future production will fall.

Our manufacturer with an output of 100 000 scooters a year can only continue to make this many if he replaces worn-out machines and plant. So he must replace these worn-out capital goods before buying extra new machines to add to his stock of capital for increased output. In much the same way a society must replace the erosion – from depreciation and obsolescence – of its stock of capital before the stock can be increased. The total production of capital goods between one date and the next is the *Gross Investment*. If the depreciation and obsolescence for the period is deducted from the gross investment, you get the *Net Investment* which is the net

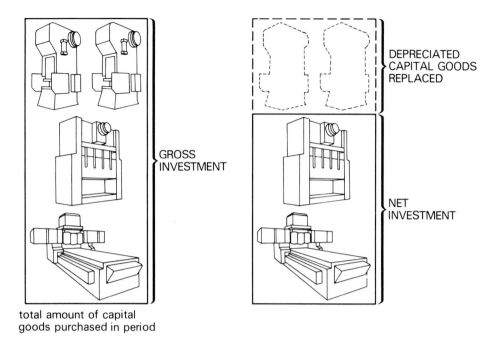

total amount of capital
goods purchased in period

Figure 3.7   Gross and net investment.

addition to the stock of capital (see Figure 3.7).

When the gross investment is insufficient to cover depreciation and obsolescence, a society is consuming capital. This may happen, for example, in war time. Such a falling level of capital stock will lead to a lower future output of goods and services.

The entrepreneur as a factor of production

The entrepreneur – enterprise and taking risks
Entrepreneurs are considered to be those who organise and combine together the other factors of production – land, labour and capital. The entrepreneur also takes risks for he must organise production of a commodity *before* he is certain that anyone will buy the good or service. This is a risk inherent in modern production where output is made in *anticipation* of demand.

Despite these uncertainties before the venture, if the entrepreneur has judged correctly the demand for the commodities now produced, he or she is rewarded by a profit (see Figure 3.8). The reward is for taking risks, for if the risk-taker 'gets it wrong' he may get no reward or make a loss. The house painter, for example, who sets up on his own is an entrepreneur. He buys ladders or hires them, and puts in time (labour) in finding customers, but he has no guarantee of continuing work. If he is successful he earns a profit – an excess of revenue over costs.

In economics these costs are taken to include 'wages' for his own labour and 'interest' on his capital as his money which is ploughed into the business, although in practice he may not separate these elements. The pure profit to him as an entrepreneur, however, does not include these 'wages' and 'interest'.

organises
voyage

profits from cargo
of silks and spices

ship sails on 2nd voyage – loses all

ship sunk
in storm

Figure 3.8   The entrepreneur – organiser and risk taker.

Who are entrepreneurs?

The factor reward to our decorator for being a successful entrepreneur was the profit he made. He also organised the work getting himself and his gear to the right houses on time among other things, and took the risks. Yet all workers must organise their jobs to some extent; the hod carrier has to get his bricks to the bricky, a teacher must organise the work for a course. Therefore many economists see the organising aspects of an entrepreneur's work as no more than a particular type of labour.

You will remember from chapter 1, the *Maxforus* philosophy emphasised the economic freedom for the individual. A part of this philosophy is that profit encourages people to take decisions and bear risks in combining the factors of production in anticipation of demand for goods and services, as our decorator did. In short: *he* will decide to run his decorating business seeking a profit. In such an economy potential profits – what our decorator hopes to earn as profit – attracts resources to cater for wants. In the *Doforall* society the emphasis is on centralised decisions taken by a planning body, calculated to achieve maximum economic welfare or well being.

Assignments

3.7 Find two examples of each of the following factors of production:

(a) fixed capital   (d) physical labour
(b) working capital   (e) mental labour
(c) entrepreneurs   (f) mineral deposits as land

3.8 What considerations should be taken into account by a business person in deciding whether or not to replace a worn-out machine?

3.9 Distinguish between gross and net investment. Construct an illustration to explain your answer.

3.10 'The entrepreneur is the essential factor of production.' Critically examine this statement and explain the role of the entrepreneur. (L 1973)

3.11 Discuss: what does the economist mean by 'capital'? What factors affect the accumulation of capital in the economy? (Based on AEB 1972)

The mobility of factors of production

Occupational and geographic

Factors of production may be mobile in two senses, occupational and geographic. This mobility is the ease with which factors can be transferred between uses or locations. Through occupational mobility, factors may be used for a different purpose from their present use – the bricklayer building homes may switch to assembling motor cars. This concept can also be applied to other factors – land used for agriculture may be used for a new town site, the factory building scooters may be used for manufacturing washing machines.

A factor may also be physically movable – have geographical mobility. Land is obviously geographically immobile. You cannot move a farmer's field, nor can you move the site on which a factory is built. But in some cases you may be able to change its use, so it has degrees of occupational mobility. The factory site may

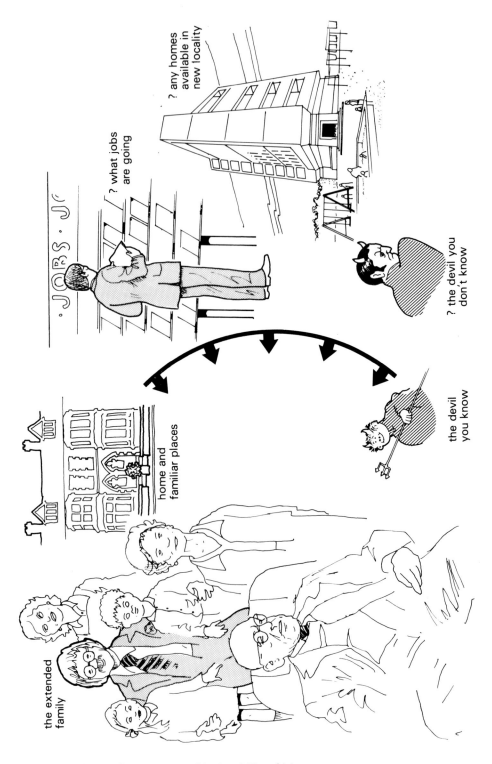

Figure 3.9   The barriers to geographical mobility of labour.

become the location for an out-of-town hypermarket, the hill-side sheep farm may become a leisure centre.

These concepts of mobility can be applied to capital, although in practice some producer goods are not readily movable. But even though you cannot move a blast furnace, you may choose to build its replacement on a new site.

Other capital goods may have been designed for a very specific purpose, railways for example. These are occupationally immobile for a railway can only be used for railed traffic. Some capital goods, however, are both occupationally and geographically mobile: a lathe may be used for making this or that, and moved from here to there.

Mobility of labour

Labour can be occupationally mobile and/or geographically mobile to a greater or lesser extent depending on a number of influences (see Figure 3.9).

The geographically mobile include some of those working in the construction or civil engineering industries who move from a major project in one part of the country to another, as did the labouring gangs and earth-moving equipment drivers in the 1960s building British motorways. There are people who are reluctant to move, however, staying in their home area even if they cannot find any employment there.

The reasons why some people are prepared to move can stem from their wish to improve their lot or because they enjoy a change of scene. In order to move from one location to another, however, people must overcome the *barriers to mobility* that keep the non-mobile at home. There are family ties, friends and the comfort of familiar places. Such ties can bind members of an extended family – those with grandparents, aunts and other relations in the group – closely to a neighbourhood. Also the familiar is often preferred to the uncertainties of change. Older people set in their ways are often less inclined to make a change. Another and important barrier to geographical mobility of labour appears to be lack of knowledge in the sense of *imperfect information* on available opportunities. In addition, the expense of moving home and difficulties in finding a suitable house are a further barrier for many people who might otherwise change the area where they work.

Occupational mobility – the ease of movement between different jobs – is sometimes limited by training. The bricklayer cannot become a motor mechanic, or the railway engine driver become a TV repairer without re-training. For some occupations this training can last several years with low pay during that time. The student qualifying as a lawyer makes financial sacrifices as does the apprentice toolmaker to become qualified. However, skilled men or women can do unskilled jobs but generally are unwilling to do this for reasons which are not solely financial.

Once trained the tool-maker and lawyer, among others, often become occupationally mobile *within* their trade or profession and more geographically mobile. Working perhaps as a tool-maker in general engineering in Huddersfield after completing an apprenticeship, a man may later move with his skills to a firm in Bournemouth making plastic mouldings where he becomes a design engineer.

Assignments

3.12 Why are workers often reluctant to change their jobs? What effect does this have on employment in different regions of the UK? (AEB 1975)

3.13 List government schemes at the time of your studies to assist individuals improve their (a) geographical mobility and (b) occupational mobility.

3.14 In many jobs women were and juveniles are paid less than men and adults for doing the same work. Discuss the economic case for and against equal pay for equal work.

3.15* Group research: find out from two local factories and/or retail organisations at least two types of machine used in each business. Which of these machines are occupationally mobile? Which are geographically mobile? Note reasons for each machine's mobility or lack of it.

3.16 What effect would increased quantity and/or quality of factors of production have on the Production Possibility Curve of Figure 1.2?

3.17 'There are four factors of production and four corresponding types of income.' Explain this statement and give examples.

Suggested further reading

C D Harbury, *An Introduction to Economic Behaviour* (Fontana, 1971), Chapter 2
Harvey, Chapters 16, 17 and 18
Powicke, Chapter 4
G Stanlake, *Introductory Economics* (3rd edition, Longmans, 1976), Chapter 3
H Williamson, *The Trade Unions* (Heinemann, 1970)

Chapter 4

Production: combining the factors

The economist's definition of production covers the making of all commodities, both goods and services (remember chapter 1?). These may be consumer or producer goods, durables or non-durables, public or private goods. We will look at the nature of demands in a later chapter, but for the moment we can assume there is a demand for the output produced.

Division of labour

Specialisation by product
Instead of everyone trying to make all he or she personally needs, we each concentrate on making a particular commodity or part of it. This specialisation is one aspect of the division of labour. The practice of each person producing a single good or a service was adopted in pre-historic times when men first lived in families or small communities. Two or three might hunt, another make spears, the women cooked. The sum of their output using limited resources (see Figure 4.1) produced more than if each man had hunted for himself, made his own spears and done the cooking.

In the 20th century, craftsmen are among the few workers who may still specialise in making a complete product. The potter may cast the clay, glaze *and* fire the pot. But most workers carry out only one in a series of processes entailed in making a good.

Specialisation by process
By splitting down the production of a good into a series of processes, workers become even more specialised. This enables them to produce more with the same resources. The group of three potters might each do all the stages in making seven pots a day, but if one moulded all the clay shapes, a second did the glazing and a third loaded the kilns firing the pots, then the three might produce 25 pots a day, four more than they could make by each doing all the processes on 21 pots (3 × 7 each). This method of specialisation by process goes back to early times and by the late 17th century families making nails in Staffordshire divided up the work. Father forged the heavier nails, his children filed points on them, while mother might cut wire into lengths ready to form smaller nails. When industry moved into factories during the Industrial Revolution, the processes of production were often further divided enabling an even greater specialisation resulting in greater output.

This benefit of specialisation was stressed by Adam Smith in *The Wealth of Nations* first published in 1776. His analysis of the division of labour in pin making (see Figure 4.2) shows the principle. Smith also believed that this division of labour

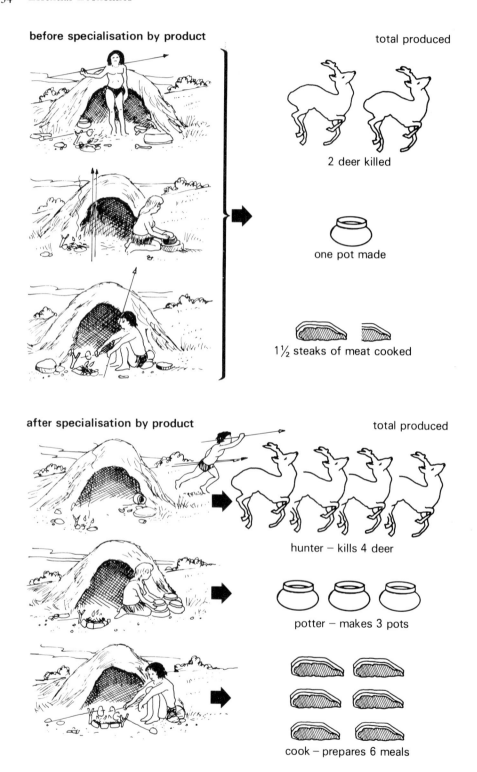

before specialisation by product

total produced

2 deer killed

one pot made

1½ steaks of meat cooked

after specialisation by product

total produced

hunter – kills 4 deer

potter – makes 3 pots

cook – prepares 6 meals

Figure 4.1   Specialisation by product.

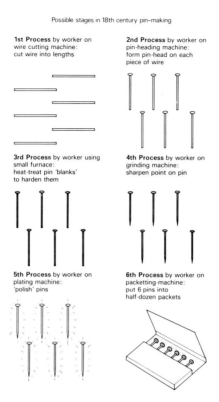

Possible stages in 18th century pin-making

1st Process by worker on wire cutting machine: cut wire into lengths

2nd Process by worker on pin-heading machine: form pin-head on each piece of wire

3rd Process by worker using small furnace: heat-treat pin 'blanks' to harden them

4th Process by worker on grinding machine: sharpen point on pin

5th Process by worker on plating machine: 'polish' pins

6th Process by worker on packetting-machine: put 6 pins into half-dozen packets

Figure 4.2   Illustration of specialisation by process.

could enable all individuals whatever their abilities, to play a part in the production process, making the best use of their abilities, and so increase a nation's output.

By the 1970s the division of labour has reached some extremes with workers spending all their working days merely guiding boxes round the curves of a conveyor shute. The monotony of this and of jobs on assembly lines, has brought the division of labour into conflict with the social desirability of job satisfaction.

Advantage of the division of labour
The advantage is a greater amount of production from given factors of production, for the following reasons:

a Practice makes perfect.
b No time is lost changing tools or re-organising work for different tasks.
c Less training is needed in learning how to do one rather than several processes.
d Special machines can be used (see below).
e Labour is potentially more mobile as a person with a particular skill – a welder, a truck driver and so on – may bring his or her special skill from production of one commodity to the production of another, possibly in a different business and/or location.
f Full use can be made of a person's natural ability; workers can concentrate on the job at which they have the greatest skills in comparison with other workers – their comparative advantage (see below).

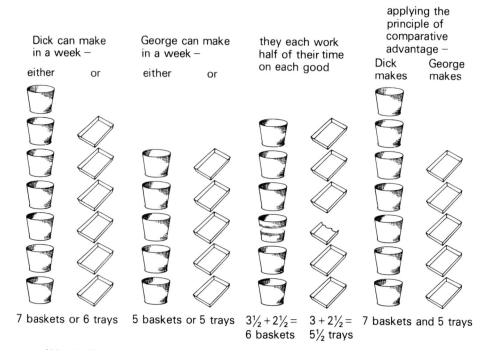

Dick can make in a week –	George can make in a week –	they each work half of their time on each good	applying the principle of comparative advantage –

7 baskets or 6 trays   5 baskets or 5 trays   3½ + 2½ =   3 + 2½ =   7 baskets and 5 trays
6 baskets   5½ trays

Although Dick is better at making both baskets and trays, the most output is obtained in a week when he concentrates on baskets, and George concentrates on trays. For Dick is 40% better than George at making baskets but only 20% better at making trays.

Figure 4.3   The principle of comparative advantage.

Specialised machinery

The breaking down of a good's production into a series of processes may show up the possibilities for a special machine not apparent when watching a craftsman make the complete good. Machines are generally faster and more precise in the jobs they do by comparison with work done by hand. Therefore a machine is often used provided there is enough work to warrant its expense, for there is no point in having, for example, a radial drill for light work taking up a few minutes a day, when this can be done with existing tools.

Comparative advantage

The concept of some people being better than others at various tasks can be developed further (see Figure 4.3). If each worker concentrates on the tasks he or she performs 'best,' higher ouput can be produced from given inputs. This is known as the Principle of Comparative Advantage.

Let's look at an example. Fred and Charley work together making chairs. How can they maximise their output? For example, Charley may make 100 chair legs a day, and Fred only 50. But Charley is also able to make 60 chair backs a day to Fred's 20. Although Charley is better at both jobs, he is *three* times as effective at making chair backs but only *twice* as good as Fred in making legs. Charley has an *absolute advantage* in making both items, and a *comparative advantage* – three times compared to twice – in producing chair backs. Looking at the position from Fred's point of view, his comparative advantage lies in making legs as he is only a third as effective as Charley in producing backs, but half as effective in making legs.

According to the Principle of Comparative Advantage, the highest level of output is achieved if each worker specialises in the task at which he or she is 'relatively better' than others – according to his or her comparative advantage.

Disadvantages of the division of labour
Despite the advantages of increased output through specialisation there are drawbacks, both social and economic:

a   Monotonous repetition on a single task can lead workers to lose interest in the quality of what is produced.
b   Fewer skilled operators and craftsmen are needed – although more machine designers and maintenance technicians may be employed.
c   Greater interdependence occurs between stages in a production process, between processes, and in an economy as a whole, for example – when a car component factory is shut down, factories producing cars may close when stocks of these components have been used up.
d   Slow workers in a team or on a production line have difficulty keeping pace with others doing different processes in a sequence.
e   Risk of unemployment may be greater for the worker with a single skill is less likely to find other work if (say) new machines or techniques are introduced, unlike the craftsman whose skill can be used perhaps in many different production processes. (But note the advantage of shorter or no training for one skill offsets this.)
f   A greater standardisation of products results in most households having the same type of taps or TVs or whatever, although this can be less harmful than some aesthetes believe.

The standardisation of products, although disliked by some, enables many people to have things otherwise not available to them – the mass-produced family car or the domestic refrigerator, for example. Standardisation can also lead to improved design and quality of the product because greater attention can be focused on design and quality control of standard goods produced in large numbers.

Limits to the division of labour
When production in a community is broken down among 'specialists', our two or three hunters, the spear maker and the cooks, each person chips in his or her work and increased output results. However, this output must be divided in some way between these 'specialists'. In modern societies this usually – although not necessarily – entails the use of money (see chapter 14) with workers paid in money rather than kind. This money can then be exchanged for the goods they want.

Division of labour between processes is impractical if only a few articles are being made for a small market. Custom-made individual surf boards, for example, are usually assembled by one person. Only where there are many customers creating a *large-sized* market can mass-production techniques with division of labour be applied satisfactorily.

Where a service is of a personal nature – the hair-stylist, the portrait photographer are examples – the work cannot be easily divided. The stylist is the only person to cut your hair although someone else may wash it. The photographer is the only one who actually takes your portrait although someone else may develop the film.

Assignments

4.1 Give at least three examples of the division of labour by product and/or process in your home or college.

4.2 Construct a simple example to show that maximising output for a day's labour by two workers is obtained by organising their efforts according to the Principle of Comparative Advantage.

4.3* Group research: list the stages in manufacture for two or three finished goods – either from production in local industries or from books in your library. Illustrate these stages with a flow chart showing each stage in sequence as   ① ⟶ ② ⟶ ③   ... briefly describing each stage, noting the division of labour.

Production

Inputs for outputs
We have seen that there are limits to the principle of division of labour. There are also other important features of production introduced in Figure 4.4.

Fixed and variable factors
The producer in Figure 4.4 has certain factors of production (inputs) the quantity of which does not alter no matter what level of output(s) is achieved. The amount of land, machines, the buildings and other fixed capital goods does not change whether the boat builders are making 15 or 40 boats a week. These factors of production are therefore *fixed factors*. The builders in the diagram pay the same local government rates, rents and interest on capital whether or not they make any boats.

The amount of plastic resin, timber strengtheners, fibre glass and other materials used in making the boats varies according to how many are produced – 3500 kilograms of resin for 10; 35 000 kilograms for 100 and so on. The amount of labour needed to laminate fibre glass with resin also varies with the number of boats. As the amount of such factors fluctuates with the volume of production, they are called *variable factors*. And the amount spent on these varies with output.

Period of production
The distinction between whether a factor is fixed or variable arises only in the 'short term' (see Figure 4.4). We will come in a moment to the definition of short term. For producers, having ensured that their existing variable factors are used to the full, have two different decisions to make when the demand for their products changes. For example, as more people want to buy the builder's boats of Figure 4.4, the firm will employ more labour and get more materials to increase the amount of output. This is a fairly straightforward decision to increase the variable factors when increased demand is not a flash-in-the-pan. However, once the factory and machines are fully employed, the output reaches an optimum level from the given fixed factors. A point explained in more detail in chapter 5.

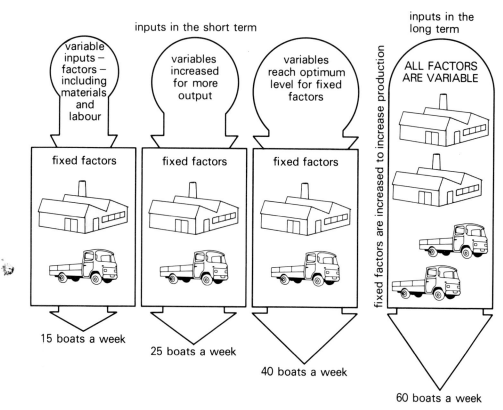

Figure 4.4   In the short term there are fixed and variable factors of production; in the long term *all* factors are variable.

The more difficult decision has now to be made. Should more machinery and/or buildings be put into the business? That is: should the fixed factors be increased? If the producer is confident that the increased demand will be sustained, he will increase his fixed factors.

However it takes time to install new machines, to put up buildings and otherwise increase the fixed factors – even renting a factory takes time to arrange. In the life of a business these decisions are made in the circumstances described above, and when fixed factors are due to be replaced. (One boat builder has increased factory floor space five times in a decade.) The amount of fixed factors can therefore be regarded as variable over a long period and be adjusted to suit the level of production.

For this reason all factors become variable in the long term, and fixed factors can only occur in the short run (or short term). The short run is then defined as the period over which fixed inputs cannot be varied. The other inputs in this short term are variable. Also in the short run there are corresponding fixed and variable costs. The long run in this context is the period over which all factors may be freely varied.

How long is 'long run'?
No exact period of time – months, year or decades – can be set to distinguish the long run from the short run. These periods vary from industry to industry, according to time needed to alter the amount of fixed factors. In generating electricity, for

example, ten years can elapse between the decision to increase such fixed factors as power stations and these units beginning to generate electricity. In this case the long run is ten years.

In a small engineering shop, however, fixed factors might be increased in a matter of weeks. A new standard machine from the machine makers' stocks might only take a couple of weeks to buy and install. So this period of weeks will be the long run for this production.

The Law of Diminishing Returns

Most people are familiar with the problem of too many cooks. For once you have so many cooks, an extra helper can only make a smaller addition than the man joining before him, in the number of loaves baked. Eventually there are so many people in the kitchen that when more helpers arrive, making any bread becomes impossible. They need a second kitchen or in other words: to increase the fixed factors.

For production in the short run a producer must decide what is the most suitable proportion of fixed to variable factors. The farmer producer of Figure 4.5 needs to know how many man-weeks of labour to employ in his field – a fixed amount of land. (A man-week is the work of one man for a week; two men's work for a week or one man's work for two weeks is two man-weeks and so on.) But once a certain amount of labour has been used on the farmer's field, each additional man-week's labour will give a smaller increase in output than the previous man-week employed.

The inevitable fall in the 'marginal product' is described by the *Law of Diminishing Marginal Returns*, more shortly and usually called the *Law of Diminishing Returns*, or sometimes: the *Law of Variable Proportions*. This shows the way the marginal product varies as different amounts of a variable factor are combined with a given amount of a fixed factor. Therefore this law only applies in the short run.

Marginal returns

Output does not usually vary directly with increases or decreases of variable input. Therefore producers in general and our farmer of Figure 4.5, in particular, ought to know how much increase there will be in output for each additional unit of variable input employed. The farmer knows that sowing seeds densely will not necessarily give him a better crop. In much the same way difficulties can arise when employing labour on the field. Too many men get in each others' way, but too few are unable to get the best results from the field.

The amount of increase in output for each additional unit of variable input is not constant, however, over a range of input levels. One man working for the equivalent of a week, digging, sowing and later weeding and reaping the crops in Figure 4.5, produces 1 tonne of wheat. Therefore the first 'additional' unit of labour produced a tonne of wheat. Employing two men who are able to follow the principle of division of labour, raised output from 1 to 3 tonnes, an increase in output or *Marginal Product* of 2 tonnes. Each additional unit of a variable factor employed gives an *increase* in the addition to output until seven men are employed. With six men the total output was 21 tonnes. With one additional unit bringing the variable input to seven man-weeks, output rose to 28 tonnes – a Marginal Product of 7 tonnes (28–21 tonnes).

But by increasing the input by one unit from seven to eight, the scene changes:

Total product (tonnes of wheat) col (1)	Amount of labour employed (in man weeks) col (2)	Average product (2) ÷ (1) col (3)	Marginal product col (4)
1	1	1	1
3	2	*	2
6	3	2	*
10	4	2½	4
15	5	3	*
21	6	3½	6
28	7	4	7
34	8	4¼	6
39	9	4⅓	5
43	10	*	4
45	11	*	2
46	12	*	*

*items to be completed in Assignment 4.5

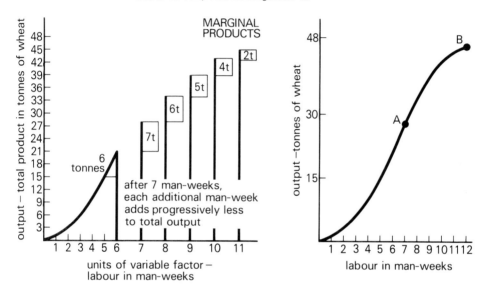

Figure 4.5   The Law of Diminishing Returns.

now the Marginal Product is only 6 tonnes. Indeed each additional unit above seven gives progressively smaller increases in output (Marginal Products), although output *in total* continues to rise. The graph in Figure 4.5 shows these smaller and smaller Marginal Products, as input rises above seven men (point A).

Until point A with seven men employed, there was more fixed factor – too large a field – than the available work force could work to advantage. Once beyond point A with more than seven men working, their Marginal Products fall for they cannot all work to their greatest effect. The marginal returns to labour or its Marginal Product decrease. This is logical for we know there are practical limits to how many people can be usefully employed in a kitchen, a field, on a machine, or with any other given amount of fixed factors.

Average Product (AP)
The Marginal Product as an addition to total output does not always tell the producer all he needs to know about production in this context. In comparing output

at different levels, the *average output per unit of input* has significance. For our farmer, when seven man-weeks are employed the output is 28 tonnes, an *Average Product* of 4 tonnes (total production ÷ amount of labour, 28 ÷ 7). Similar calculations show that 11 man-weeks of input yield on average $4\frac{1}{11}$ tonnes. But on employing a twelfth man the Average Product falls to $3\frac{5}{6}$ tonnes.

The farmer may therefore have to consider whether or not it is worth putting a twelfth man into this field.

Diminishing returns

The Law of Diminishing Returns may now be stated: as increasing amounts of a variable factor are applied to a fixed quantity of some other factor, the marginal product will eventually begin to become successively smaller. (The increase in the proportion of variable factors to fixed factors gives rise to the law's alternative name as the *Law of Variable Proportions*.)

As fixed factors only arise in short-run production, the Law of Diminishing Returns only applies in the short run.

To summarise these points: what the producers need to know in the short term is the increase in output for each *extra* unit of variable input employed. This increase in output is the *Marginal Product*, the marginal return to a variable factor of production. The Marginal Product of a factor is defined as: the addition to output (or product) resulting from the employment of one additional unit of the variable factor. The Law of Diminishing Returns describes the variation in marginal product as the amount of the variable factor is increased. You have also seen that average product eventually decreases. An understanding of these principles is important in deciding on the most profitable level of output.

Assignments

4.4 Which of the following types of labour should be classified as variable factors: (*a*) bricklayers paid by the hour; (*b*) salaried managers supervising factory work; (*c*) assemblers of electric fires paid on piece-work rates; and (*d*) a swimming bath attendant? Explain your answers.

4.5 Complete the * items in columns (3) and (4) of Figure 4.5, by calculating the Marginal Product for these missing items.

4.6 Plot on the same axes the two graphs for Average Product (column (3)) and for Marginal Product (column (4)) from the figures in Figure 4.5. What do you notice about the point where the Marginal Product graph crosses the Average Product graph? Can you explain this result?

4.7 What values is the Marginal Product likely to take in Figure 4.5 at levels of variable factor usage in excess of 12 man-weeks (that is: to the right of point B)?

4.8 What do you understand by the long run? Illustrate your answer with two examples showing how the length of the run differs between industries.

Production costs

Fixed and variable costs

So far we have looked at inputs and outputs in terms of quantity, so many hours for so many tonnes, so many hectares of land for so many tonnes of a crop. The relationship between such inputs and outputs may be expressed as production costs – the £:p for labour, for raw materials and other factors. A producer wants to know what an extra unit of output will cost him, in the price he pays for extra labour, extra raw materials, etc used to produce it.

To work out these costs the inputs are classified in two groups, those that are fixed and those which are variable. The fixed costs must be paid whatever production is achieved. They are the fixed *overheads* including rent, rates and some salaries which have to be paid even if the producer's factory is closed. They correspond to the fixed factors of production. But note from Figure 4.6 that the more units produced for a given total of fixed costs, the smaller the fixed cost per unit. In other words, the better the spread of overheads.

Economists include *normal profit* in fixed costs. This is the amount which a producer must earn to be persuaded to stay in a particular industry, and is the amount he could earn in the next best alternative production. (This normal profit is described as a form of transfer earning.) Any excess over 'normal profit' is called super-normal profit or excess profit, and is an example of the economic rent described on page 37. As a transfer earning, normal profit is an opportunity cost. For example: there is income sacrificed on using land for a house rather than agriculture. Normal profit is, therefore, determined by the amount which could have been earned in the alternative use – agriculture, in this example.

Producer's costs

Output quantity	Fixed costs	Variable costs	Total costs	Average variable costs	Average total costs	Marginal costs
		(see note 1)	(Col (2) + (3))	(Col (3) ÷ (1))	(Col (4) ÷ (1))	(see note 2)
(1)	(2) £	(3) £	(4) £	(5) £	(6) £	(7) £
0	50	0	50	—	—	—
1	50	80	130	80	130	80
2	50	110	160	55	80	30
3	50	130	180	$43\frac{1}{3}$	60	20
4	50	190	240	$47\frac{1}{2}$	60	60
5	50	300	350	60	70	110

Notes: 1. Variable costs are those varying directly with output – the cost of variable factors used.
2. Marginal cost is the increase in total cost as output is increased by one unit. For example, the increase in output from 3 units to 4 raised total costs (column (4)) from £180 to £240, a marginal cost of £60.
3. Average costs measure *costs per unit of output* – unit costs. The average total cost equals 'total costs' (column (4)) divided by output (column (1)). In the same way 'average variable costs' are calculated by dividing 'total variable costs' (column (3)) by output (column (1)).

Figure 4.6   Production costs.

Variable costs fluctuate with the level of output, in our example (Figure 4.6) they include costs for labour, raw materials and any other variable factors. These costs are determined by the prices of factors and the amounts they produce. They are, therefore, sometimes also called *direct* or *prime costs*. The more goods produced, the greater the total cost of raw material and other variable inputs consumed in production will be. The variable costs per unit of *output* are determined not only by these input costs but also by the average and/or marginal product (see Assignments 4.9 and 4.10). Nevertheless the distinction between fixed and variable costs is made according to whether or not they vary with output (see Figure 4.6). But do not forget that in the long run all factors and associated costs are variable.

Average and marginal costs
The calculation of average and marginal products described above can be used to calculate in £:p the average and marginal costs. The average costs are calculated – for total, variable or fixed elements – by dividing these costs by the quantity produced. Marginal cost is the *increase* in total costs incurred when output is increased by one unit (see Figure 4.6).

Assignments

4.9 A producer has £50 of fixed costs. Plot a graph with 'Average Fixed Costs' on the vertical axis and 'Quantities produced from 1 to 20 a week' along the horizontal axis. What will happen to Average Fixed Costs as output becomes very large?

4.10 Plot graphs of the Average Variable Costs, Average Total Costs, and Marginal Costs from columns (5), (6) and (7) of Figure 4.6, on the similar *axes* as in 4.9 above, with £:p on the vertical and output on the horizontal axis. What do you notice about the points where the Marginal Cost curve cuts the Average Total Cost curve? Can you explain this?

4.11 Calculate the increase in variable costs for each unit of increased output shown in the table of figures in Figure 4.6. How are these increases related to the Marginal Cost shown in column 7? Can you explain this relationship?

4.12

Successive units of output	Total cost (£)	Average cost (£)	Marginal cost (£)
1	20	20	20
2	32		
3		14	
4			6
5	50		

Use data in the above table to calculate: (*a*) Total cost at an output of 4 units; (*b*) Average Cost when Marginal Cost is £12; and (*c*) Marginal Cost when Average Cost is £10. (AEB 1972)

4.13 The following figures refer to output and total cost of a manufactured commodity:

Output	Total cost (£)
0	100
1	120
2	134
3	144
4	152

(a) What are the fixed costs?
(b) (i) What is Average Cost when total cost is £152?
    (ii) What is Marginal Cost of the third unit?

(AEB 1972)

4.14 Twenty-five workers, each earning a weekly wage of £25.50 for a 5-day working week are employed by a small manufacturing firm. During a certain week they produced 7500 articles. Other costs incurred by the firm during the week included:

	(£)
Power	90.00
Raw materials	310.00
Interest charges on capital assets	40.50
Rent and rates	52.75

Calculate:
   (a) the *Variable Costs* incurred during the week;
   (b) the *average daily output* per worker. (AEB 1973)

Suggestions for further reading

J Hanson, *A Textbook of Economics* (6th edition, MacDonald and Evans, 1972).
   Chapter 3
Harbury, Chapter 2
Stanlake, Chapters 4, 5 and 6

Chapter 5
Large- or small-scale production?

Having looked at combining the factors of production, we can now look at what happens when the size (or scale) of production changes. Entrepreneurs must somehow decide on what scale to produce. If production is for profit – some may work for personal satisfaction rather than gain – you would expect the entrepreneur to aim at the scale of production where unit costs are lowest for the output produced. You will remember there were fixed and variable factors to consider in the short term, but in the long term all factors are variable. In this long term, therefore, the entrepreneur can decide his scale of production.

Economies of scale

How big?
As all factors are variable in the long term, the relation of inputs to outputs varies as a matter of scale. If the producer doubles all his inputs and this doubles his output, there is a direct relationship between the size or scale of this production process and

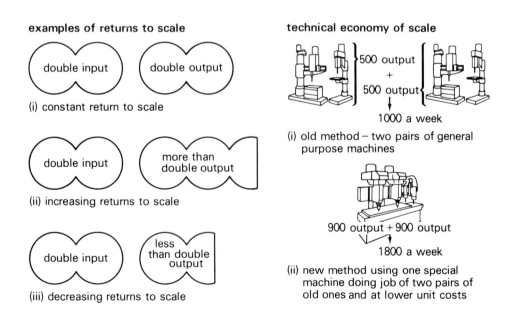

examples of returns to scale

double input   double output

(i) constant return to scale

double input   more than double output

(ii) increasing returns to scale

double input   less than double output

(iii) decreasing returns to scale

Figure 5.1*a*   Returns to scale.

technical economy of scale

500 output
+
500 output
1000 a week

(i) old method – two pairs of general purpose machines

900 output + 900 output
1800 a week

(ii) new method using one special machine doing job of two pairs of old ones and at lower unit costs

Figure 5.1*b*   Technical economies of scale.

its output. With this direct relationship of inputs to outputs, the producer is operating under *constant return to scale*. But on doubling the inputs the producer may get more than double the output. Then he is operating under *increasing returns to scale* with decreasing long-run average costs. Or he may double inputs and get less than twice the output, operating under *decreasing returns to scale* (see Figure 5.1).

In deciding the optimum scale of production, after establishing the likely demand for his output, an entrepreneur may take account of economic and other considerations. The owner of a one-man business may prefer to turn away work rather than have the worry of running a bigger organisation. But economic considerations have a habit of asserting themselves over other notions, for his customers may drift away to his rivals who can produce more cheaply on a large scale.

There are both economies and disadvantages (diseconomies) of large-scale production. We will look first at the economies and return to the diseconomies on page 75.

These economies of scale fall into two categories. The first are internal economies which the entrepreneur can plan to achieve by increasing the scale of production. A firm may decide to increase its factors of production – staff, machines, buildings, perhaps – and produce more output of (say) tobacco pipes. The second category is external economies through the growth of the whole industry in which this or any firm operates. For if the industry expands because pipe-smoking in general becomes more fashionable, there may be external economies of scale benefiting the individual firm, but arising from the growth of the whole industry.

Internal economies of scale
Internal economies of scale fall into five groups – technical, managerial, commercial (or marketing), financial and risk bearing.

1. Technical economies of scale. These economies are brought about because different techniques and equipment can often be employed in large-scale production which cannot be adopted by small-scale producers.

In the larger unit there may be a greater degree of specialisation or division of labour (see Figure 5.1). Special machines may also be employed: equipment that cannot be used to advantage in small-scale production for there the special machines would not be used to the full. That is, they might run for only 20 hours in a 40-hour week. Since there is no way to install half a machine economists regard such factors as indivisible. However, the larger producer will be able to keep it fully occupied. He may also be able to undertake stages in the production process previously undertaken by others. For example, he may install die-casting equipment to make castings rather than buying these.

Technical economies of scale will also arise because the cost of machinery does not vary in direct proportion to its capacity. Neither the purchase price nor the running costs of a 32-tonne lorry, for example, amount to as much as twice these for a 16-tonner. The large-scale producer benefits in this case moving 32 tonnes of goods at a lower unit cost (cost per tonne kilometre) than the producer using a 16-tonner on the same run. The labour costs per unit carried can also be lower with the same driver and mate needed on a 16-tonne vehicle as on a 32-tonner.

Large-scale producers may link processes where these are separated – often in different organisations – in small-scale production. This linking of two or more processes can save waste and handling costs, including the labour for moving output from one process to the next (see Figure 5.1). But there are often less obvious savings especially in processes which can be continuous when on a large scale (that is, processes which take raw material through several connected stages running without a stop in making a finished good). In a continuous process making sheet steel, for example, there is much less wasted heat – and the power to create it – if ore converted to iron passes to the stage making this into steel ingots and these are passed straight on to the mills rolling the sheets. When these stages in making steel sheets were at different locations there were reheating processes in making iron into steel and again before the steel ingots could be rolled into plates. And there were greater transport costs between each stage.

In large-scale production there is also an economy in those costs that do not fluctuate much whatever the output. Design and development are a clear example. They are similar to those fixed costs which can be spread over production in the way explained on page 63.

2. Managerial economies of scale. As the scale of production increases, an organisation may employ more and different specialist managers – a form of division of labour. A personnel manager might be appointed, perhaps trained to interview and select the right employees for jobs rather than a general manager doing this. In small-scale production many managers have to be Jacks (if not Kings) of all trades.

3. Commercial economies of scale. Specialist buyers and salesmen may be employed in large-scale production units, with advantages akin to those given above for specialised management. But the major marketing economies of scale lie in the purchase, handling and distribution of goods in greater quantities. Raw materials may be bought in bulk at lower unit costs than to a small producer. The bulk quantities may also be shipped to the large-scale producer at favourable rates, for transport costs do not increase proportionally to weight for most materials.

In marketing commodities on a large scale, goods may be sold in big consignments. These are often cheaper to pack per unit and to transport to customers, than smaller consignments. Heinz beans, for example, are sold in several family sizes, the most popular being $7\frac{3}{4}$ oz and $15\frac{3}{4}$ oz tins. They also sell large tins of 28 oz and 92 oz for use in cafés and other catering organisations. The price per ounce in these larger tins is about 20% less than for the smaller tins. Also the salesman selling 10 cases of beans can take as long for a visit and travel as far to see a customer as the man selling 100 cases.

There are also other administrative advantages in large-scale operations. It frequently costs as much to process an invoice of £10 as one of £10 000. The same can be said of other paperwork – processing customers' orders, requisitioning (documenting requirements from) stock, preparing consignment notes and other shipping documents and so on. For these reasons many small-scale orders are charged at a minimum price – £5 perhaps – although the goods are priced at less than this in the firm's catalogue.

4. Financial economies of scale. Large-scale producers can borrow money more easily and cheaply than smaller producers, because bankers and others often prefer to lend £1 million to a reputable firm with assets of £100 million, rather than lend £50 to a one-man business of unknown repute. The large-scale producer also gets his loan at lower interest rates because of his reputation through the size of his firm. There are, however, other considerations than the scale of an enterprise taken into account when making a loan or borrowing (see chapter 8).

5. Risks bearing economies of scale. The large-scale producer benefits from spreading the risks – risk bearing economies – in both the supply of his raw materials and possible changes in customers' demand. By buying raw materials from different sources, diversifying the sources of supply, the large-scale producer has a safeguard against shortages. If one supplier fails to deliver materials, in all probability the others will keep the producer supplied. For this reason large-scale chocolate manufacturers buy cocoa beans from several countries. Then the blight on one crop does not entirely cut off their raw material supply of these beans.

The large producer can to some extent also spread the risk of customers changing their tastes, by producing a range of products. Many tobacco manufacturers have therefore diversified into food processing, cosmetics and other businesses. Then a fall in demand for cigarettes can be offset in part at least by sales of other goods. An example is the Imperial Group Ltd. In 1975 they owned not only tobacco companies like W D & H O Wills and Players, but also breweries (including Courages), soft drink manufacturers (Cantrell & Cochrane), the Golden Wonder potato crisp company and the Ross companies producing frozen foods, eggs, poultry and seafoods.

This diversification of a business can take several forms, all of which are easier in large-scale production than in small. A firm can diversify into different types of product as above, or diversification may be in the range of one product – selling small *and* big cars, perhaps. The large business may also diversify its markets, selling in many countries to even out fluctuations in the home country's demand.

In short: the large-scale producer can to some extent reduce the risks to both his supplies and sales by producing a variety of goods. However, the larger the producer's operations, the harder his fall might be should he get the scale of his production and other decisions wrong. On the other hand, the same financial decision – buying a £1000 machine, say – is less of a risk for the big producer than for the small.

External economies of scale

While the internal economies – technical, managerial, commercial, financial and risk bearing – are all within the control of the entrepreneur, external economies are outside it. These external economies arise from the growth of an industry of which a producer is part (see Figure 5.2). These, therefore, occur outside the individual firm and are of three different types – concentration, information and disintegration.

1. External economies of concentration. When several firms in one industry grow larger in a locality, the concentration of their needs for special services attracts these to the area. The individual specialists and special services may range from experts in branches of a local bank with special knowledge of the industry's financial needs, to special transport facilities – part of the locality's infra-structure of roads, rail links, etc – designed to serve the industry's needs.

The area will also build up a work force skilled in the industry's processes and used to its conditions – as miners are used to shift work or maintenance engineers to weekend working. In turn this work force will be helped by local college and training

Examples of some external economies of scale for furniture manufacturers in High Wycombe

Through concentration:

120 furniture factories in or near the town of High Wycombe produce 75% of the UK's output of wooden chairs, among other furniture.

This concentration of producers has attracted experts to the locality including the Forest Products Research Laboratory and the Timber Research Association.

The local workforce of 9000 in furniture and allied trades includes apprentices and other trainees attending the local technical college, with its 'unrivalled facilities for instruction in all aspects of the furniture industry'.

By 1865 the area had a reputation for its furniture with 20 factories selling chairs etc to London and the Midlands, creating a demand for the town's furniture which brought more manufacturers to the area to meet the increased demand.

Through economies of information:

Specialist publications of the furniture trade include the quarterly bulletin of the Furniture Industry's Research Association. Information and other services are provided by the High Wycombe Furniture Manufacturers' Society, an association that also has played a part in the good relations between the local manufacturers and their workers in the Furniture, Timber and Allied Trades Union.

Through economies of disintegration:

Some firms who at one time made a range of furniture now specialise in making particular types of furniture with, say, laminated tops. Other manufacturers may then place this work with the specialist and so buy in the laminated table tops they need in making kitchen furniture.

Figure 5.2   External economies of scale.

centre courses to prepare people entering the industry.

Another feature arising from the geographical concentration of firms of one industry is the development of local manufacture of special machines used in it. Having a local source for such machines has advantages in servicing, in exchanging ideas between a machine's builders and those operating it, and other contacts where machine makers and their manufacturer customers come together. In this way the British United Shoe Machinery Company Ltd provide specialised shoe making machinery for the boot and shoe industry in Leicester and Northampton.

The concentration of firms and supporting services leads to the locality developing a reputation for the industry's products. This helps these producers to sell their goods by establishing a market for this locality's goods (see Figure 5.2).

A firm having a high concentration of an industry's output may also benefit with sales increased to a larger extent than its rivals, when the industry's sales increase. This gives that firm an external economy of concentration whether or not its production is geographically concentrated.

2. External economies of information. Firms need a whole host of facts and figures – next year's likely crops for raw materials, possibly; foreign governments' regulations affecting both supplies and sales; the cost of borrowing money; trends in wage and other cost rates. While this information may all be available in some form from Government and other sources including overseas magazines, a large industry can set up or attract others to set up special information services for its producers. For example, many industries have trade magazines like the *Building Trade Journal* and *Chemical Age*. These give not only facts and figures of interest but also informed comment on their implications for the industry, and details of new equipment and techniques. Similarly institutions like the Motor Industry Research Association and the Production Engineering Research Association provide facilities for exchanging ideas and joint efforts in research.

3. External economies of disintegration. This economy of scale is not the contradiction it might appear, for as the industry grows the benefits of specialisation can be extended to particular producers of parts or processes. Firms may then develop to specialise in doing a particular process or making a particular component for other firms in the industry. This specialisation enables this firm to get economies of scale through the size of its production of this one part or process. This is generally known as 'vertical disintegration'. For example, when the motor industry grew, firms like Joseph Lucas specialised in making motor car lamps and electrics, while Girling specialised in components for brakes and clutches.

Assignments

5.1 (*a*) Describe some of the economies which can be achieved through large-scale production. (*b*) What external economies of scale attract firms to locate their business in the south-east of England? (JMB 1975)

5.2 What is meant by internal and external economies of scale? Explain (*a*) how a steel works may obtain internal economies, and (*b*) how a West Riding woollen manufacturer may obtain external economies. (L 1972)

5.3* Group research: trace two trade magazines for industrial or agricultural activities, and note three examples from each in advertising or articles on current information of importance to these producers.

5.4* List and explain examples of (*a*) external economies of concentration, and (*b*) external diseconomies of concentration, in any area with which you are familiar.

Horizontal and vertical integration

Specialisation or diversification?
You have seen that there are advantages in *specialisation* and that there are also advantages in *diversification*, a dichotomy often seen in the strong conflict of views between works managers and sales managers! The works managers' preference is often for expansion with little or no variety of size, colour and so on in the goods made. The sales managers usually want as great a variety as possible in the output of goods, which widens the range of customers.

Almost every producer faces a similar problem: does he continue to specialise or diversify into other markets? Does he maximise the benefits of specialisation or diversify the risks? In both cases the entrepreneur is looking for economies of scale. These may be brought about by a single firm growing larger, or by amalgamations and mergers. These takeovers of one firm by another can happen because the

instigator of the deal is motivated by economies of scale. Or – as you will see later –
he may want to achieve a degree of monopoly by supplying a larger slice of the
market.

Forms of growth

A firm may grow by increasing its sales through attracting more customers, the most
usual way for small firms to reach medium size. Once of medium size or possibly
earlier in its growth, the firm or business may expand by acquiring other firms (see
Figure 5.3). If these firms are in the same type of production, bringing them together
is known as *horizontal integration*. But if the businesses acquired are suppliers to the
expanding firm, or distributors of its products, the merger is *vertical integration*.
Other forms of integration are *lateral* and *conglomerate* integration, as we shall see
below.

Horizontal integration

In acquiring businesses producing very similar goods (Figure 5.3) an expanding firm
expects to gain the benefits of large-scale production. Only one sales force will be
needed, one head office and probably fewer factories to produce as much as the two
firms previously made together.

   Horizontal integration also reduces the amount of competition, achieving some
degree of monopoly: we will come back to this topic, but the now larger business
may perhaps reduce the variety of goods sold. Then customers have less choice as
they have only the monopolist – or at least fewer suppliers – to buy from. So with a
larger integrated business the producer tends to run less risk of losing customers to
competitors.

   While the horizontal integration of businesses is illustrated above in terms of
manufacturing producers, this integration may also be between producers in service
industries. Retail shops, garages, professional and other firms may each be horizon-
tally integrated in their particular service industry. For example: the National
Provincial Bank's merger with the Westminster Bank was a horizontal integration
forming the National Westminster Bank.

Lateral integration

Merging two businesses which produce similar products but not perfect substitutes
is known as *lateral integration*. The difference between lateral and horizontal integration is one of degree. Horizontal integration – as we have seen – is a merger of firms
producing close substitutes. But when the Brooke Bond Company merged with the
Oxo Company to form Brooke Bond Oxo Limited, this was a lateral integration. For,
although tea is a beverage, it is not a close substitute for beef extract.

Vertical integration

We have seen that many products are made in stages – textile threads are spun, then
woven into cloth, dyed and then made into clothes. Each stage can be and often is
carried out by separate firms. These may have originally come into existence as an
industry grew and the economies of disintegration were sought.

   An expanding firm may join together two or more of these production stages in a
vertical integration. The linking of these processes may bring about economies of
scale. For example in 1946 British Leyland (then BMC) acquired the car body

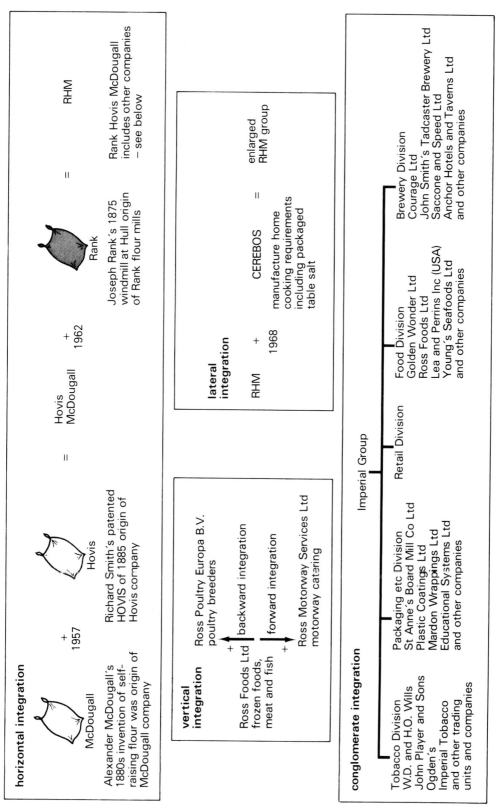

Figure 5.3   Examples of integration.

building Pressed Steel Company, as Fords acquired the Briggs Motor Bodies Company. As the instigator integrated a supplier into the business, this vertical integration was 'backward'. Backward, that is, along the chain of supply towards basic raw materials.

When the producer takes over a distributor as petrol refiners might do when they buy a chain of garages distributing their petrol, the integration is 'forward'. Forward in the chain of supply towards the market – in other words nearer the point of sale to customers. This forward integration can provide more retail outlets obliged to sell (tied to) the expanding producer's goods.

Backward vertical integration is often made to secure an expanding business' sources of supply or at least some of them. Securing supplies in this way, the producer can also get better control over the quality, quantity, availability and cost of these raw materials. Cadbury Schweppes bought cocoa plantations and Brooke Bond Liebig own tea plantations for this reason.

Conglomerate integration
Sometimes an expanding firm may acquire businesses which are not in any way connected with its present activities. This course – conglomerate integration (see Figure 5.3) – is followed to diversify a business. We saw this in Figure 5.3 with Imperial Tobacco, who integrated food processing and other businesses with their tobacco business to form the Imperial Group. Another example was the merger between British Match Corporation and Wilkinson Sword Ltd in 1973.

Elimination of waste
One of the economies of scale achieved by integration is the elimination of waste, since the resulting larger business has – or more precisely its managers have – more opportunity after horizontal integration to rationalise production. They may reduce the variety of products made and cut out wasteful duplication. Where two transport fleets of 16-tonne lorries have been operated, these might be replaced by one fleet of 32-tonners.

Waste may also be eliminated in vertical integration through linking processes as you have seen. It may also reduce duplication in other ways, for there should be less paperwork between what are now probably departments than there was between firms.

Assignments

5.5 Distinguish between horizontal and vertical integration. What motives might prompt a firm to integrate vertically? (IWMC 1971)

5.6 From articles or advertisements in newspapers and/or on television select two examples of conglomerate mergers. List the likely advantages to the firms involved.

5.7 Mergers are often reflected in the names of companies. Next time you visit a supermarket or from the telephone directory Yellow Pages select four to six examples – Rank Hovis McDougall Ltd is one example, Cadbury Schweppes Ltd another. Which type of integration took place in your examples? List the likely benefits to the firms involved.

5.8* If firms experience diminishing returns, why is it that economists often assume that they operate under conditions of economies of scale? (CAFC 1975)

Limitations to size

Limits to mass production

We have seen in chapter 4 that the size of a market limits the extent of division of labour. The market for a product – the number of potential customers who might buy it – equally sets a limit on the size any business may grow to produce it. Also when each item has to be made to meet customers' individual needs, the different specifications of size, shape and perhaps of colour, mean that these goods must be made individually.

Since there are limits to mass production, opportunities arise for small firms to produce in small quantities and to produce the one-off (a single special) product for a customer.

Diseconomies of scale

Big is not necessarily better. The disadvantages of large-scale production arise in part from the inefficiencies that creep into any large organisation. The more people a firm employs, the more difficult they become to organise so that the right decisions are made *quickly*. Also once a decision is made in any large organisation, there are problems in ensuring that it is carried out quickly and efficiently.

The man running his own small business, although he delegates work, knows everybody in the firm. He can physically check by going to look at what happens in the factory or shop. An employee with a complaint can approach the boss as he walks round the factory or shop. But once the firm has more than 500 or so employees, the top people cannot know everybody in the organisation. As the firm or other organisation grows, committees are formed to take decisions and departments are created on the principle of division of labour. These must be consulted about their departmental interests in any decision.

Decisions are often caught up in this web of bureaucracy and the large firm may be slow to respond to any change. Most important of these are the changes in demand for the firm's products. By not responding quickly to customers' new tastes, the large-scale producer can continue producing goods no longer in demand. By comparison the small boutiques, for example, are quick off the mark when fashion changes.

In large businesses such internal inefficiencies can all too easily go undetected despite everyone working hard. Decisions can take too long to make and to put into practice. At the same time customers may resent the lack of personal attention when they are dealing with an apparently faceless organisation, and the business may lose their customers' goodwill.

The employees, remote from the management in a large organisation, can become discontented. Decision-making is out of their hands and they feel that no one listens to their complaints. Then the employees do not feel part of the business, and are less motivated to work hard.

External diseconomies

A further diseconomy of scale arises from sources outside the organisation. These external diseconomies of scale are the opposite of external economies of scale, arising from the growth of an industry. Firms in a growing industry may suffer public displeasure which can turn to social action. Perhaps the industry's effluent (waste)

Size (number employed)	Number of establish- ments	%	Net Output £ million	%
1–24	52 403	56·88	NA	NA
25–99	17 185	18·72	1 573	10·29
100–199	6 137	6·69	1 499	9·80
200–499	5 007	5·46	2 850	18·64
500–999	1 653	1·80	2 313	15·12
1000–1999	789	0·85	2 313	15·13
2000–4999	329	0·36	2 080	13·57
5000–9999	66	0·07	994	6·51
10000 & over	14	0·02	474	3·10
Not available	8 205	9·15	1 193	7·84
	91 788	100·00	15 289	100·00

75% of firms *employing* employ less than 100 people. 1·3% of firms produce 38% of output.

Source: *Census of Production* (HMSO).

Figure 5.4   Distribution by size of manufacturing establishments in the UK 1968.

disposal pollutes the atmosphere, or their heavy vehicles – especially in areas where the industry is concentrated – may eventually congest roads. All these are social costs, the costs to a society having the industry in its midst. Unlike private costs appearing in the individual firms' books, social costs are borne by society as a whole. When the social costs grow large, society may act and laws be passed to make the industry stop the nuisance, often a costly job for large organisations.

Predominance of small firms

Definitions of a small *firm*
The size of a production unit or factory is often as significant as the size of the organisation of which it is part, for as you will remember, a firm may have several identical production units or several units producing different goods. However comparisons between the size of organisations are often useful.

Size may be measured in several ways – by annual sales (turnover), by its stock of capital or assets, and by numbers of employees (see Figure 5.4). Comparisons by 'numbers employed' is a convenient and quick method of judging the size of organisations. But these comparisons must be treated with caution. For 300 employees may be the total work force in a chemical plant with sales of £100 million, while 350 can be employed in a small department store with sales worth only one-hundredth of this amount.

Small firms in the United Kingdom
Despite the limitations of comparisons by numbers employed, these can be useful indicators of an organisation's size. Figure 5.4 shows among other things that 75% of UK manufacturing firms in 1968 each employed less than 100 people, whereas only 1.3% each employed 1000 or more. These large employers, however, produced 38% of the total output, against 10% from all the firms employing 100 or less.

Why so many small firms?

Some small-scale production units and small firms exist because they are already at an optimum size. That is, they are producing goods at the minimum unit cost for their industry by making use of all the possible economies of scale available to them. A supermarket is an example of a small-scale production unit – production in the sense that retailing is a service produced by these shops – that often has no further economies of scale open to its owners. There is no point in making it any larger nor in carrying more stocks because the costs of operating the supermarket are as low as they can be. This supermarket, however, may be one of many small production units within one business like Tesco's.

There are also firms which are small because they produce for a small specialised or local market – the Lotus motor-car company and the village shop are examples. The type of products produced – those one-offs referred to earlier – may also limit size. This is particularly important where personal services are given – the hairdressing salon, the bespoke (hand made) tailor and similar trades. Other firms may be small because they are at an early stage in their development. They may be larger firms in the making.

Whatever the reason for a business being small, it usually survives because it avoids the diseconomies of scale. Those running it are able to react quickly to changes in demand as there is 'the right proportion of Chiefs to Indians' and not a bureaucracy. Most of these Chiefs working for themselves tend to work effectively by necessity. There are, therefore, usually good relations with employees and customers – the important element of goodwill.

Assignments

5.9 In view of the advantages of large-scale production, why is it that many businesses still operate on a small scale? (L 1971)

5.10 In spite of a general trend to large-scale units the small firm continues to survive in the United Kingdom. Why is this so? Give examples of some industries in which the small firm plays an important part. (AEB 1972)

5.11 List two or three occupations of relations or friends. Can you account for the size of the organisations in which they work?

5.12* Group research: using the telephone Yellow Pages for your locality, trace the total number of taxi firms and number of building contractors. You may limit your study to particular districts or a town in large telephone directory regions. Compare for the districts or town selected these total numbers, with the number of public swimming pools and/or Central Electricity Board's power stations in the same locality. Account for the difference in total numbers of each.

Suggested further reading

J Hanson, Chapter 7
Harvey, Chapter 4
Paish and Culyer, Chapter 8
Stanlake, Chapter 7

Chapter 6
Location and distribution

Where to produce

The pros and cons

Almost every choice of site for a factory or other production unit is a compromise between advantages and disadvantages. Social and political considerations may be as important as economic considerations. From the economic point of view, the most suitable location is the one with the lowest costs for producing goods and getting them to consumers. For our purposes at the moment this assessment is made in terms of the producer's private costs, the figures in his books. However the economist may make a separate calculation adding *social* costs and benefits into the reckoning, for a government study, perhaps. When these social costs and benefits are included in the calculation, a completely different site may be the most suitable.

Historic associations

Economic reasons of cheaper production costs led over the recent centuries to some industries being concentrated in particular areas while others were widely scattered. In the early days of the Industrial Revolution production of manufactured goods had to be carried out near sources of power. In those days water power was the only practical way to drive numbers of machines, and so factories had to be sited near fast-running streams. It was for this reason that Richard Arkwright set up his water-frame making thread at Cromford, Derbyshire in 1771, using water to power the machine's rollers.

These early manufacturers could also get cost advantages by being near their sources of raw materials. The pottery manufacturers in Staffordshire used clay found in local deposits. Beer was brewed where the water was suitable – at Burton-on-Trent, Staffordshire, famous since the early 1700s for its ales.

The development of the first practical steam engine in 1776 and its later improvement as a power source for machinery drew industry near the coalfields as coal is bulky and expensive to transport.

Other producers had to be near their customers. As milk went sour quickly in the days before refrigeration, there were cows in towns with many in London dairies until the cattle plague of 1865–7. Market gardeners supplying fresh vegetables were within a day's journey by cart from the city markets. These producers, needing to be near their customers, were therefore scattered throughout the United Kingdom.

These historic causes for location can still be seen in the siting of certain industries today (see Figure 6.1). Others are still dependent on climatic conditions as we will see in chapter 16. But the bulk of modern industry's location is influenced by transport costs.

Location	Historic natural advantage	Brief history	1970s
High Wycombe	Beech trees grew easily on nearby chalk hills, providing timber suitable for shaping into chairs and similar furniture.	In early 1800s chairs' legs and other components turned on primitive lathes by chair bodgers. Rush and cane seating at that time made by women in their homes. This furniture was assembled in a few factories and sold by carters carrying their stocks along coach roads. By 1920s stained and polished beech widely accepted as suitable for cheap chairs.	Furniture of many modern types produced by 9000 people in this trade.
Teeside	Local ironstone grid found in 1850 enabled local iron founders to expand production. This had started in 1839 in a foundry that took advantage of good rail and sea communications bringing in Durham coal, Weardale limestone and Scottish pig-iron. The heavy goods produced were shipped by sea and later by rail to customers.	For 50 years until 1900 these natural advantages enabled this region to be the World's leading iron producer. By-products of iron making included coke oven gas, and the distillation of crude benzole and tar, processes that led to the development of a chemical industry in the region. This was expanded after 1939 when home-produced fertilisers and other bulk chemicals were required in World War II.	The chemical-producing complexes have often to be integrated, so the production of one product attracts the production of others (not necessarily by the same firm). Use is made of North Sea gas and oil in making fertilisers, plastics and other petrochemicals.

IN BRIEF:

Location	Historic natural advantage	Brief history	1970s
East Anglia	Flat high quality farm land, when adequately drained.	Proved ideal for carrots, peas, and similar crops.	Flat open land enables large machines to harvest these crops for freezing or canning factories.
The Clyde	Deep water estuary near iron and coal deposits.	Ship building and associated heavy industries developed, using these natural advantages.	Oil-rig and similar structures built using shipbuilding skills.
Aberdeen	Natural harbour developed for fishing and conveniently placed for North Sea oil development.	Since 1960s has become the oil capital of Northern Europe.	Many oil industry firms based in the town.
North Wales	Slate in abundance.	Quarries provided roofing slates for most late 19th and early 20th century buildings.	Slate no longer used in any quantity, quarries now a tourist attraction.
Lancashire	Water power, later coal, and suitable climate for spinning cotton shipped through deep water ports on the Mersey.	A major centre for cotton spinning in late 19th and early 20th century. The cotton industry providing a key part of the region's industry.	Inherited know-how and skills of cotton workers familiar with machinery and factory work, employed in making electronic products as fewer employed in textiles.

Figure 6.1   Origins of natural advantages and current location of some UK industries.

Transport costs

By the 1930s power to run machines could be distributed more conveniently if not always as cheaply in the form of electricity rather than coal. The National Grid provides adequate power for most types of manufacture anywhere in the United Kingdom. However a few manufacturers still have to be near sources of cheap power, such as aluminium smelters who use vast quantities of electricity.

The cost of transporting other raw materials, not only those used to power machines, can still be high enough to force producers to use sites near the sources of

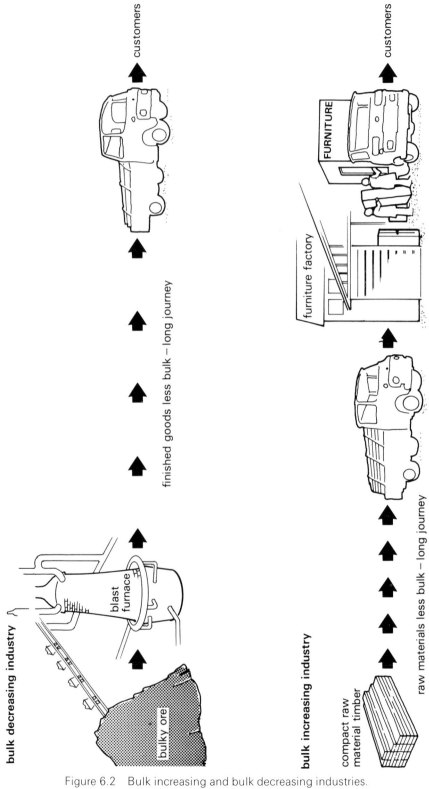

Figure 6.2   Bulk increasing and bulk decreasing industries.

materials. These are called *bulk reducing* industries as their output is substantially less in weight and volume than the materials which made it (see Figure 6.2). Consequently they can transport their output more cheaply than the raw materials.

On the other hand there are *bulk increasing* industries with output more expensive to transport than raw materials. Furniture makers, clothes manufacturers and makers of domestic appliances, among others, have relatively bulky outputs. Timber is cheaper to transport than furniture made from it, cloth cheaper to carry than clothes, and steel plate cheaper to handle, in transport or around a factory, than finished washing machines or fridges. Many of these producers also assemble a variety of components supplied from several locations. Therefore these bulk increasing industries are sited near their customers (see Figure 6.2).

Outlets to customers
The historic reasons have been explained for the scattered units of some types of production. The advantages in low costs for these have in some cases become less significant as technical innovations brought cheaper transport, refrigerated trucks and improved road communications. Nevertheless most service and some other industries providing goods and services for individuals must be near their customers. Hairdressers, restaurants and retail shops have to be where people may easily visit them. Producers of products with a short 'shelf life' – i.e. goods that cannot be stored for long – must also be near their customers. Bakers of cakes therefore spread their factories around the country so the goods are delivered within 24 hours of baking and still have three of their four days shelf life in which they can be sold.

These service industries and producers of goods with a short shelf life are dispersed according to the distribution of their customers. This leads to their concentration in or near towns, as were the dairies of former times.

Natural and acquired local advantages
The cost advantages of particular locations can be seen as being natural or being acquired.

Natural advantages lie in the availability of such factors as coal, raw materials, sources of power, and in the climate. The location of materials and power sources are particularly important in bulk reducing industries. Another natural advantage is the proximity of markets, especially important in bulk increasing and service industries.

Such natural advantages, as we have seen, were of considerable importance historically in the choice of location of many industries and services. Today they are still important for some producers. For instance asparagus of special flavour can only be grown in the Vale of Evesham, because of traces of particular mineral salts in the soil there.

Acquired advantages in a location may come from past concentrations of an industry in an area which benefited from this external economy of concentration. In the past, knife makers settled in Sheffield where charcoal from the woods, hill streams to power water wheels, and local millstone grit for their grinding wheels, as well as local iron ore were available. Now through new technology there is no longer any need for charcoal nor for local millstones in knife making. But these natural advantages have led to acquired advantages such as those of skilled labour and a reputation for the industry's goods, that continue to attract producers – with 160 cutlery firms in Sheffield in 1976 – although there are no longer *natural* advantages.

Disadvantages and social costs
While there are advantages from growth and large-scale production in particular localities, there are also external diseconomies of scale such as congested roads and pollution. There is also a risk of high local unemployment if many firms in one area are all in the same industry and that industry declines.

Many social costs are not realised or quantified and do not appear in the producer's calculations when deciding which site gives the lowest production costs. This can be a tricky point in cost comparisons between regions in different countries. Social costs often fall on those living near the source of nuisance, the factory, but are not often taken into account. When a producer takes account of these, however, the customer is likely to pay higher prices: the National Coal Board's customers pay – in the price of coal – for the repair of properties damaged by subsidence.

Government influences
British governments have taken steps to influence industries in the redevelopment of certain areas. Since World War II, during which British industry had been largely controlled by government regulations, successive governments have exercised varying degrees of influence and control over its location. This has occurred especially because of the decline of the cotton textile, ship building and other industries concentrated in regions where originally they had natural advantages. Look back at Figure 2.6 to note the distribution of population. By the 1930s the decline of these industries in areas such as Clydeside, Merseyside, Jarrow and other north-east towns, and South Wales left unacceptable social conditions. The unemployment in Jarrow, for instance, was well above the national average in 1931. There was not only the misery and waste of high unemployment but also the waste of social capital.

Unemployment and location of industry
In trying to improve the regional balance of employment successive British governments have offered financial incentives to producers to move to areas where industry has declined (Figure 6.3). Governments have also limited expansion for producers in certain areas of high employment. This can be done by refusing permission for the extension of factories and new production facilities in these regions.

The intention of financial inducements – grants, special reliefs from taxes, and subsidies – is to draw production to regions of high unemployment. This will increase the prosperity of the area, perhaps enabling derelict buildings to be repaired, land use to be improved and places of entertainment and other amenities to be re-opened. Coupled with better job opportunities, these improvements stem the pressures on the local population's net migration, improving the area's appeal to new industries, as the young – the most geographically mobile – are less likely to leave.

The name given to these regions with problems of unemployment has changed from time to time. No doubt there will continue to be periodic changes of terminology, not only for the regions with the so-called 'regional problem' but also for the forms of government assistance they receive. You should therefore update your information on this study.

An example of government policy
In the spring of 1976, the British Government policies to encourage producers to move to regions with problems included several inducements. The basic policy had

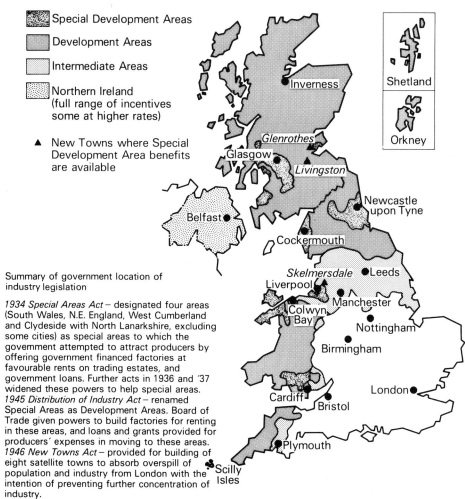

Special Development Areas

Development Areas

Intermediate Areas

Northern Ireland
(full range of incentives
some at higher rates)

▲ New Towns where Special
Development Area benefits
are available

Summary of government location of
industry legislation

1934 Special Areas Act – designated four areas
(South Wales, N.E. England, West Cumberland
and Clydeside with North Lanarkshire, excluding
some cities) as special areas to which the
government attempted to attract producers by
offering government financed factories at
favourable rents on trading estates, and
government loans. Further acts in 1936 and '37
widened these powers to help special areas.
1945 Distribution of Industry Act – renamed
Special Areas as Development Areas. Board of
Trade given powers to build factories for renting
in these areas, and loans and grants provided for
producers' expenses in moving to these areas.
1946 New Towns Act – provided for building of
eight satellite towns to absorb overspill of
population and industry from London with the
intention of preventing further concentration of
industry.
1947 Town and Country Planning Act – producers
had to obtain an Industrial Development
Certificate (IDC) before building any factory
except the smallest in size. The Certificates were
readily given in Development Areas but difficult
to obtain in areas with little unemployment. The
system still operates in the mid-1970s.
1960 Local Employment Act – replaced the large
Development Areas with smaller Development
Districts to channel assistance more precisely to
locations of high unemployment. Various
government grants and loans made available to
Development Districts.
1963 Budget – provided investment incentives to
producers in Development Districts, with
increased grants and tax concessions allowing
producers favourable terms for claiming
depreciation.
1964 Office Developments – controls introduced
on building office premises in London and
some other areas.
*1967 Introduction of Regional Employment
Premium* – a grant was payed to employers in
Development Areas at so-much per employee per
week. Designed to attract labour intensive
industry to these areas rather than capital
intensive ones with relatively few employees for
output from chemical plants etc. Financial
assistance also given to employers for training
workers. The premium and training grants in 1975
ranged from £3 per week for men over 18 to 47½p
per week for part-time girl employees under 18,
and £10 a week towards training.
1969 Intermediate Areas – a category introduced
for areas needing similar although not complete
assistance offered to producers in development
areas.
1970 Tax Incentives – the policy between 1966
and·1970 had involved cash grants, these were
replaced by tax incentives with the intention of
assisting only efficient and therefore profitable
firms – liable to tax – in Development Areas. (This
was a change of emphasis through a change of
government.)
1972 Industry Act – extended the tax benefits
introduced in 1970 to all producers in the U.K.,
and Regional Development Grants were
introduced for Assisted Areas – see text.

Figure 6.3   The Areas for Expansion – UK Spring 1976.

been laid down by the White Paper *Industrial and Regional Development* (1972) with some supplementary amendments. This White Paper created Areas for Expansion. Broadly these were Scotland, Wales, the North and the North-West of England, Yorkshire and Humberside, Cornwall and parts of Devonshire, Nottinghamshire and Derbyshire. While they all had common problems at that time, they suffered these in different degrees. Therefore three categories of Areas for Expansion were created: *Special Development Areas* – where the problems were most acute; *Development Areas* – with a high degree of unemployment; and *Intermediate Areas* where the degree of unemployment was high but not to the same degree as in the *Development Areas*.

A system of Regional Development grants provided money towards the cost of plant, machinery and buildings. Unlike earlier grants these were not limited to projects creating employment, for the intention was to improve the social capital of these problem regions. Some years earlier the Government had introduced some reliefs from taxation nationwide, which encouraged *all* producers to increase their capital 'stock' of machines, buildings and so on. The grants introduced in 1972 did not alter the favourable tax position where these grants were paid in Areas for Expansion (see Figure 6.3). There the producer could get the whole cost of a machine set against his taxable profits *and* the grants. In Special Development Areas the grants amounted to 22% of the costs of both buildings and land. In the Development Areas they amounted to 20% of these factors – buildings and land, while in Intermediate Areas the 20% grant was paid only on buildings.

There were also Derelict Land Clearance Areas given some of the help available in Intermediate Areas. Although this gave inducements to clear unsightly relics of older industries for only a limited number of years up to September 1974, the effects were dramatic. The landscape around old spoil tips in Staffordshire was changed from an unsightly moonscape to gently rolling grassed spaces with facilities for leisure.

The effect of these policies in Areas for Expansion is brought out in the Assignments below. There were also in 1976 some arrangements for regional aid from the European Economic Community (EEC). These are described in chapter 17. Broadly speaking they provide funds to aid UK Areas of Expansion, supplementing the funds available under UK government policies.

Assignments

6.1 'The assembly of motor vehicles is mainly concentrated in certain areas, whereas bakeries are generally more widely distributed.' Explain this statement giving reasons for these differences in location. (L 1971)

6.2 Choose *one* of the following industries: textiles, iron and steel, electricity supply, motor vehicles. Describe, with appropriate examples, the factors determining its location. Comment on the relative importance of these factors at the present time and indicate how their importance has changed since 1930. (L 1973)

6.3 Examine the arguments for and against 'taking work to the workers and taking workers to where there is work'. Summarise the pros and cons in a page of notes.

6.4 Update the examples of Government and EEC policies for improving the balance of regional employment.

6.5* Discuss: the social costs of producer 'A' are estimated at £10 a TV set, those of producer 'B' at only £1. Examine by discussion the case for and against government legislation requiring them to each pay a levy to compensate the community for these costs.

6.6* Add to your notes on examples listed for Assignment 5.11 on page 77 the reasons why these organisations are located where they are.

6.7* Group research: each group should select one industry. If your group were entering this industry as a producer, where would you locate your factory or production unit? Explain your choice of location.

The distribution of goods

Chain of supply
Division of labour can provide economies of scale from specialisation in distribution (see Figure 6.4). (*Note:* there is a difference between the meanings of distribution in

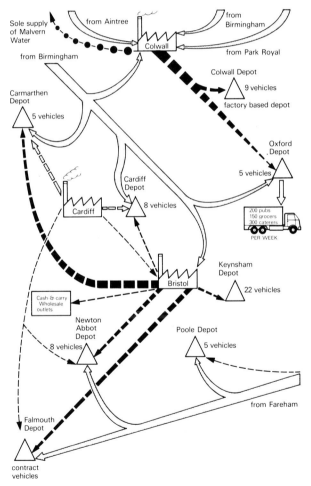

Figure 6.4   Chain of distribution – an example based on a representative part of the Schweppes distribution system.

the sense of 'getting goods to customers' and distribution of industries, etc by geographic or other areas.) The compromises determining a producer's location often leave him with customers widely dispersed geographically. Before looking at the way distribution takes place in supplying consumers, we must understand that many producers' output is an input for other producers – cars are assembled from many supplier-producers' components.

The *chain of supply* is the link between the producer and the eventual user of his product. Two important elements are *wholesalers* and *retailers* as shown in Figure 6.4. While these may be conveniently considered as firms specialising in these different functions, wholesaling and retailing can be carried out by departments of the firms making the goods as shown in this figure.

Wholesalers and wholesale markets

There are sometimes advantages for manufacturers selling through wholesalers acting as a go-between between them and shops (or other retail outlets selling to the public). A wholesaler may buy from several producers, store the goods in his warehouse, and then distribute them in relatively small quantities to many shops. We will see in a moment the advantages of this system.

Where the goods are perishable they cannot be stored and the wholesaler needs a quick turn-round. That is: he must sell quickly the goods he takes from producers. There have therefore grown up wholesale markets for perishable foods. Here major wholesalers and some producers have stands selling to smaller wholesalers and some retailers.

Wholesalers in general buy goods in bulk and by selling these in smaller lots to the retailer, help to keep down distribution costs. For the producer to call on, say, 200 shops in a region would cost say £2 a delivery. But the wholesaler can deliver the goods from several producers for about the same cost. He takes a case of soup, ten cartons of potato crips, nine boxes of dried peas, perhaps, and other items to one shop. To the next he delivers a different load. If the manufacturers had each delivered their own products – the soup man, the crisp man and so on, each making drops to these shops – the cost of delivery would have been higher. Wholesalers can also get the advantages of specialisation from the use of equipment made possible by the division of labour. Each shop's goods may be carried on the lorry on special trolleys left for the shop to unload when convenient, so the lorry is not delayed.

As the wholesaler carries (holds in stock) many producers' goods, retailers may order all these different goods at one time – a saving in paper work and time putting one order to the wholesaler, rather than one to each producer. They also can get a choice from the wholesaler's stocks of various manufacturers' goods.

Wholesalers' stocks

The wholesaler's warehouse holds stocks with advantage to both producers and retailers. Retailers do not want to use the space or tie up cash by holding stocks of every item in adequate quantities to meet a sudden increase in a particular demand. The corner shop does not carry more than a few dozen bottles of ant killer, adequate for customers' needs in a normal year. But in a year when there is a plague of ants in the area, this shopkeeper could get a large stock quickly from his wholesaler.

The producer prefers to make a regular quantity of goods each week, avoiding peaks that involve overtime and other extra costs. But many commodities are not sold in the same quantity from week to week, or are bought at different seasons. However, storage for stock is expensive, so if the producers can sell their output regularly to wholesalers, this eases their storage problems.

Wholesalers' ancillary jobs
There are a number of jobs wholesalers sometimes carry out as part of wholesaling. Goods may be re-packed and occasionally re-labelled in smaller quantities than are worthwhile for manufacturers. The goods may be graded – most of the tomatoes in Guernsey produced by professional growers go to wholesalers who grade them. The retailers can then buy quantities at the different grades to suit their likely customers.

Wholesalers often import and export goods when they must ensure that these have been produced, packaged and labelled to meet local laws. They arrange 'clearance through customs' getting the documents and facts that Customs Officers require, and may arrange shipment from abroad and certainly work with the overseas producer in getting the goods to a UK warehouse. They may also organise a service of maintenance and repair.

Wholesalers provide information for retailers – which goods are most suitable for the shopkeepers' needs, different ways the goods can be used by the retailers' customers and warn when supplies will be short. This help is given as the wholesaler and the retailer both stay in business by satisfying their respective customers.

As mentioned earlier the wholesale functions may be carried out by departments in the organisation producing the goods. There are also a number of specialist organisations with many of the features of wholesalers: distributors – buying goods like motor cars from one or two manufacturers for distribution to retailing garages; cash and carry wholesalers, described below; and discount warehouses offering near wholesale prices to the public (see below).

Retailers
The retailer is the last link in the distribution chain. He or she sells to the public and therefore must usually be located near them. There are a number of different types of retailer distinguished by the sort of goods sold and/or the degree of personal service offered.

The Corner Shop. The corner shop is the most localised form of retailer, and offers the highest degree of personal service. The shopkeeper will know many of his customers personally, and because he will often be the owner of the business, will be prepared to stay open late, and sometimes even open on Sundays. However, because his turnover will be relatively small, his prices are likely to be higher than many other forms of retail outlet.

Specialist Retailer. The specialist retailer sells just one type of product. Examples are butchers, greengrocers and hardware stores. These specialists also include retail outlets for *services* such as garages, cafés and hotels.

The Supermarket. These originated in the USA during the 1930s slump when producers could not sell to shops who had no cash to buy stocks, so they piled their goods outside their factories and customers helped themselves having paid for the goods. The idea caught on. In Britain the early supermarkets were almost all self-service food shops. But by the 1970s they have tended to carry a wider range of goods, with the emphasis on low prices rather than personal service. Supermarkets are of at least 2000 sq ft selling area and have self-service as their main feature. Although the self-service idea has spread to many outlets from local shops to city department stores, it has some limits as we will see later.

The Chain Store. Where one organisation runs ten or more shops in different places these are known as chain stores or multiples. They may be specialist shops, Dewhurst, the butchers for example. Or they may sell a variety of goods like Woolworths and Marks & Spencer. Whatever type of goods sold, many of these chain stores are, in part, supermarkets and often they sell their own brands of goods. These own-brand goods can be cheaper than manufacturers' brands partly because they do not incur high advertising costs. Chain stores also offer lower prices because they buy in bulk at lower unit costs – a commercial economy of scale. They can organise their warehousing and distribution effectively. However, some smaller shop-owners – inspired by wholesalers – have banded together to get the benefit of bulk buying and more efficient distribution from warehouses. Mace and the VG stores are examples of these 'voluntary groups'. One of the greatest advantages chain stores often have over other shops is their strict control of stocks – how much is held at each shop, and what particular lines of goods are carried. This rationalisation – a scientific reorganisation – cuts costs. But the small shopkeeper, anxious to give that extra bit of personal service, may carry more lines than are worthwhile, with storage costs and waste through deterioration of unsold items.

Department Stores. These offer personal service, sales on credit and delivery to customers' homes. They provide under one roof a number of different 'shops' each set up as a department of one organisation. Since 1950, however, department stores have made increasing use of self-selection, although still giving customers advice and guidance when required. Many of them by the 1970s were in groups of stores run by organisations like Debenhams and the House of Fraser.

Limitations of self-service
Where the risk of pilferage is high, as in jewellery stores, self-service is impractical. Although other retailers accept some $1\frac{3}{4}\%$ of the sales value of their turnover being stolen, losses could be much larger for small goods of high value. Where personal service is often required by customers buying cameras, hi-fi's, sewing machines and similar articles, the shops also remain relatively small or as departments in larger stores, with trained staff to serve customers.

Cash and carry and other developments
Some wholesalers apply the self-service principle for their retailer customers. This enables these customers to buy in quantities at relatively low units costs because there is no credit or delivery from the wholesaler. The cash and carry wholesaler usually sells strictly to retailers only, who have been issued with identity cards. But some members of the general public can obtain cards under arrangements made with societies, unions and clubs.

From this cash and carry wholesaling developed the *cash and carry discount ware-house.* This offers goods at close to trade prices to the public. Discount warehouses can sell domestic and similar appliances at these low prices to the public, because a warehouse without expensive displays and demonstration facilities involves fewer day-to-day costs than a shop of similar size. With the increased domestic use of deep-freezers, the principle has been applied to food sales. A customer may then buy more cheaply in larger quantities, storing the food for daily use.

Another development from the USA is the *hypermarket*, more common in France than Britain. Selling virtually everything from matches to a mink coat all under one roof, these hypermarkets are built on the outskirts of towns. Here land is cheap and customers can drive easily to the hypermarket with its large car park.

Shopping precincts, especially those in covered buildings, have all the advantages of historic markets – you can wander round to compare prices, you can see goods you may need, and other goods you had not thought of buying. But the precinct avoids the smells, wet weather and other discomforts of earlier markets. Like hypermarkets, these precincts tend to draw shoppers to one place albeit in the town centre.

Catalogue and mail-order sales

Another form of retailing is the mail-order firm. These originated mainly in America, where in the early days the population was widely dispersed, so for many people it was not possible to shop at big stores. There grew up, therefore, catalogue and mail-order businesses like Sears, Roebuck and the Army and Navy Stores. The customers saw anything they needed, from barbed wire to pianos, in the catalogue and could order it from the retailer. From this developed the mail-order business of the 1970s with the retailer supplying many easily packaged articles sent by post or van delivery.

Assignments

6.8 What is meant by (*a*) specialisation and (*b*) economies of scale? Show how each has affected the organisation of firms in the retail trade. (L 1972)

6.9 There are two phrases frequently used to describe different types of price for exported or imported goods: Carriage, Insurance and Freight (CIF); and Free on Board (FOB). Trace the exact meanings of these terms and give two – real or made-up – examples. This practice in finding out the meaning of commercial and similar terms should lead you to sources for such information and ways of discovering things for yourself.

6.10 List four to six examples of different types of retail outlet in your area. Give the advantages and disadvantages of each type of outlet from the customers' point of view.

6.11 Trace the stages in the flow of distribution of fresh fish from the time when it is caught to its sale to the final consumer. Show how the division of labour facilitates distribution. (L 1971)

6.12* Describe how the methods of distribution of two of the following products have changed in the last two decades and account for these changes: (*a*) food; (*b*) clothing; (*c*) motor vehicle accessories; and (*d*) books and records. (L 1973)

6.13 What part does the middleman play in the flow of goods from manufacturer to the final consumer? Choose examples to illustrate your answer. (L 1972)

6.14 'Distribution is part of the process of production.' Explain this statement and indicate the functions of the wholesaler and the retailer in this process. (L 1971)

6.15* Describe and account for changes that have occurred in the occupational distribution of the population of the United Kingdom during this century. (Revision) (L 1971)

6.16* Review your study notes and cross-reference linked topics like the occupational distribution of the UK population, location of industry, and government policies. Discuss: what topics so far have direct links? (Future additions to your notes should include such cross-references.)

Suggested further reading

Hanson, Chapter 8
Harvey, Chapters 7, 10, 11 and 12
Stanlake, Chapters 11 and 12
P Donaldson, *Guide to the British Economy* (4th edition, Penguin, 1976), Chapter 7

Chapter 7

Firms, companies and other financial institutions

Words used to describe the legal form of companies have precise definitions as shown in Figures 7.1–7.3, 7.5 and 7.6.

The legal organisation and the activities of a firm can be considered separately, although very often the nature of the work determines the most suitable legal form.

Business organisations

Business names

Names in business have to conform to certain rules to avoid possible confusion, and are registered. The name often includes the word 'Company' or 'and Company' (& Co) but these have no more significance than the descriptive word 'firm'. You will find one-man businesses and partnerships with titles including '& Co'. A Limited Company is a different matter as we will see later in this chapter, with the important part being the word *Limited* in a company name.

Limited companies have to register their names along with other details when they are first formed. The law also requires details to be sent to the Registrar of Companies at least once a year and when debenture loans, new share issues and other events occur affecting a company's financial and/or legal structure.

Sole proprietors

Sometimes called 'one-man firms' these are owned and controlled by one person, with all the advantages and disadvantages of small-scale production referred to on page 77 (see Figure 7.1). Among these are many chiropodists, small shopkeepers and window cleaners.

They have, however, two major disadvantages. The individual seldom has sufficient finance for expansion on more than a modest scale. And if the business goes bankrupt, being unable to pay the sums it owes, then the owner has to sell his *personal* possessions including his home and car, to help pay what the firm owes (its debts).

Partnerships

Two or more persons can form a partnership but in the UK there cannot be more than 20 partners in each partnership and only 10 in a banking business. You choose a partner more carefully than a wife, or so people say, because he or she can cost you more dearly and be harder to 'divorce' from your own financial affairs. Figure 7.2 shows a typical partnership which grew from a one-man firm. The profits are shared on an agreed basis but there are legal rules for sharing profits when there is no formal

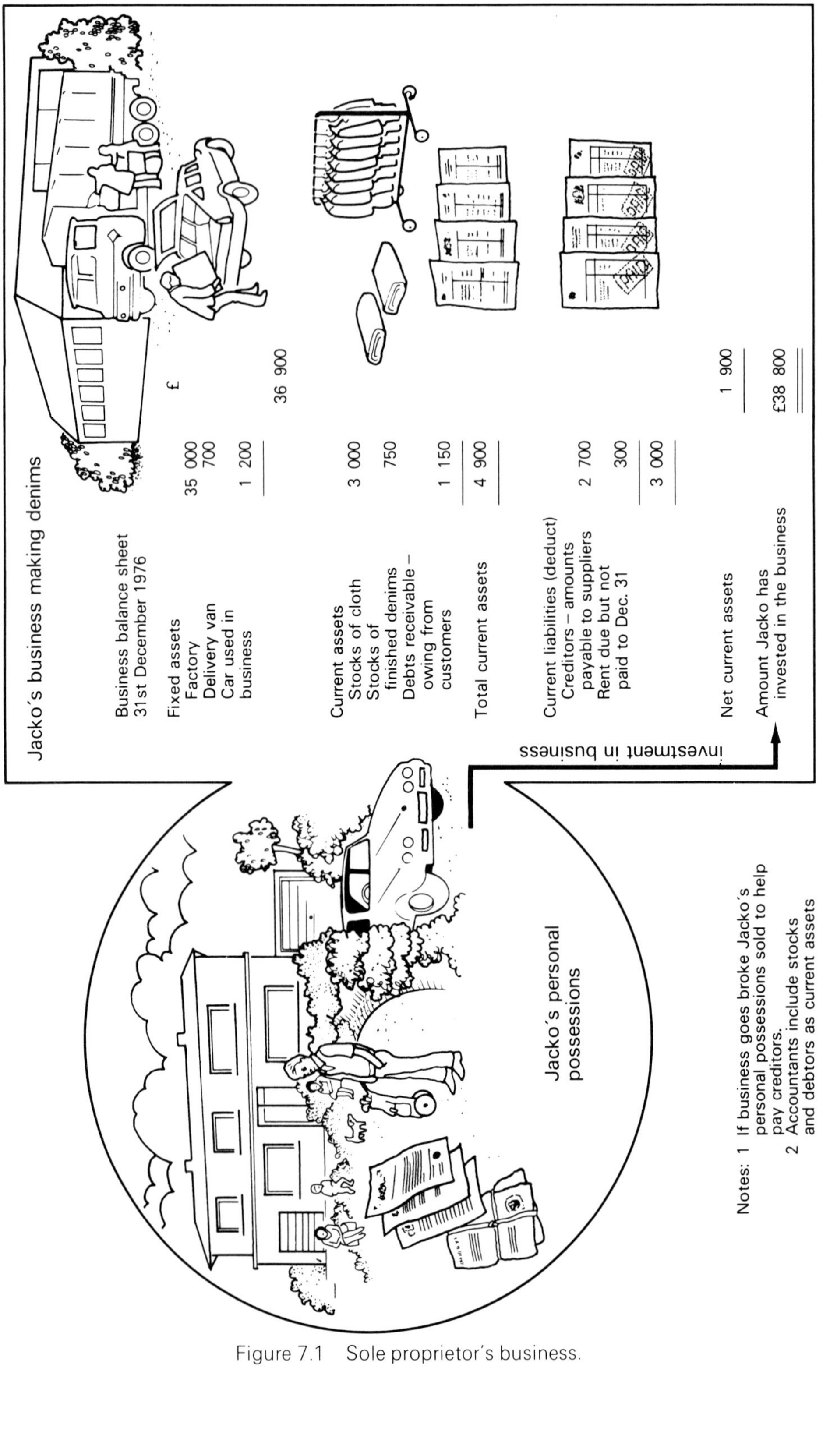
Jacko's business making denims
Business balance sheet
31st December 1976
£
Fixed assets
Factory 35 000
Delivery van 700
Car used in business 1 200
36 900
Current assets
Stocks of cloth 3 000
Stocks of finished denims 750
Debts receivable – owing from customers 1 150
Total current assets 4 900
Current liabilities (deduct)
Creditors – amounts payable to suppliers 2 700
Rent due but not paid to Dec. 31 300
3 000
Net current assets 1 900
Amount Jacko has invested in the business £38 800
investment in business
Jacko's personal possessions
Notes: 1 If business goes broke Jacko's personal possessions sold to help pay creditors.
2 Accountants include stocks and debtors as current assets

Figure 7.1 Sole proprietor's business.

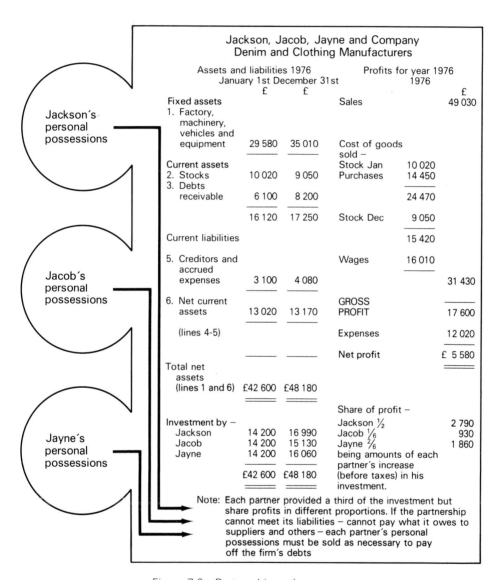

Figure 7.2 Partnership and accounts.

partnership agreement. There is still the flexibility in response to change that the one-man firm possesses. In addition, with two or more people providing the capital as finance to set up the firm, it can usually expand further than a one-man business, although it may still be limited in its potential size through lack of funds.

Partnerships, like one-man firms, may take all the partners' private resources to pay off the business debts should it go broke. What is more harrowing for a partner is that he or she may have to pay all the firm's debts if the other partners have no personal possessions, or if these are insufficient to pay their share of business debts.

However a partnership can be set up so that some partners have 'limited liability'. That is they can be called upon to pay no more towards the firm's debts if it goes bankrupt than the capital they originally agreed. But in England there must always be one partner with unlimited liability.

Where a partner only puts up capital but takes no active part in running the business, he or she is a *dormant* or *sleeping* (in the business sense) partner. The dormant partner nevertheless may take a share of the profits under the partnership arrangement.

Dissolving a partnership

Any partnership is automatically dissolved in the UK on the death or bankruptcy of any one of the partners. This can cause difficulties for those partners wishing to continue the business because they may not find anyone suitable or with the funds to buy the late partner's share of the firm. They may not even have the money to buy it themselves. Partnerships – especially those of doctors, lawyers, and other professions – therefore usually take out life insurance on each partner against this eventuality. At the same time they make arrangements to provide for the time when older partners wish to retire; a new partnership will be then formed to carry on the business. Partnerships may also be dissolved by arrangement under the terms of the partnership agreement.

Joint-stock companies

The fascinating aspect of these companies is their legal identity which is separate from those who own and/or manage them. The people who own the business are shareholders (see Figure 7.3) and *as shareholders* do not take part in the day-to-day running of the business. Their liability to contribute to the company's funds on bankruptcy is also limited to the £:p amount of their shares. Whatever happens to the company, the original shareholders cannot be asked to pay in more to pay creditors (those owed money), nor can anyone buying these shares be asked to do so. Figure 7.4 explains this with the nominal value of shares. This is the principle of *limited liability*.

Because shareholders have this limited liability, the word *Limited* appears in the company's name in all but a few very special cases. The laws including the Companies Acts 1948 and 1967 regulate the actions of those putting money into limited companies and those operating them. These laws also protect the small investors attracted to put up money for shares, as the limited liability encourages them to risk a known amount of their savings. The number of shareholders can be several hundreds of thousands in a large limited company. The Imperial Group Ltd had over 226 000 shareholders and about 90 000 employees (including 3000 seasonal workers) in October 1975.

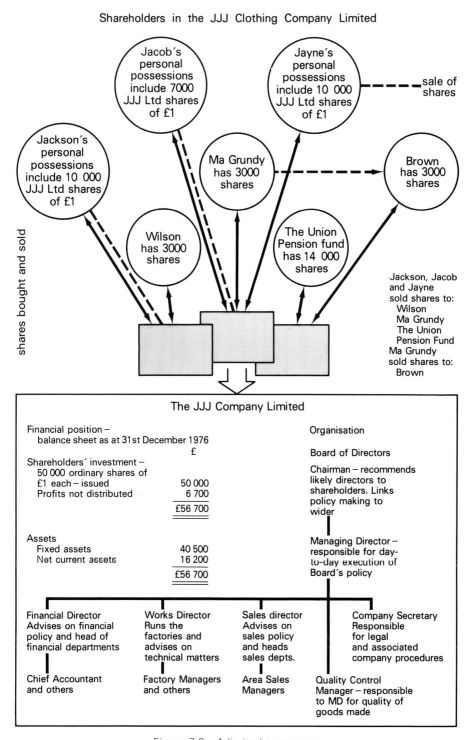

Figure 7.3   A limited company.

SHARES

Shares and dividends

All shares are initially issued to subscribers (those putting up capital) for a limited company. But a shareholder cannot be called on to subscribe more than the nominal value of his or her share.

Shareholders' rights to any profits, dividends, or repayment on liquidation, are always subject to the interest on and loans made by debenture holders and others being paid first. Dividends can only be paid in the normal course out of profits, the terms varying as explained below. They may be declared as a percentage of nominal value, or as so many pence per share, and be paid over a year as one or more interim-dividends and a final dividend.

Stocks

These are un-numbered shares; £1 shares numbered 1 to 1000 may be redesignated '£1000 of stock'.

Share capital

The total nominal value of *all* shares issued is a company's *Issued Capital*. Its *Authorised Capital* is the £:p amount of shares on which the company has completed legal and other requirements for issue or subsequent issue, and may therefore be greater than the Issued Capital.

Types of Share	Degree of risk	Dividend	Share of profits	Ranking on liquidation
Ordinary Shares As amounts of profit (after paying all interest etc) *and* preference dividends may fluctuate with the company's fortunes, these ordinary shares are 'risk capital'.	High – if company fails, ordinary shareholders likely to lose his/her investment	As approved at annual general meeting	All that is left after paying preference dividends	Received any surplus ranking after repaying preference shareholders
Undistributed profits, however, are part of the ordinary shareholders' investment – the 'equity capital'.				
An Ordinary Shareholder with one vote per share has an influence on the company's policy decisions, according to the proportion of shares he/she holds. The business cannot be sold or merged without the ordinary shareholders' approval, nor can new shares be created. They can dismiss directors.				
Preference shares Holders receive only a fixed rate of dividend (set at time of issue) because they are subject to less risks of loss, having preferential treatment over ordinary shareholders. Votes only when dividend in arrear (unpaid).	Less than ordinary shares but greater than loans	Fixed rate out of profits (if any) each year	Dividends only	Before ordinary shares but after debentures and other loans
Redeemable preference shares Issued on terms for repayment after some years. These are the only shares on which a holder may be repaid their investment without a company going into liquidation	As above	As above	Dividends only	As above *or* when due for redemption
Cumulative preference shares Similar to other preference shares, but if no profits in any year dividends due are carried forward – accumulated for payment when profits available.	As above	Fixed rate for each year accumulated if necessary till profits available	Dividends (and accumulated) only	As for other preference shares but plus arrears of dividend
Participating preference shares – similar to other preference shares, but in addition to fixed rate may receive an extra dividend from any profits remaining after paying Ordinary Shares' dividends.	As above	Fixed rate plus extra	Dividends only	As for preference shares

DEBENTURES AND LOANS

	Degree of risk	Interest	Ranking on liquidation
Debentures These are a form of loan usually secured (see text) – like a mortgage – with first claim on funds available on 'selling up' assets in liquidating a company. Their holders are repaid before general creditors.	Least risky of any investment	Interest payable at rates set when loan made whether or not company makes profits	First claim after certain legally preferred claims for wages etc
Loan interest is payable whether or not the company makes profits.			
No votes in company's affairs until it cannot pay its debts.			As for general creditors, before any shareholders
Unsecured loan Holders receive interest and have similar claims for repayment as suppliers of goods have when company is liquidated.	Similar to risks of a supplier of goods on credit		

Note: This summary simplifies a wide variety of types of shares, debentures and loans.

Figure 7.4   Types of company shares, debentures and loan stock.

Limited company's shares can be sold (see Figure 7.3) by a shareholder without disturbing the company's organisation. This enables a shareholder to sell the shares to anyone willing and able to buy them.

Public and private limited companies
A private limited company must have at least two shareholders and not more than 50 shareholders. Although employees may be shareholders in unlimited numbers, the private company must not offer its shares to the public. A limited public company, however, can have an unlimited number of shareholders and must have at least seven.

Following the usual practice in talking or writing about limited liability companies, having established that we are talking of *limited* companies, we refer to them simply as companies. But in other contexts be sure that you distinguish between limited companies and businesses merely with company in their titles (see page 91).

Private companies are often family businesses and far more numerous although generally smaller than public ones. Because they cannot ask the public to subscribe for their shares, private companies rely on borrowing or keeping profits in order to finance expansion. They do not make as detailed returns on their financial affairs as public companies must send to the Registrar of Companies. Nor can their shareholders sell their shares without the approval of the directors of the company.

Shareholders in public companies may sell their shares without prior reference to the company. This is usually done through the Stock Exchange (see chapter 8).

Types of share and loan capital
Figure 7.4 sets out the various types of *shares* and their characteristics. Note the different methods of determining dividends on these shares. A dividend can only be paid out of profits in the ordinary course of events, but loan interest has to be paid

whether or not the business is making a profit. The *debentures* – described in Figure 7.4 – are loans, and in the event of the company going into liquidation must be repaid before most other creditors and any shareholders get any cash. If the debentures are *mortgage debentures* they may have to be repaid either out of money from the sale of particular buildings, for example, or before creditors get any funds on a general selling-up of the business. There are, however, certain creditors given by law a claim on the funds available before paying even debenture holders.

The terms *capital, share capital, assets* and *liabilities* are introduced in Figures 7.1 to 7.4 showing how these words are used in a business context. Note the way assets are classified in accounts, particularly 'circulating capital' which is conventionally shown as current assets in accounts. So far as these are used in the day-to-day business of the organisation, accountants regard them all as assets realised (sold) in day-to-day trading.

Limited companies in the economy

The concept of Joint-Stock Companies, to give Limited Companies their somewhat old-fashioned name, has helped to promote economic development in several ways. It has allowed companies, public companies especially, to obtain capital for expansion. In this way large organisations have been created with small subscriptions for shares from many people, who would not have been prepared to risk their money if liability was unlimited. Individuals' savings through insurance companies and pension funds, the premiums and contributions paid regularly for some future benefit, are often invested in industry and commerce. The producers, manufacturers, retailers and others forming public companies or expanding existing ones, can attract funds from these institutions discussed later in Chapter 5. The managers of a pension or similar scheme must be sure that businesses using these pension funds – the contributions of subscribers – are properly regulated. The laws relating to limited companies go a long way towards ensuring this.

You have seen that limited companies have separate entities. They continue when any of their owners – shareholders – withdraws by selling his or her shares. In many smaller companies and a few large ones, the owner-shareholders are *also* managers and run these businesses in much the same way as any small firm is run: the boss as owner makes all the important decisions. Most limited companies, however, employ professional managers. The effect of shareholders owning a business in which they take no other part divorces the control of the day-to-day running from ownership.

Organisation

This divorce of ownership from the day-to-day running of the limited company is shown in Figure 7.3. The precise duties of senior directors and managers can only be shown as an example in the diagram, for these vary from company to company. Nevertheless directors in general are elected or re-elected periodically by shareholders.

The board of directors decides matters of policy, whether the business should expand in this direction or that, how much finance should be raised and where it might come from, and whether or not the company should follow one or another course to achieve its aims and objectives. The managing director is responsible for the day-to-day execution of these policies.

Co-operatives and co-operative societies
Retail Co-operative Societies are customer-owned businesses. The first one on the lines of societies today was formed by weavers in the 1840s in Rochdale. They banded together for – among other aims – buying in bulk at wholesale prices and sharing the profit which would otherwise have been earned by shopkeepers. The profit was distributed as a 'divvy' (dividend paid according to the amount you spent, maybe 6p in £). By 1975 there were 10 765 000 members of retail Co-operative Societies in the United Kingdom operating through networks of chain stores, supermarkets and local shops, with a retail turnover of £2075 million (see Figure 7.5). For some years retail societies have given trading stamps rather than divvy, as the stamps show a more immediate benefit to customers than dividends paid half-yearly, and are less expensive to administer.

Retail Co-operative Societies are run by elected committees of members. In 1862 a number of the retail societies got together to set up the Co-operative Wholesale Society (CWS). The CWS is owned by the retail societies, and supplies goods and does some manufacturing on their behalf. If a Co-op fails, the CWS also steps in to prevent that society from defaulting on repayments to members.

Worker co-operatives
The idea of workers owning the business which employs them is probably very old. In modern times the idea has been tried with varying degrees of success in the USSR, China, Cuba, Israel, Yugoslavia, Denmark and in the UK among other countries. The important characteristic of co-operatives is the workers' ownership of the enterprise, although very often these are in part at least financed from government loans as was the Meriden Motorcycle Co-operative. Each worker member generally has one vote in electing the committee who organise the work of the co-operative.

Other co-operatives
A number of farmer co-operatives have been set up to market produce, cutting out some wholesalers and other middlemen. Farmers also use these co-operatives to obtain the benefits of buying seed, fertiliser and other commodities in bulk. Typical is Midland Shire Farmers (MSF), a society with nearly 8000 farmer members who own this business with its five mills for preparing animal feed – including in 1976 one of Europe's most modern animal feed mills. MSF also has depots and shops providing fertilisers, machinery and many everyday supplies for their members. They also operate an egg trading and packing depot that supplies shops in the Midlands of England (see Figure 7.6). The farmer owners are customers and sometimes also suppliers, but they do not have to sell their produce to the Society nor buy from it.

Public enterprises
The arguments for government or state intervention in the working of the economy are set out in the *Doforall* community's approach to solving the economic problem. Look again at the points summarised in Figure 1.4 on page 18.

Public enterprises in the United Kingdom
British governments have set up a number of nationalised industries or public

THE GREATER NOTTINGHAM CO-OPERATIVE SOCIETY LTD

Members (255 180 in 1976) elected 64 Council Members.

The seven areas covered by the Society each elect a number of Council Members according to the food-trade sales in each area. This Council meets at least four times a year, elects the Board of Directors from Council Members, elects representatives to various committees, receives reports and makes recommendations to the Board 'on the affairs of the Society'.

Financial Position as at 31 Jan 1976

	£000s
Fixed Assets	
Land, buildings, etc	17 086
Less depreciation	8 665
	8 421
Investments	955
Net Current Assets	
Stocks, debts & cash	10 601
Less trade creditors, amounts due to banks, & unredeemed dividend stamps	4 746
	5 855
Total Assets	**£15 231**
Financed by:	
Share Capital	5 564
Reserves — mainly accumulated revenue account surpluses	2 699
Loans	6 968
Total Funds	**£15 231**

Board of Directors

Controls all the business of the Society, appoints staff, sets pay rates and makes contracts. The Board may and does delegate part of their powers to senior executives and other employees of the Society. All committees of the Society are subject to the Board's decisions.

Various committees are formed to work with consumer groups, cultural groups, the Co-operative Party, and others.

Revenue Account for 1975/6

		£000s
Sales (including VAT)		60 042
Cost of goods sold and expenses		58 068
Trading Surplus		1 974
Dividend stamps		1 017
		957
Prior yrs' Milk Margins		326
Interest etc recd		91
		1 374
Interest paid	984	
Provision for employees' grants, etc	166	1 150
Surplus for year		224
Surplus on sale of Assets		28
Allocated to Reserves		£252

Figure 7.5   A retail co-operative organisation and accounts.

MIDLAND SHIRE FARMERS LTD (known as 'The Society')

Brief history — Worcestershire and Warwickshire Societies (the parent co-operatives) merged in 1968 to form MSF Ltd. Their origins included a growers' co-operative to give an even flow of vegetables to the local market and factory canteens in World War I. Since 1921 the Society has run Worcester Produce Market under a charter from the local Council. The Society bought egg packing stations, opened depots and set up its first mill by 1958; this processes cereals from growers into feed for cattle. By 1976 the major part of the Society's trade was in animal feed from its 5 mills including some of the best equipped in Europe. It markets vegetables, fruit, eggs, grain and meat, runs grain driers and seed units, sells fertilizer, fuel and all manner of goods needed by farmers. It supplies in 12 counties through 14 depots and shops. Many deliveries are in the Society's own vehicles with 80% of feed delivered in bulk. It builds and sells agricultural machinery nationwide.

Members — some 8000 farmers and grers of fruit and vegetables, each with 50 shares of 25p in the Society. They do not *have* to sell to or buy from the Society.

The Board of 12 member farmers are elected as part-time directors who make the regulations for running the Society's affairs, and appoint managers.

Organisation — the General Manager is responsible to the Board and has 10 managers responsible to him for Finance, Production, Publicity, Sales, Machinery-production, Garden Shops, Egg Packing, Wholesale Fruit & Veg, Seed Testing and Fuel Departments.

Financial Position — 31 October 1975	
	£000s
Fixed Assets	
Land, plant etc less depreciation	1 151
Investments	85
Current Assets less	
Liabilities	1 928
Total Assets	£3 164
Financed by:	
Share Capital	1 305
Reserves & Deferred tax	1 378
Loans	481
	£3 164

Profit and Loss (P & L) Account 1974/5	
	£000s
Sales	19 098
Less costs and expenses	18 607
Profit before tax	491
Corporation tax	61
Profit after tax	£430
Allocation of profits:	
To members	330
To reserves	100
	£430

Figure 7.6   A farming co-operative organisation and accounts.

The National Coal Board

Set up in 1946 to take over virtually all the UK coal mines, has subsequently managed and developed the UK's coal resources, producing 125·2-million tons in 1975 and 123·8-million tons in 1976.

British Steel Corporation

Created by the Iron and Steel Act (1967) to take over 14 major steel producing companies in the UK. The Corporation has to supply iron and steel at prices and in the quantities that will reasonably satisfy demand.

British Railways Board

The railways were nationalised in 1947 and the Board set up by the Transport Act (1962) and subsequent legislation to operate the railways with 28 700 miles of train routes in late 1976.

British Gas Corporation

Created in 1949 to take over the gas supply industry, at that time including a number of gas works owned by Local Authorities. By late 1976 some 97% of the gas sold was natural gas mainly from the North Sea.

National Freight Corporation

Created by the Transport Act (1968), the Corporation provides integrated road and rail freight services. The Act requires the Corporation to make the best use of rail services where this is possible after taking account of the type of goods carried and customers' requirements.

British Airways

Established in 1972 under the Civil Aviation Act (1971) which merged the intercontinental operations of the nationalised British Overseas Airways and the British European Airways Corporation. The Corporation has some 200 aircraft.

Electricity Authorities

These in 1976 included the Central Electricity Generating Board responsible since the late 1940s for generating electricity and operating over 130 power stations selling electricity to twelve Area Boards. These are each responsible for the supply of electricity to customers in their areas.

British Aerospace Corporation

Created by the Aircraft and Shipbuilding Act (1977) to take over certain aircraft and guided weapon manufacturing companies, the Corporation controls the major part of this industry.

British Shipbuilders Corporation

Created under the Act mentioned above, this Corporation has taken over all major shipbuilding yards in the UK.

British Transport Docks Board

Set up under the Transport Act (1962) to own and operate 19 ports, the Board run most of the major dock facilities in the UK.

British National Oil Corporation (BNOC)

Set up in 1975 to take over offshore oil and gas interests of the *National Coal Board* from early 1976. BNOC also holds the interest under licences the government has issued to companies exploring for and/or producing oil from British areas of the Continental shelf. It may also explore for, produce, refine, distribute and sell oil products and provide advisory services to those who are involved in the oil industry. BNOC requires government approval, however, to carry out any specific exploration or other activity abroad.

British Airports Authority

Set up under the Air Ports Authority Act (1965) to own and manage several airports the Authority runs Heathrow, Stanstead, Prestwick and Aberdeen airports among others.

Other public enterprises

Reference is made in the text to the National Enterprise Board. There are also motor car and vehicle production companies including Rolls Royce (1971) Ltd and Leyland, bus operations in some areas and on inter-city services, canal services, nuclear power developments, Cable & Wireless Ltd, the Milk Marketing Board, the Bank of England and the Post Office with activities in the economy that can be described as public enterprise. Whitakers Almanak is a source for updating this information and finding the correct titles of the public organisations carrying out these activities at the time of your study.

Figure 7.7   The principal public sector trading organisations in the UK May 1976.

corporations. A corporation in this sense is not unlike a limited company but in America and occasionally in the UK the term 'corporation' is also used for private concerns. Public corporations, including nationalised industries, are run by boards whose members are appointed by the Secretary for Trade and Industry. Although his or her title may change from time to time, this politician is a member of the Cabinet. Details of the main public corporations in industry are given in Figure 7.7 with summaries of their aims and organisations.

A major period of nationalisation occurred just after World War II with the nationalisation of the coal industry in 1946, of railways in 1947, electricity supply industry in 1948 and the gas industry in 1949. (For other dates see Figure 7.7.) The original shareholders of businesses in these industries received compensation in government securities paying a fixed interest – these can be sold for cash as we will see later.

The government sets targets for the nationalised industries' performance, outlined in White Papers from time to time. But the day-to-day running of each business is in the hands of its board. These nationalised industries – as mentioned earlier – are run in part at least with social as well as financial objectives. Over the years, however, there have been changes in government policy towards the running of the industries and pricing policies have been altered (see Assignment 7.2 below).

Assignments

7.1 What is the principle of limited liability? What are its advantages to (a) investors and (b) firms? (AEB 1973)

7.2 Update Figure 7.7 – listing public corporations and their aims at the time of your study.

7.3 Distinguish between private and public enterprise and compare the advantages of each as forms of business organisation. (L 1971)

7.4* Discuss: 'Partnerships and sole proprietors are suitable forms of organisation for professional work but are unsuitable for manufacturing industries.'

7.5* Group research: select four particular businesses with a different form or organisation for study by each group. Note the likely advantages and disadvantages of each organisation in the particular business's activities.

7.6* Group research: draw up a chart showing the organisation of two local social or sports clubs. How are their committees elected? What are the duties of each club's officials? How is information obtained for decisions to be taken?

Suggested further reading

Donaldson, Chapters 4 and 5
Hanson, Chapter 6
Harvey, Chapters 5 and 6
Stanlake, Chapter 9

Chapter 8
Raising finance

Whatever the form of organisation from a one-man business to a public corporation, those running it will need to find cash to finance its operations. There are wages, bills for materials and other expenses to be paid *before* any revenue comes in from the sales of output. The firm probably also needs machines and other producer goods before it can start manufacturing any output. You will later see that there are different ways of raising this money, according to the type of business and its particular needs.

Sources of finance

The need for finance

You will remember that fixed and variable factors must be brought together for production. In practice this means finance is needed not only for week-to-week operations but also on a longer term.

Short-term borrowing needed to finance variable factors is met (raised) in the expectation that it can be repaid reasonably soon – in three months, perhaps. But in business, as with your own income, if you borrow on a short-term basis to finance a long-term need, you are in trouble. The motorcyclists with only enough cash each month to pay small instalments towards the cost of a machine would be foolish to buy his bike with a loan repayable in three months. A businessman, for similar reasons, does not borrow on a short-term basis to buy machines, for these will take a number of years, probably, to earn sufficient return from which to repay money borrowed to buy them. (This 'return' is the net revenue after deducting running costs.) But short-term needs – buying raw materials to manufacture this month and to pay wages for such work – may be financed with short-term loans, because these should be repaid when the output is sold later in the month (see Figure 8.1).

Undistributed profits

Before looking at the institutions providing finance, the 'savings' made by firms themselves must be considered, for owners of a business may 'keep the profits in the business'. Rather than draw out or distribute profits as salaries for owner-managers or dividends to shareholders, the profits can be left undistributed.

Future expansion can be financed from these retained profits. But in so far as they are used to finance long-term needs of the firm, they cannot always be drawn out at a later date (see Figure 8.2).

long term borrowing for investment in fixed capital

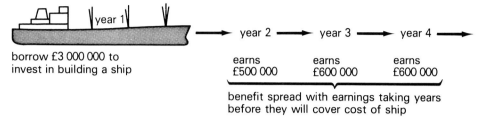

borrow £3 000 000 to
invest in building a ship

year 2 ⟶ year 3 ⟶ year 4 ⟶

earns
£500 000

earns
£600 000

earns
£600 000

benefit spread with earnings taking years
before they will cover cost of ship

short term borrowings for investment in working capital

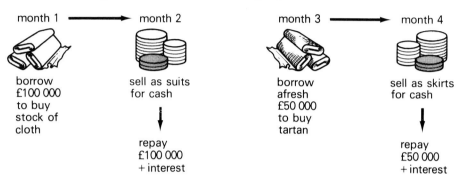

month 1 ⟶ month 2

month 3 ⟶ month 4

borrow
£100 000
to buy
stock of
cloth

sell as suits
for cash

↓

repay
£100 000
+ interest

borrow
afresh
£50 000
to buy
tartan

sell as skirts
for cash

↓

repay
£50 000
+ interest

Figure 8.1   Long-term and short-term borrowing for investment.

Money and Capital Markets
Something of the way the savings find their way into industry is shown in Figure 8.3. Note how the institutions handling these monies (funds) are generally speaking from part of the Money Market for short-term loans, and the Capital Market for medium- and long-term finance. These are explained in more detail in chapter 14.

Finance from banks
The commercial banks hold money from individuals and firms. They also lend money in different ways to suit customers' particular needs (Figure 8.4). A customer who is moving house may need a short-term loan to cover the purchase price of the new house before being paid for the old one. This loan like any other bank loan is only made against some security should anything go wrong. Or the bank will have at least reasonable assurances – guarantees, perhaps – that the money will be repaid as agreed.

The simple bank loan, like most loans between individuals, is made for a specific period. The borrower repays it with interest. So if Jack borrows £100 from Jill for three months at an agreed rate – say 10% per year – he repays £100 plus $\frac{3}{12}$ of the 10% payable in a full year: £2.50 ($\frac{3}{12} \times \frac{10}{100} \times$ £100). If Jack borrows a sum repayable in two equal amounts, then the interest may be charged on only the amount outstanding: £10 on the first year – 10% of £100; and £5 for the second year – 10% of £50. Whichever way it is calculated, interest is the return to the lender's financial capital and paid to induce Jill and others to lend it, foregoing current consumption. Therefore on the £100 Jill lent, she earned interest to compensate her for not currently spending this cash herself.

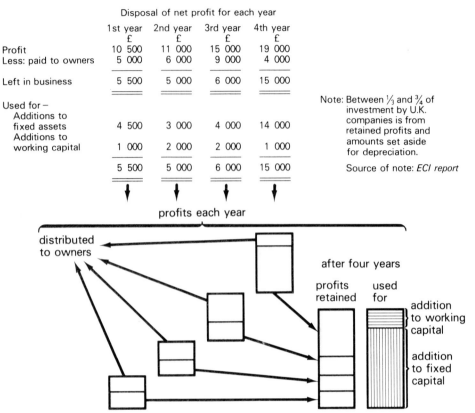

Disposal of net profit for each year

	1st year £	2nd year £	3rd year £	4th year £
Profit	10 500	11 000	15 000	19 000
Less: paid to owners	5 000	6 000	9 000	4 000
Left in business	5 500	5 000	6 000	15 000
Used for – Additions to fixed assets	4 500	3 000	4 000	14 000
Additions to working capital	1 000	2 000	2 000	1 000
	5 500	5 000	6 000	15 000

Note: Between ⅓ and ¾ of investment by U.K. companies is from retained profits and amounts set aside for depreciation.

Source of note: *ECI report*

profits each year

distributed to owners

after four years

profits retained   used for

addition to working capital

addition to fixed capital

Figure 8.2   Retained profits used in a business.

Bank overdrafts
In the United Kingdom bank overdraft facilities – the arrangements for overdrafts – are perhaps the most convenient and usually the least costly form of short-term borrowing. The bank agrees that the borrower may draw money up to a maximum sum borrowed at any one time. However, actual sums borrowed will vary from day to day as the borrower pays money back into the account. On a Monday the overdraft of a firm might be £10 200 (written in an account with a minus sign: −£10 200). But on Tuesday £10 000 may be paid in and only £225 paid out of the account, leaving a balance of −£425 on Tuesday night (−£10 200 + £10 000 − £225 = −£425). Wednesday may bring only withdrawals for £375 increasing the overdraft to −£800 (−£425 and −£375 = −£800) in the 'red' (as sometimes overdrafts are printed in red).

With an overdraft the borrower uses only the amount of loan he (or his firm) requires on any day, while the bank charge interest only on the amount outstanding from day to day. In our example the interest is then paid for one day on each sum £10 200, £425 and £800.

Personal loans
To meet the needs of some individuals, a form of loan was developed called a 'personal loan'. This is a method of borrowing which has parallels with buying goods on hire purchase; like HP regular instalments are repaid.

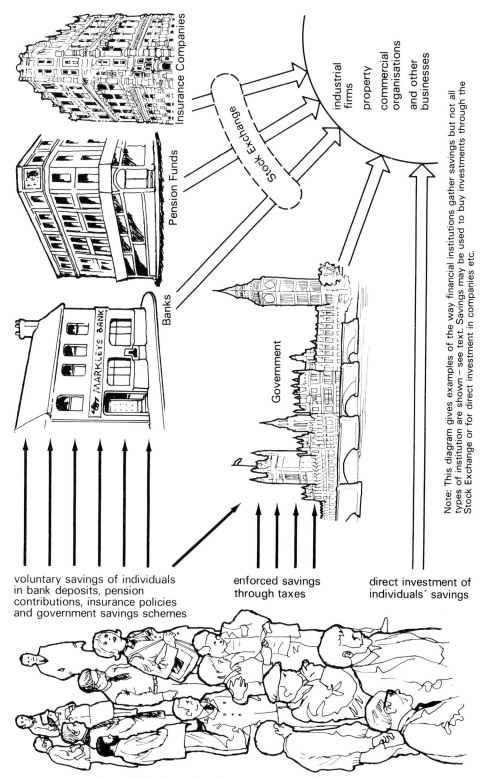

Insurance Companies

Pension Funds

Banks

MARKLEY'S BANK

Stock Exchange

Government

industrial firms
property
commercial organisations
and other businesses

Note: This diagram gives examples of the way financial institutions gather savings but not all types of institution are shown – see text. Savings may be used to buy investments through the Stock Exchange or for direct investment in companies etc.

voluntary savings of individuals in bank deposits, pension contributions, insurance policies and government savings schemes

enforced savings through taxes

direct investment of individuals' savings

Figure 8.3   Examples of sources of funds for investment.

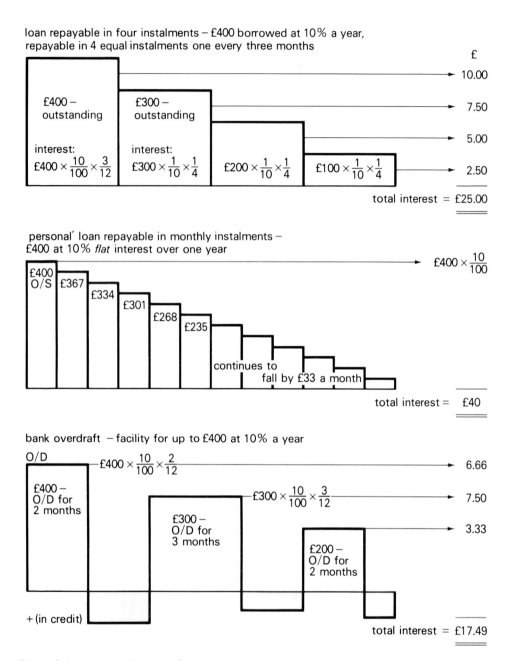

Figure 8.4   Loans and overdrafts.

The charge for personal loans is based on what is called a flat rate used to calculate the interest on the loan. So a flat rate of 10% a year on a £100 loan for two years gives an interest charge of £20 (2 × 10% of £100), regardless of the fact that instalments paying off the loan will reduce the sums outstanding at the end of each month. Note that there is a difference between this and a *true* rate of interest calculated on the amounts owing at the end of each month, the true interest rate is approximately twice the flat rate (see Figure 8.4).

Institutions making personal loans in the UK after 1974 have had to include the true interest rate, as well as any flat rate given in the document setting out an agreement between a borrower and lender, under the Consumer Credit Act.

Credit from suppliers

Firms receive credit from their suppliers who normally do not expect payment until the month following the month-in-which-goods-were-delivered. Sometimes longer credit can be arranged. This enables the producer to process materials and possibly collect cash from his customers, before the raw material supplier has to be paid. However, the law is strict in its regulations against abuses of credit from suppliers, for all too easily a firm can delay paying these bills.

Uses for short-term finance

Short-term finance is used for day-to-day purposes including the purchase of variable factors in anticipation of sales revenue. Also the sudden upsurge of business for a seasonal demand, the extra-large contract from a customer, the unexpected delay in a customer paying what is due, are all sound reasons for increased short-term borrowing. Any of these are requirements which will be met in a reasonably short time out of revenue coming into the business from its sales.

Long-term finance is a more complicated matter covered in the last part of this chapter. Therefore the following Assignments include some revision on 'limited companies' structure and share capital.

Assignments

8.1 List the steps necessary for you to open a bank account – see any commercial bank's brochures for details.

8.2 Which is cheaper, a personal loan of £500 repayable in monthly instalments with interest at 10% 'flat', or a two-year loan of £500 repayable in four equal 6-month instalments with a 'true' interest of 18%? Record your calculations.

8.3 Three friends each hold a third of the share capital of a limited company. One dies. What may happen to (a) his shares and (b) the value of his friends' shares?

8.4 Construct an example to show how a £100 overdraft at (say) 15% pa interest may compare in terms of interest paid with a loan at 10% pa of the same amount repayable in twelve monthly instalments by someone with a regular salary.

8.5* Group research: find at least two ways of financing the purchase of a specific tape-recorder or assemble-it-yourself greenhouse or a motor-car. Each group may take one article for study. Record cash price, interest and other (if any) charges, with comments on total outlay and periods for repayment. Among the six or more calculations from details in advertisements, enquiries at shops and at banks, should be at least one example of HP, of store's budget-account, of a personal loan, and of a bank loan.

8.6* Discuss: if a workshop lathe costs £2500 to buy and lasts ten years, what considerations would influence your decision as a businessman on whether or not to invest in this machine?

Long-term finance

Funds 'locked' into the business
The one-man firm or the partnership cannot readily draw out funds already spent on fixed factors of production as we saw in Figure 8.2, with long-term finance invested in machinery and buildings or retained profits employed for this. Nor can shareholders get cash dividends if all retained profits become locked into the business when financing long-term needs.

Limited companies may raise money from time to time by share issues in anticipation of further expansion, as well as making these when the company is first set up.

Whatever the method of raising long-term finance, the costs of the operation – fees to advisers, stamp duties on total share or debenture values and other charges – amount to thousands of pounds. Therefore long-term finance is generally only raised in large amounts.

Long-term finance for individuals and partnerships can come from financial institutions as well as from the owners' personal funds. But since these financial institutions are mainly concerned with larger organisations the following paragraphs deal mainly with limited companies.

Share offers
Private companies, unable to offer shares to the public, can nevertheless raise money through share offers to institutions. But the issue of shares by a public company can follow four different avenues. The *public issue* of shares is made by advertising for people to subscribe. The documents offering the shares must include a prospectus giving facts and figures of the company's history, its directors and its operations. Preparation of this and other formal documents are part of the procedure conducted by an Issuing House for the company. *Issuing Houses* are institutions which specialise in making share offers and also advise the company on when and on what terms an issue may be most successful.

The issue may be *underwritten*. An underwriter agrees to take any shares not taken by the public. Although the underwriters are paid a fee whether or not they have to take up shares, having an issue underwritten is a wise precaution for most companies. It is a form of insurance.

Another method of issuing shares is an *offer for sale* in which the Issuing House buys the shares. (On a sale to the public the House only advises on the terms, etc of the issue.) These are then sold by the Issuing House to the public who are entitled to much the same information as when shares are issued directly to them.

The share may be *placed*. This method is used when the company, or Issuing House acting for it, contact institutions or individuals who each take a sizeable portion (block) of shares. The company get their long-term capital without involving themselves in the risks and expense of a public issue. A *placing* is made normally only in raising funds for relatively small companies. But the sponsors of such shares to be sold on the Stock Exchange (see page 115) must make sure a certain proportion is available for this market.

Sometimes existing shareholders may be given the opportunity to subscribe for new shares. This is known as a *rights issue* – so called because existing shares carry a right to so many new ones. The rights issue may be made on favourable terms, giving existing shareholders the opportunity to take a further stake in the company, or to sell these rights while keeping their original shares.

The choice of method depends on a variety of circumstances, among the most important of which is the need to maintain the value of existing shares. The timing of an issue is also important, one reason for making an *offer for sale* to an Issuing House. The company may need the money now, but a public issue might be inappropriate so that the House buys the whole issue of shares and then sells them in small lots over a period.

These are only a few of the permutations of terms, reasons and methods used in issuing shares. No matter what method is followed, any share issue brings in long-term finance.

Investors

Mention has been made of the way institutions gather the savings of individuals and channel them into industry and commerce among other investments; look again at Figure 8.3, page 107. Insurance companies are a major channel for these funds. They hold premiums on life and fire insurances and policies against all manner of risks. While holding the life premiums the insurers want them to earn a return – keeping down the premiums and in part making profits for the insurance company when this has shareholders. And as they expect to hold the funds for a long time, they can be used to provide long-term finance. Insurance companies' actuaries calculate tables showing the likely time before pay out. The fire insurance premiums must also be held to pay out those policy holders unlucky enough to have a fire. This and other accident premiums can be invested for shorter periods – a year or two.

Another major group of investors are pension funds. These may be schemes set up by private or public companies and by other institutions for their employees. The trustees – those responsible for seeing that the pension fund is properly run – look for investments which maintain their value and give a good return in interest or dividends. As most contributors to these funds will have made twenty or more years' contributions before drawing a pension, the pension funds can be invested on a long-term basis.

Two special forms of investment companies are those known as *Investment Trusts* and *Unit Trusts* (see Figure 8.5).

Investment Trust companies buy and sell shares in other companies, using the profits from this and the dividends (received from shares held) in part to pay their dividends, and to subscribe for new shares in other companies. As experts in investment, managers of these Investment Trusts expect to do better from dealing in shares than shareholders dealing as individuals.

Unit Trusts sell a 'unit' of stock representing its holder's portion of a wide collection of shares (a portfolio). Although complex organisations, Unit Trusts offer to the public a means of investing in industry and commerce in small amounts, spreading the risk over many different companies' shares. The Unit Trust will buy back units at any time the holder wishes to sell, if he or she does not want the bother of selling these units to others. The re-purchase price of a unit is fixed by a formula related to the value of the underlying portfolio, but the units' holder may get a better price if he or she can find another buyer.

Finance for Industry Ltd (FFI)

This company owns two financial institutions established in the mid-1940s: the

INVESTMENT TRUST CO LTD
Financial position

	£000s
Assets	
Investments mainly in ordinary shares of different companies	£20 000
Bought with funds from:	
Shareholders in the Investment Trust Company	10 000
Debenture or loan holders	10 000
	£20 000

Profit for a year (tax not shown)

Dividend received from investments		2 700
Less: Management expenses	80	
Interest paid to Debenture holders	1 000	1 080
		£1 620

Notes: 1 Shareholders' risks are spread as Trust Co's investments usually in different industries and countries. A third of the £4000-million in some 250 Investment Trusts was invested abroad in 1975.

2 Management expenses in many Investment Trusts was less than 0·4% of assets in 1975.

3 Special tax arrangements have led to realised profits on sales of investments being re-invested during the mid-1970s.

4 Shareholders in this simplified example, and often in practice, get the benefit of 'gearing', as a fixed percentage of interest is paid on debenture or other loans, yet these funds may be used by the Investment Trust to buy ordinary shares (equity) paying a higher return. The difference goes to the benefit of the Investment Trust's shareholders.

UNIT TRUST

Shareholders – provide funds to set up business with offices etc.

Managers – bring together a portfolio of shares, for example:

Car Motors Ltd	100 000 at £1
Malay Tin Inc	50 000 at £2
British Zinc	250 000 at 20p

and so on with perhaps 30 or more different shares in all worth £200 000. Trustees – by law are independent of the Managers, and hold the cash and shares for Unit holders under a Trust deed.

Units – an example – 800 000 units at 25p each, sold to the public who then have an interest in the underlying portfolio according to the number of units each person holds. These may be bought and sold and the Managers will buy them back at a price – see text.

Notes: 1 Units are often easier than shares for the investor to buy.

2 The Unit holder spreads the risk of his/her investment because of the spread of shares in the underlying portfolio.

3 Unit Trusts are operated under strict rules to the directions of the Dept of Trade & Industry.

4 The Managers make a charge for operating the Unit Trust, as do the Trustees. A sum to cover these costs and the Unit Trust shareholders' profit is included in the Managers' price for a unit. They also deduct a small fee from the income of the portfolios. Many Unit Trusts operate several different portfolios and matching units.

5 Income Tax is deducted from the 'dividends' paid on units, and Capital Gains tax is paid by a Unit Trust under special arrangements relieving the Unit holders of Capital Gains tax on unit sales.

Figure 8.5   Investment Trusts and Unit Trusts.

Industrial and Commercial Finance Corporation Ltd (ICFC), and the Finance Corporation for Industry (FCI).

ICFC provides long-term finance with amounts from £5000 to £1 million or more for smaller businesses. FCI provides medium-term loans mainly for larger enterprises borrowing £1 million to £25 million. The group also provides financial and management advice, and funds for entrepreneurs developing businesses based on new technology.

ICFC, since its formation in 1945, had provided over £450 million for more than 4000 companies by 1976. In financing the development of small- and medium-sized businesses, ICFC may make loans, subscribe for shares, or in other ways provide financial assistance suited to a firm's needs. FCI makes loans for periods usually of ten years or more. These are at interest rates that may be fixed when the loan is made, or they may vary according to the prevailing levels of interest – the general rates for loans, etc (see page 207).

The FFI is owned by the English and Scottish clearing banks (85%) and the Bank of England (15%). It is *not* a government agency although it works in close cooperation with the government and other European institutions. In March 1976 FFI had some £107 million in shareholders' funds, £437 million in loans, and could call on other facilities – promises by banks to provide the FFI with further loans if required.

Large sums
The large sums involved in some investments are often difficult to relate to everyday events. But for every £1 000 000, you could build nearly eighty average-priced houses in 1976. For £25 million you would require £500 from every spectator in a crowd of 50 000 at a football match.

The National Enterprise Board (NEB)
The NEB – set up under the Industry Act 1975 – has a similar status to a nationalised industry and provides government funds mainly for the modernisation and reorganisation of manufacturing industry in the private sector. These financial resources supplement other institutions' funds available for investment in industry. Its aims include the safeguarding of productive employment, and the improvement of industrial efficiency and profitability not only through promoting reorganisation but also by investing in particular firms from time to time. As an industrial holding company, the NEB owns subsidiaries like British Leyland Ltd and Rolls-Royce (1971) Ltd, formerly direct holdings of the government. From time to time the Board may set up new enterprises and take part in joint ventures with one or more other organisations. On all these activities, the Board ensures the companies it owns and its other investments provide a proper return to the public as their indirect owners.

In providing such financial and managerial help to manufacturing industries, the NEB follows government guidelines for a long-term strategy. These include the requirement that it should exercise commercial judgement in seeking an adequate return on its investments. However, as an important element of government policy in the mid-1970s, it takes a broad view of the benefits flowing from each investment and not merely the likely return in purely financial terms. It has a special responsibility for stimulating investment and employment in areas for expansion and regional development that were described in chapter 6.

When providing financial and managerial help to firms, the NEB has no special privileges over financial institutions in the private sector. Its policies must follow those in the capital market on fair trading and on mergers, and it may not subsidise the interest rates charged to borrowers. Usually the NEB takes ordinary shares (see Figure 7.4, page 96) although it may make medium- and long-term loans. Also on occasions the government may direct the Board to give short-term financial and managerial help to specific firms.

The amount of funds available to the NEB is decided by the government. Under the Industry Act (1975) the overall limit is £1000 million, but this may be increased through further legislation. Part of these funds are to be in loans at rates of interest broadly the same as for government borrowing, and part in *public dividend capital*. The government set an appropriate return to be earned on this public dividend capital in the light of the Board's future investment plans. These are likely to include investment in manufacturing companies which might otherwise not have survived a difficult time. Under the NEB's wider responsibilities, the government may ask the Board to help in following up some matters of reorganisation and with joint ventures arising out of *planning agreements*. These are medium-term agreements between the government, trade unions and major industrial companies about future developments in their industries. Introduced under the Industry Act (1975) the agreements are being discussed with a number of companies in 1976.

Equity Capital for Industry Ltd (ECI)
The ECI was set up in May 1976 with a capital of approximately £41 million provided by the capital market institutions including insurance and pension funds. (For tax reasons the pension funds' investment is in the form of a unit trust.) The institutions formed ECI to make equity and equity-type investments in industrial companies (and others) that have sound long-term prospects. But since some years may pass before a commercial return is received, one institution's support on its own for a firm might be inappropriate because of the risks involved. The companies needing support are not aggressively sought by ECI, but are brought to its attention by institutions. Then a full investigation is made by ECI sometimes leading to recommendations for the company to be reorganised possibly with management changes. Subsequently ECI monitors the company's performance until it is restored to a sound position. ECI can also advise and assist institutions with investments in companies.

ECI shares and units will initially be held only by institutions who may buy and sell them between each other.

Industrial investment
In 1976 with the NEB and the ECI being formed, and other moves to supplement traditional sources of finance for industry, the British took steps to strengthen the allocation of resources to productive industry, for without adequate industrial investment there can be no sustained economic growth – an outward shift in the production possibility frontier (the PPC curve of Figure 1.2, page 14) that can improve living standards described in detail in chapter 13.

Sources of UK public companies' finance
Figure 8.6 summarises the sources of investment from which UK public companies draw their equity finance.

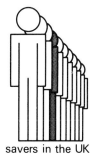

savers in the UK

In 1973 nine out of ten adults had savings of some kind. About 2½-million had invested directly on the Stock Exchange, and 22½-million invested indirectly through life insurance, pension schemes, etc.

Ownership of quoted ordinary shares in UK
31st December 1973

	£-m	%
Individuals, executors and trustees resident in UK	17 010	42.0
Charitable and similar non-profit making bodies	1 780	4.4
Insurance companies	6 550	16.2
Pension Funds	4 950	12.2
Investment Trusts	2 640	6.5
Unit Trusts	1 390	3.4
Banks and other institutions not listed separately	4 090	10.1
Overseas investors	2 110	5.2
	40 520	100.0

Source: *Stock Exchange*

Figure 8.6   Notes on sources of funds for UK public companies.

The Stock Exchange

The share market

Shares in public companies can be bought and sold through a stock exchange. This is a market like any other although regulated by rules drawn up for the public's safeguard and conforming to relevant company laws. If there were not a market for shares, investors would be less likely to invest, for they cannot – as we have seen – get their money back from companies at any time they might need it.

Although a shareholder may make any deal (subject to company law) he wishes with others, a stock exchange is the most likely place to find a buyer or seller of particular shares (see Figure 8.7). As we will see later in chapter 14, many government securities are also dealt in on the London Stock Exchange. It is described below although shares may be bought and sold (dealt in) on the provincial and the Irish Republic exchanges all with links to the London Exchange. The shares of some British public companies can also be bought and sold on stock exchanges overseas, in much the same way as some foreign companies' shares and other foreign stocks may be bought and sold in London.

The London Stock Exchange's 1972 annual turnover was the world's third largest after the New York and Tokyo exchanges, while it was second to New York in the total value of investments in which brokers might deal. These include government securities, local authorities' and nationalised industries' loan stock, and many public companies' shares and debentures, with over 10 000 stocks and shares of all types.

Before a public company can have their shares dealt in (and quoted) by the Stock Exchange, the company must satisfy the Council of the Stock Exchange on the adequacy and accuracy of information provided to the public, including details of management, promoters and past profits. Once accepted, the company's shares are quoted in the daily list published by the Stock Exchange giving market prices of shares. If shares are only occasionally bought and sold they may be in a second list published monthly. We will come back to the way the Exchange does business but first we need to understand something of the way share prices are determined.

your broker takes order to buy 1000 Sapsadd ordinary shares

Settlement date – all transactions in company shares and stock are settled at the end of two or sometimes three week *Account Periods*. Settlement for government stocks is usually the day after the transaction took place. On settlement day a broker pays the jobbers what is due by the broker's clients and collects what is due to his clients for sales. Buyers pay the broker a day or so before Settlement Day. A computerised system – *Talisman* – is being developed in 1976 with the intention of reducing the half million or so documents used to link buyers to sellers at the end of an Account Period.

jobbers buy from and sell to brokers

offer bid

offer bid

offer accepted

new share certificate for you to your broker

offer bid

jobber buys 2000 'Sapsadd' and sells 1000 of them to your broker, and keeps 1000 on his – the jobber's – books for the next buyer

offer bid

prices displayed

share transfer documents to Sapsadd Co Ltd from Harry's broker

Harry's broker asked to sell 2000 'Sapsadd' shares

Sapsadd Co Ltd enter your name as shareholder and adjust share register for Harry's sale of Sapsadd shares

Figure 8.7   Stock Exchange transactions.

Notes:
1. The yield here is shown for a dividend related to the price paid for a share.

2. Quoted prices include the right to any dividend unless given as 'ex-div.'

3. Earnings per share of a company – usually greater than dividends paid – may also be shown as a percentage of a share's price.

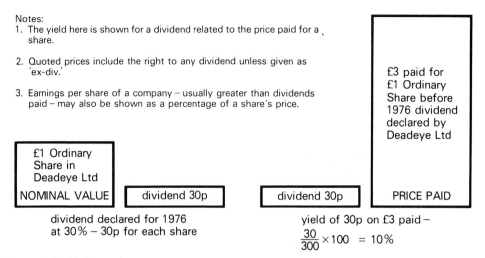

dividend declared for 1976
at 30% – 30p for each share

yield of 30p on £3 paid –
$$\frac{30}{300} \times 100 \ = 10\%$$

Figure 8.8   Yield on shares.

Share prices and yields

The price of any share is determined by how many people want to buy it and the numbers of this share offered for sale at any one time. Without getting involved for the moment in details of demand and supply forces, clearly if investors took a gloomy view this morning of prospects for British industry, then share prices would tend to fall. This happens because people are reluctant to buy and others may be keen to sell, fearing a fall in share prices.

The amount of dividends paid in the past and estimates (or more probably informed guesses) of future dividends affect the demand for a share. This dividend or expected dividend can be related (see Figure 8.8) to the current market price for a share, to give the yield. This is expressed as the percentage you get or expect to get on the price of the share. Several facts are taken into account when considering a share, but the yield is usually the most important for the ordinary investor. He or she may also want to know how many times the total dividend is covered by profits – paying £100 000 in dividends out of £400 000 profits means that the dividend is covered four times. There are also formulae used by experts to assess the worth of a particular company's shares. But remember that the price of a share is determined by the demand for it and its supply – how many of this share people are willing to sell.

Organisation of the Stock Exchange

Members of the public cannot deal direct through the Stock Exchange but must approach a stock broker – look again at Figure 8.7. The system of having stock brokers who deal with the public, and stock jobbers who deal with the brokers, is intended to smooth out prices. The jobber does not know on whose behalf the broker is acting, and his prices are not therefore influenced by the customer's size or related considerations, while his anticipation of demand or lack of it is reflected in his prices.

With jobbers specialising in particular types of shares the broker can approach several who deal in the shares you want bought for you. The jobber gives two prices, not knowing if your broker wants to buy or to sell. There is a top price at which the jobber will sell and a lower price at which he buys. From the difference between his prices the jobber makes his 'turn', the profit from buying low and selling more dearly. However, on a single transaction the difference between these two prices does not necessarily represent a profit to the jobber, for he does not always have the stock he sells, and must then 'go into' the Market to buy shares to cover this sale. If he sells shares at 152p each, he may have to pay 153p or more to get shares for delivery against his original sale, and paying a 1p more a share means he makes a loss on the original sale. The sum of his profits and losses on each deal during a period is his total profit or loss for that period.

Having decided which jobber offers the best deal, the broker then buys on his client's (your) behalf. The shares are then 'off the jobbers books' and on your broker's. A sale is made in the reverse way.

Jobbers' prices are determined through their response to demand and supply, taking account of the shares they hold 'on their books'. They may therefore mark-down (reduce) prices on a morning they felt investors took a gloomy view of British industry's future; this discourages sellers and attracts buyers. On the other hand when jobbers mark up prices this encourages selling and discourages buying. In this way prices fluctuate hour by hour, or even minute by minute.

A number of indices or indicators are published showing the movement in share prices each day. The most famous British one is the *Financial Times* (FT) Index. The FT Index is calculated on the movement in selected shares that give a guide to the overall movement of prices in the Market. There are also published price indices for groups of shares in gold mining, industrial companies and so on. In the USA, the Dow Jones Index serves much the same purpose, giving investors and others an idea how the Market has moved.

Influences on share prices
We have seen how a company's shares may be considered in terms of yield or expected yield, and the effect of changes in investors' expectations for industry and commerce's future prospects. So changes in prices reflect in part the changes in confidence among investors. The FT Index is therefore a useful barometer of the climate of opinion among investors. Any event which causes uncertainty – wars, some change in government policy, any bad news of a particular company – may sap investors' confidence and, other things being equal, tend to cause a fall in share prices or the price of shares in the company affected.

Speculation
Some people buy shares in anticipation that these will rise in price and can be sold in a short time for a profit. Although there is an element of chance in buying any share as its price can change, the speculator looks to profit from the price change rather than the future dividends usually considered by investors.

Speculators who buy shares in anticipation of prices rising are known as 'bulls'. Others can sell shares when prices are falling or expected to fall and are known as 'bears'. They may even sell shares they do not yet own, a curious feature of Stock Exchange dealings.

Importance of the Stock Exchange
Despite the criticisms levelled at the Stock Exchange for the activities of speculators, there are a number of important functions it performs in the economy as we have

seen. In particular through its facilities the *small* as well as the large investor is able to channel funds through shares into industry and commerce. Its broker members also provide expert advice, while the Stock Exchange rules protect investors' transactions. And as a by-product of its activities some indicators are provided on conditions in the economy.

This concludes our short study of the mechanics of business organisation and raising finance for these operations. The Assignments below enable you to extend these studies if necessary for your course, before going on to the economics of supply and demand in the following chapters.

Assignments

8.7 Show how the existence of (*a*) limited liability, and (*b*) the Stock Exchange help public companies to obtain finance from the public. (L 1971)

8.8 In what ways may (*a*) a nationalised industry, (*b*) a public company, and (*c*) a retail cooperative society obtain capital? How does each dispose of its profits? (AEB 1974)

8.9 If you wished to set up a small manufacturing business, what sources are available from which you would be able to raise finance? (AEB 1974)

8.10 A shopkeeper in a city centre wishes to open a small branch in the suburbs. By what methods can he raise the necessary finance? (AEB 1975)

8.11 How does an ordinary share differ from (*a*) a preference share and (*b*) a debenture? What would be your rights as an ordinary shareholder compared with those as a debenture holder? (AEB 1974)

8.12 In 1976 Finance for Industry Ltd, the National Enterprise Board and Equity Capital for Industry Ltd provided finance for manufacturing industry in particular. At the time of your study update your information on the activities of these and any similar institutions.

8.13 Describe how the principle of division of labour is applied in the Stock Exchange. What are the advantages of this specialisation? (L 1973)

Suggested further reading

Donaldson, Chapter 1
Stanlake, Chapter 10

Chapter 9

How prices are determined: an introduction

In simple terms the price of any good or service is determined by the interaction of the forces of demand and supply – the quantities that consumers wish to buy and that producers offer for sale.

Demand

Types of market

Before looking at these forces, we need to understand the meaning of the economist's term '*market*'. This is defined as an area or a situation in which buyers and sellers negotiate the exchange of a particular commodity. A market for *any particular good or service* can take various forms. For example, it may serve a geographical area – 'local' for a town's fruit and vegetable market, 'national' for machine tools in the United Kingdom or other country, and 'international' for worldwide trade in wheat or other commodities. Buyers and sellers need not necessarily meet face to face in their market-place dealings but can use telephones, telex, letters and so on.

The market for any specific good may vary in the degree of competition which exists. Almost all local vegetable markets for example have a common characteristic in the large numbers of both buyers and sellers dealing in tomatoes – many shoppers looking round many stalls to find the best buys, with each stallholder competing for the shoppers' custom. Such local vegetable markets, therefore, can be described as markets with a high degree of competition. At the opposite end of the scale are markets with little or no competition. Here when there is only one seller – a monopoly situation – buyers cannot shop around; or when there is only one buyer in the market – a monopsony – then sellers have only one potential customer. In the same way, the sole employer of skilled labour in a town is a monopsonist for its skilled labour.

These single seller or single buyer – monopoly and monopsony – situations are types of market studied in chapter 11. In this chapter we are going to see how price is determined in competitive markets. In practice the degree of competition will vary, but our starting-point is the *perfectly competitive market*. These are markets where a large number of buyers and sellers operate, and no one by his or her actions can influence the prevailing price, because each buys or sells only a small fraction of the total quantity traded. In conditions of perfect competition, therefore, there is no degree or element of monopoly on either the demand or supply sides of the market.

Demand and supply

In these competitive markets two forces interact to determine the price of a good or a service. But before looking at this interaction the characteristics of each force – demand and supply – must be understood.

The meaning of demand
'Demand' is the desire to possess a particular commodity, coupled with a willingness and ability to pay a certain price for it. That is: what you – or someone else – wants, are willing to buy, and have the ability to pay a given price for. Since demand in this sense implies an ability to pay, it can be described as *effective demand*, since our desires – several large cars, a couple of houses and a private yacht, perhaps – are almost invariably greater than our limited incomes run to.

Demand must also be related to a time period, otherwise it is unclear what is meant. A demand for 100 pints of milk means little unless you know whether it is for 100 pints a week or a month. Demand therefore is regarded as a flow with so many units demanded in a period of time: loaves, pints of beer, tonnes of soya bean, motorcars, demanded per week, per month or any other period, at a given price.

The demand for any particular commodity is often considered at three levels – demand from individuals, from households, and from the community or the market as a whole. Since households are comprised of individuals and communities of households, any study of demand involves an understanding of people's behaviour as individual consumers. How they are likely to react to the change in the price of a good, their changes of taste and other behaviour which influences their demand for a good or service must now be considered.

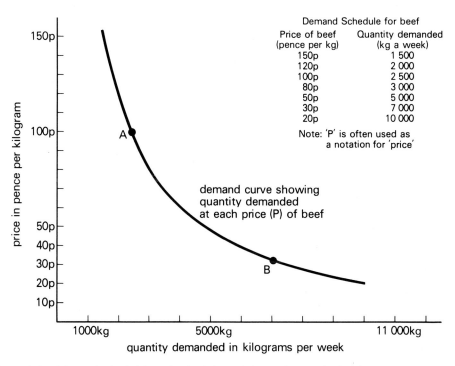

Demand Schedule for beef	
Price of beef (pence per kg)	Quantity demanded (kg a week)
150p	1 500
120p	2 000
100p	2 500
80p	3 000
50p	5 000
30p	7 000
20p	10 000

Note: 'P' is often used as a notation for 'price'

demand curve showing quantity demanded at each price (P) of beef

Figure 9.1   A hypothetical demand schedule and demand curve for beef.

Price and demand
The demand for a good will generally vary as its price changes. In general the quantity demanded increases as the price falls and vice versa. Figure 9.1 shows an example of this for beef demanded in kilograms per week by a community, at various price levels. This is known as a *demand schedule*. The information may also be used to draw a graph known as a *demand curve*. Figure 9.1 illustrates the usual shape of such a curve falling from left to right and indicating that as the price (measured along the vertical axis) falls, the quantity demanded (measured along the horizontal axis) increases – note the use of the symbol 'P' as a convenient notation for price.

Other influences – the conditions of demand
So far we have seen the influence of price on demand. When the price of beef (Figure 9.1) falls from £1 a kilogram at point A to 30p at point B, the quantity of beef demanded increases from 2500 kilograms to 7000 kilograms per week. Such a movement *along* the demand curve shows changes in the quantity of beef demanded as price – and *only* price – changes. Demand curves show the relationship between quantity demanded and the good's price when all other influences on demand remain unchanged.

The other influences – the conditions of demand – may be grouped conveniently in the case of individuals' behaviour under three headings: the price of other goods, taste and income. Two other influences – population and distribution of income – must also be taken into account when considering the total or market demand for any commodity.

The price of other goods
The price of other goods is important, for a decrease in the price of lamb may mean that at any price-per-kilogram for beef less of it will be demanded. This happens because consumers tend to eat lamb in preference to beef, now that lamb is cheaper than it was. In other words they will tend to substitute lamb for beef in their diet, as lamb has become *relatively* cheaper.

Since lamb and beef are acceptable alternatives for most of us, a change in the price of one is likely to have a marked effect on the demand for the other. There are similar pairs of goods that are close *substitutes* – where the price of one influences the demand for the other – cod and halibut, frozen and fresh vegetables, tea and coffee, cotton fabric and cloth from synthetic fibres, coal and oil generating electric power in dual-fired stations. Figure 9.2 shows the effect of a change in lamb prices on the demand for beef. Now that the price of lamb has fallen, the community demand for *beef* has fallen. This shows that consumers are substituting lamb for beef. Similarly at every price for beef the demand has decreased, resulting in a leftward shift of the beef demand curve.

There are also goods in joint or *complementary* demand – cars and the petrol to run them, beds and bed clothes, machine tools and coolant liquid (preventing cutters over-heating), housing and sewage-disposal equipment. Changes in demand for the first of these jointly demanded items affect the demand for the second. Thus a fall in the price of motor-cars with a consequent increase in demand for them, *also* leads to an increased demand for petrol at each price per litre. Conversely a rise in the price of cars leads to a decrease in demand for petrol at each price.

demand for beef when
lamb is £1.00 a kilogram

original demand curve for beef

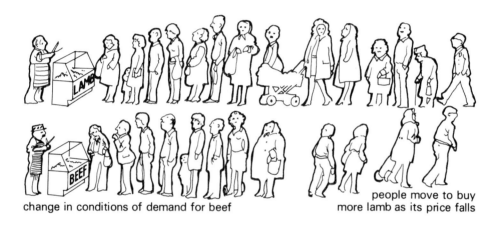

change in conditions of demand for beef

people move to buy
more lamb as its price falls

with lamb prices down, there is a
new condition of demand for beef

this change in condition affects
the demand for beef at each
beef price giving a new demand
curve for beef

new demand curve for beef

Figure 9.2   A change in conditions of demand.

Tastes and preference
A number of goods and services – clothing, furniture and a pop group's concerts, among them – are susceptible to changes in taste. These changes may be influenced by advertising and other promotion campaigns, or by more subtle social changes. Whatever the reason, such changes of preference among consumers influence the demand for a commodity – as in the late 1960s the demand for drain-pipe trousers fell away as the demand rose for flared jeans. Such changes in taste can often occur very quickly and for little apparent reason.

Income
As consumers' incomes – more precisely their disposable after-tax incomes – alter, their demands change. This may not only lead to individuals buying different amounts of a good they have been buying, but may also cause a change in their pattern of demand. With more income to spend, the consumers may buy beef instead of sausages. But as there is a limit to the amount of everyday food and clothing the consumers require, their demand for these will not increase very much.

On the other hand an increase in incomes leads to an increased demand for luxuries. You may buy a suit off-the-peg when your income increases on taking your first job. In a few years you may have several suits and then with further increases in your income you may buy hand-made suits. Your demand for off-the-peg suits has decreased. This is a case where a good becomes 'inferior' in the sense that you demand fewer (or less) of it as your income rises, substituting a more desirable or 'superior' alternative.

In the same way the demand for any good increases initially as incomes of individuals rise. The demand usually levels off before eventually decreasing as a good becomes 'inferior' – hand-made suits taking the place of the now 'inferior' off-the-peg suits, above.

So far we have looked at individuals' and households' demands. But when considering the total or market demand, account must also be taken of population and of income distribution mentioned earlier.

Population
The total size of a community, its population, influences the demand for beef. In our example, the greater the population, the larger will be the quantity of beef demanded at any price per kilogram. As you saw in chapter 2 changes in the population structure – by sex, by age and so on – have an influence on the pattern of demand, and these changes in size and structure occur over long periods. With a population that is becoming younger in its age distribution there is an increased demand for nappies and prams. Indeed as a bulge in the birth rate works through various ages of a population, the pattern of demand changes accordingly: first nappies, through schools and record players, perhaps, to wedding outfits, homes, something to fortify the over forties, and on to geriatric care.

Distribution of income
Although the community's total income may not alter, its poorer members may get – through taxation, possibly – more income at the expense of richer members. Then the pattern of demand will reflect this, with more family saloons being demanded and fewer limousines, more homes of a modest sort and fewer country estates.

Assignments

9.1 What do economists mean by markets? List four examples and note down their main characteristics and the ways in which they differ.

9.2 What does the economist mean by *demand*? What are the principal factors affecting the demand for refrigerators? (AEB 1973)

9.3* Discuss: under what conditions may people actually demand more at a higher rather than a lower price?

9.4* List the items of which you would buy more and of which you would buy less, if your income were (*a*) to double, (*b*) to increase fivefold, and (*c*) increase one hundredfold. Can you explain the differences between your answers in (*a*), (*b*) and (*c*)?

Shifts in a demand curve

Changes in conditions of demand
A demand schedule and matching demand curve show the relationship between price and quantities demanded *when conditions of demand remain unchanged*. It shows how demand changes when the good's price and *only* its price alters. A change in any of the conditions of demand creates a new demand curve, as in the case when a change in the price of lamb affected the demand curve for beef in Figure 9.2.

Another example in Figure 9.3 shows the effect of increased income leading to increased demand for beef at each price. A new demand schedule and curve must be

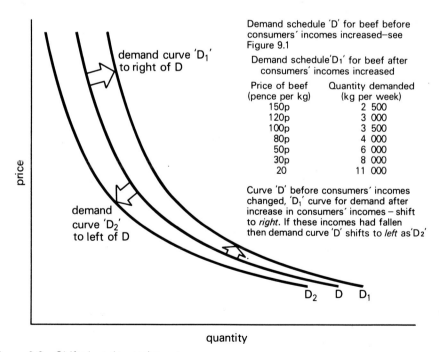

Demand schedule 'D' for beef before consumers' incomes increased—see Figure 9.1

Demand schedule'D₁' for beef after consumers' incomes increased

Price of beef (pence per kg)	Quantity demanded (kg per week)
150p	2 500
120p	3 000
100p	3 500
80p	4 000
50p	6 000
30p	8 000
20	11 000

Curve 'D' before consumers' incomes changed, 'D₁' curve for demand after increase in consumers' incomes – shift to *right*. If these incomes had fallen then demand curve 'D' shifts to *left* as'D₂'

Figure 9.3   Shifts in a demand curve.

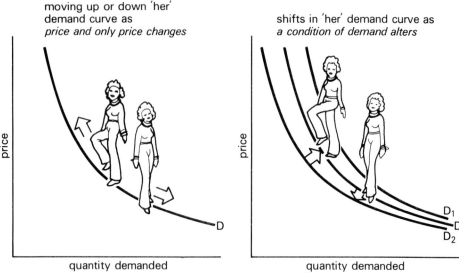

Figure 9.4   Demand – summary.

drawn to show the price–quantity relationship *under the new conditions*. When we graph this information we get a new demand curve D_1. (A convenient notation for any set of curves on the same graph is: D, D_1, D_2 ... with D here standing for 'Demand'.)

Should consumers' income fall, we get another demand schedule showing the price quantity relationship under the new conditions. The demand curve from this schedule is D_2, a shift to the left of D in Figure 9.3, reflecting the lower quantities of beef demanded at each price when customers' income falls.

Summary
We must clearly understand the difference between moving along a given demand curve *and* shifts in the position of this curve (see Figure 9.4):

1. Movements along a demand curve show changes in the quantity demanded as price – and only price – changes with all conditions of demand unchanged. The assumption that other things remain equal is known as the *ceteris paribus* assumption.

2. When any of the conditions of demand change, a new demand curve is required, its position relative to the original curve reflects the nature of the condition and the direction of its change.

3. The terminology for these movements along and shifts in a curve must be remembered:

   a Movements along a demand curve are called 'expansions' or 'contractions' of demand, sometimes referred to more briefly as 'changes in the quantities demanded'.

   b Shifts of a demand curve are called 'increases or decreases in the conditions of demand', sometimes briefly termed 'increases or decreases in demand'.

When you have worked through the following Assignment, you should be able to work out for yourself the direction of shifts in demand curves resulting from various changes in the conditions of demand.

Assignment

9.5 By copying out the following statements and completing the missing words, you can summarise the shifts of demand curves that occur when conditions of demand alter. The first statement summarises the shifts in the demand curve for beef that came about when consummer incomes alter as described on page 124. Include in these notes a copy of Figure 9.3.

1. *A change in income* – an increase in income causes an *increase* in the conditions of demand represented by an *outward* shift in the demand curve to D_1. Similarly a decrease in incomes causes a *decrease* in conditions of demand, represented by an inward shift of the demand curve D_2.

2. *A change in other prices* –
   (a) an increase in the price of SUBSTITUTES causes __ _____ in the conditions of demand represented by an _____ shift in the demand curve to __. A decrease in the price of substitutes causes __ _____ in conditions of demand, represented by an _____ shift in the demand curve to __.
   (b) an increase in the price of COMPLEMENTS OR GOODS IN JOINT DEMAND causes __ _____ in the conditions of demand represented by an _____ shift in the demand curve to __. A decrease in the price of compliments causes __ _____ in conditions of demand, represented by an _____ shift in the demand curve to __.

3. *A change in taste or preference* – an increased preference causes __ _____ in the conditions of demand represented by an _____ shift in the demand curve to __. A decreased preference causes __ _____ in conditions of demand, represented by an _____ shift in the demand curve to __.

4. *A change in population* – an increase in population causes __ _____ in the conditions of demand represented by an _____ shift in the demand curve to __. A decrease in population causes __ _____ in the conditions of demand, represented by an _____ shift in the demand curve to __.

Note: a change in the distribution of income with incomes becoming more equally distributed leads to an increased income for some of the population and a decrease for others. These changes can lead to an increase in the conditions of demand for beef but a decrease in the conditions of demand for sausages, an increase in conditions of demand for family saloon cars but a decrease in conditions of demand for limousines.

Supply

The meaning of supply

Supply is the amount of a commodity (a good or a service) which producers are willing and able to offer for sale at a particular price. Supply, like demand, is a flow concept being related to a time period. A supply of 20 litres of milk means little unless we know that this is 'per week' or 'per month'. Supply can be considered at the level of the individual producer or for an industry as a whole; but as any competitive industry is made up of many producers, the study of supply involves understanding the behaviour of individual producers.

Price and supply

The supply of a good will vary with its price, with the quantity supplied increasing in general as its price rises, since you would expect a producer to increase the quantities supplied as prices rise, since he or she is in business to make a profit.

Figure 9.5 gives the supply schedule and curve for beef, showing the amount of beef in kilograms-per-week which beef producers are willing to supply at various prices. This supply curve illustrates the usual shape of such curves running upwards from left to right. The shape indicates that as the price (measured on the vertical axis) rises, the quantity supplied (measured on the horizontal axis) increases.

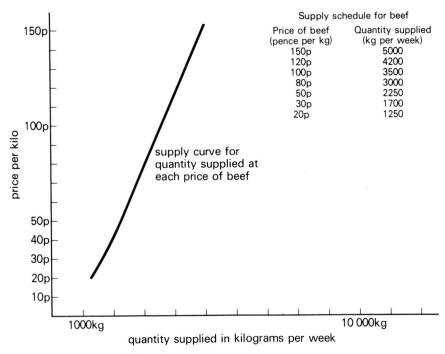

Supply schedule for beef

Price of beef (pence per kg)	Quantity supplied (kg per week)
150p	5000
120p	4200
100p	3500
80p	3000
50p	2250
30p	1700
20p	1250

Figure 9.5   A supply schedule and curve.

Other influences – the conditions of supply
A movement along the above supply curve shows changes in the quantity of beef supplied as price – and only price – changes. But price is not the only influence on supply. As with 'demand', the supply curve shows the relationship between the quantity supplied and the good's price when all other influences on supply remain unchanged.

Other influences – the conditions of supply – fall under four headings: the prices of factors of production; techniques of production; the weather and other phenomena outside man's control; and taxes and subsidies from governments.

Factor prices
Prices of factors of production – raw materials, labour and other factors – change. This in turn affects the cost of production, as the 1970s increase in the price of oil led inevitably to higher costs in manufacturing products derived from oil.

Such a change in the conditions of supply requires a new supply curve (Figure 9.6) that falls to the left of the original one drawn before production costs rose. This indicates that producers are only willing to supply the same quantity at a higher price, or what is the same thing: they are willing to supply a smaller quantity at any given price. When production costs fall, as these did for jam when sugar prices fell in 1975, producers are willing to supply a greater quantity at any given price.

The effect of such changes in a factor's price varies with the importance of the factor in the total cost. Where wages are a major part of the good's cost in labour-intensive industries like clothing manufacture, changes in labour cost have a marked

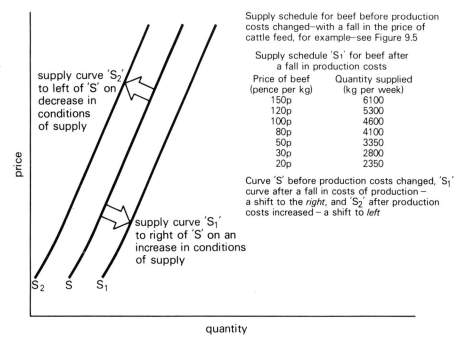

Supply schedule for beef before production costs changed—with a fall in the price of cattle feed, for example—see Figure 9.5

Supply schedule 'S₁' for beef after a fall in production costs

Price of beef (pence per kg)	Quantity supplied (kg per week)
150p	6100
120p	5300
100p	4600
80p	4100
50p	3350
30p	2800
20p	2350

Curve 'S' before production costs changed, 'S₁' curve after a fall in costs of production – a shift to the *right*, and 'S₂' after production costs increased – a shift to *left*

Figure 9.6   Shifts in a supply curve.

effect on production costs. In contrast in capital-intensive industries – using machines rather than manpower – wages form a low proportion of total costs. Therefore a given increase in wages in this case has a much smaller effect on costs. With six men using large machines to produce 1000 tonnes of fertiliser a week, the cost per tonne of fertiliser is increased only marginally if each man gets an extra £6 a week. The shift in the supply curve brought about by this change is correspondingly small.

Techniques of production
New inventions and techniques – improvements in technology – leading to improved methods of production, decrease costs of a given output. When Henry Ford introduced his first moving assembly line the time for assembling a model-T Ford fell from over 12 hours a car to just under 6 hours, and with further improvements before the 1930s the time had come down to 93 minutes a car. Such improvements enable a producer to supply a larger quantity, as producers did in Figure 9.6, at any given price. Or the producer may do the equivalent: supply the same quantity at a lower price.

Changes outside man's control
The state of the weather is important for some industries' production – agriculture and building are major examples. The weather affects harvests, while disasters such as floods, droughts and major storms set back production from many producers dependent on consistent if not fair weather. In times of adverse weather, producers are able to supply less of a commodity at any price than when weather conditions are

favourable. This change for the worse in supply conditions results in a leftward shift of the supply curve. The effect was seen in the hot dry summer of 1975 after a late frost in the UK when potato growers produced crops only 77% of their previous five years' average yield per hectare.

Taxes and subsidies
Taxes and subsidies are considered in later chapters. However the imposition of certain taxes on a producer has the effect of increasing his costs of production with any level of output costing more to supply. Prior to the tax, a producer will be willing to supply (say) 100 units at £1 each. After the imposition of a tax at 8% of the price of each unit sold, he will now be willing to supply 100 units at £1.08 each. That is: £1 as before to the producer and 8p to the government. Therefore any given quantity will only be supplied at a higher price. The imposition of excise duty on motor fuels leads to producers only being willing to supply the same quantity at a higher price, causing a shift in the supply curve to the left.

Conversely the payment by governments of subsidies – for example those on milk in 1975 – received by a producer lowers his production costs. So at any price level he is willing to supply a greater quantity than before.

Shifts in a supply curve

Changes in the conditions of supply
In a similar way to 'demand', a supply curve shows the relationship between prices and the quantity supplied *when the conditions of supply remain unchanged*. Whenever a condition of supply alters, a new supply curve must be drawn to show the relationship between price and quantity supplied under the new conditions. As we saw in Figure 9.6, changes in the conditions of supply lead to shifts in the supply curve to either the right (S_1 – Figure 9.6) or left (S_2).

Summary
The differences between movements along a given supply curve and shifts in the position of this curve must be understood:

1. Movements along a supply curve show changes in the quantities supplied as price alters with all conditions of supply remaining unchanged.

2. Whenever the conditions of supply change, a new supply curve is required *either* to the left *or* right of the original curve, its new position reflecting the nature and direction of the change.

3. The terminology for these movements along and shifts in a curve must be remembered:

a Movements along a supply curve are called 'expansions' and 'contractions' of supply – more briefly: 'changes in the quantities supplied'.

b Shifts of a supply curve are called 'increases or decreases in the conditions of supply' – more briefly: 'increase or decreases in supply'.

Assignments

9.6 By copying out the following statements and completing the missing words, you can summarise the shifts of supply curves that occur when conditions of supply alter. The first statement summarises the shifts in the supply curve for beef that would come about when factor prices alter, as described on page 128. Include in these notes a copy of Figure 9.6.

(a) *A change in the price of factors of production* – an increase in the price of a factor of production used in beef production, causes a *decrease* in the conditions of supply represented by an inward shift in the supply curve to S_2. And vice versa.

(b) *An improvement in technical knowledge causes* __ _____ in the conditions of supply represented by an _____ in the supply curve to ____. (See also Assignment 9.7.)

(c) An unfavourable change in the weather causes __ _____ in the conditions of supply represented by an _____ in the supply curve to __. And vice versa.

(d) The imposition of a tax on producers causes a _____ in the conditions of supply represented by an _____ in the supply curve to __. And vice versa.

9.7 Consider what effect a 'loss' of technical knowledge might cause in the conditions of supply. Might this occur in the future as it did in the Dark Ages?

9.8 What influences affect the amount of labour supplied by a household? (Includes revision)

9.9* Discuss: must supply always equal production or can it exceed production?

Suggested further reading

Harbury, Chapter 3
Harvey, Chapter 8
Paish and Culyer, Chapters 12, 13 and 14
Stanlake, Chapter 14

Chapter 10

Demand, supply and price

So far we have considered the separate forces of demand and supply. In order to see the way they interact to determine price, the demand and supply curves for a good or service are plotted on the same price-quantity graph. Figure 10.1 shows this for our beef example using the schedules shown in Figures 9.1 and 9.5

Interaction of demand and supply

Price determination

When we plot the demand curve and the supply curve for any good on the same graph, with price on the vertical axis and the quantity demanded with the quantity supplied on the horizontal axis, these curves will in general intersect at one point. In this way the two curves cross – point E in Figure 10.1. This happens because the demand curve falls from left to right, while its matching supply curve rises from left to right. The point of their intersection is called the *equilibrium point* because at this

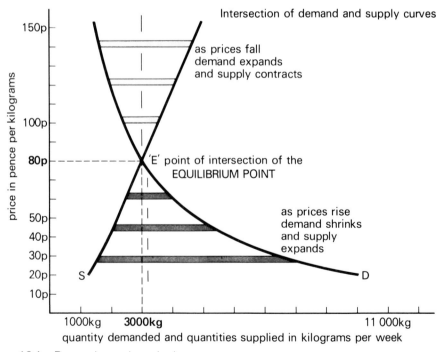

Figure 10.1   Demand, supply and price.

point supply equals demand. That is: the quantity producers are willing to supply is equal to the quantity which consumers demand at this price.

In the example, Figure 10.1, this equilibrium point E is where beef at 80p a kilogram is demanded in the same quantity as the quantity supplied – 3000 kilograms per week.

If prices were above 80p a kilogram, say at £1.50, then the amount supplied at 5000 kilograms (see Figure 10.1) exceeds the amount demanded of 1500 kilograms. Producers find there is an *excess supply* of 3500 kilograms. Because of this 'excess supply', the unsold goods, prices will tend to fall encouraging an expansion of demand and a contraction of supply. When prices fall to £1-a-kilogram excess supply has shrunk to 1000 kilograms – look again at Figure 10.1. Should the price fall to 50p a kilogram, there will be an excess of demand over supply, with consumers demanding more beef than is available for sale. Prices will then tend to rise as sellers find demand exceeds supply. This rise causes the excess demand to shrink by contracting demand and expanding supply, until at 80p these are in equilibrium – there is no excess demand nor excess supply.

Therefore when the price of beef is 80p a kilogram there is no tendency for the price to alter, since the quantity supplied equals the quantity demanded. This can be seen in the shrinking of excess supply as prices fall at levels above the 80p price of Figure 10.1, and the shrinking of excess demand as prices rise at levels below 80p.

Two further examples illustrate this tendency. Late in the day when market traders are about to close their stalls, if they have any unsold tomatoes they lower the prices. On the other hand there is always an excess demand for tickets at their *issue* prices to watch the FA Cup Final. As a result of this excess demand, ticket touts can charge an 'equilibrium price' balancing demand and the touts' supply.

In a case of excess demand – look at Figure 10.1 – we can see an important function of price. As a price increases demand contracts, rationing the available supply – a rationing by price, because fewer customers are willing to buy at the higher price. The queue of customers, in other words, at the butchers' stalls shrinks from the many who stood in it when beef was 30p a kilogram, to the smaller number willing to pay higher prices. The queue will continue to shrink as more people leave unwilling to buy at higher prices, until the time when butchers have raised prices to 80p and the demand queue equals available supply.

The following Assignment is another example of price determination.

Assignment

10.1

Price (£) per unit	Quantity demanded	Quantity supplied
7	90	200
6	110	170
5	130	130
4	140	110

(a) What is the equilibrium price in the market to which the above demand and supply schedule refers?

(b) If the government imposed a tax of £1 on each unit, how many units would the suppliers be prepared to offer at a market price of £6 per unit? (AEB 1971)

The theory
The above examples of particular cases illustrate the way in which prices in competitive markets will be determined. However the theory of price determination is very versatile and applied in a wide variety of situations for the price of goods, services and factors of production – including wages, the price of labour.

The theory can now be stated in more exact terms: prices are determined by the point of intersection of demand and supply curves, since at this point the quantity supplied equals the quantity demanded and hence there is no tendency for prices to alter.

Uses of demand and supply analysis
Many economic problems can be analysed by plotting demand and supply curves. Following through the example on beef supply and demand illustrates one simple application of the technique. What effect would an increase in consumers' incomes have on the price of beef? As we know, this *change in a condition of demand* requires a new demand curve on the right of the original one in Figure 10.2 as D shifts to D_1.

The original equilibrium point (E) was 80p with demand equalling supply at 3000 kilograms a week. At the higher level of income, more beef is likely to be demanded at each price. Families may now have it roasted on Sunday and grilled steaks in the week instead of 'inferior sausages'. The new demand curve D_1 intersects the supply curve S when the price of beef is £1 a kilogram. This new equilibrium point E_1 shows that producers are willing to produce and sell 3500 kilograms of beef, equal to the amount customers are willing to buy (demand) at £1 a kilogram, now that their incomes have increased. In short: the increase in consumers' incomes has led to a rise in beef prices to £1 a kilogram and an increase in the supply of beef raising it from 3000 to 3500 kilograms a week.

The importance of time
Changes in demand can occur quickly and may even change almost overnight as in the fashion trade. But producers usually take a longer time to increase supplies than it took for demand to increase since they often physically have to bring together extra inputs of materials, find additional labour and so on, that is: increase their use of variable factors. These are all steps which can take days if not weeks or longer to complete.

The distinction has already been made between production in the long- and short-run periods (see page 58). In the short term output can only be varied by increasing the variable factors (or reducing these) used with existing fixed factors. In the long term, all factors are variable. There is a third time period to consider in analysing a demand-and-supply situation. This is the ultra short or *momentary period* when supply is fixed because only a limited amount of a commodity is available for sale.

At any moment in our beef example, supply is limited to say 3000 kilograms no matter what the price is. This may come about because there is only this amount butchered ready for sale in the shops. So a vertical line – SM in Figure 10.2 – may be drawn to represent this supply 'curve', the momentary supply curve. Perhaps a sudden increase in other meat prices led to this change in demand for beef. Sellers now find an excess of demand over their supply of beef at their original 80p, on this change in demand conditions. Therefore prices will tend to rise. Drawing this vertical line for the 'momentary supply' curve on the graphs in Figure 10.2 cuts the

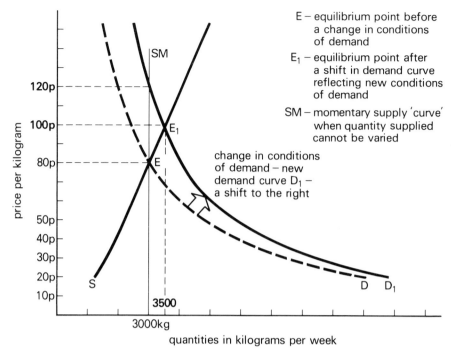

Figure 10.2   Analysis of beef prices when demand conditions change.

new demand curve D_1, showing that prices rise in the 'momentary period' to £1.20, effectively 'rationing' by price the available supply of 3000 kilograms. We will come back in a moment to the precise meaning of this interaction, but clearly the price differs from the 'new' equilibrium of £1.

When other demand and supply conditions do not change, this momentary supply is likely to be soon supplemented. This is done first by depleting stocks – as sides of beef are brought from cold stores, perhaps. Second, production is increased from existing fixed factors – more cattle are put through the slaughter house. However, the length of a 'momentary supply' period depends on the time needed to bring together additional factors, as we have seen. It may be as short as one day, its duration perhaps in the beef market; but often it is longer, as when the demand for a moulded plastic toy increases suddenly, organising a night shift to run the machine making this may take two weeks.

Instantaneous effect of demand changes
Coming back to our example in Figure 10.2, the momentary supply curve SM for 3000 kilograms of beef cuts the new demand curve D_1 at a price of £1.20 a kilogram. So the immediate effect of a sudden upsurge in demand is to raise prices to this level. Producers respond to this by increasing the quantities supplied according to their supply curve S. The movement *along* this supply curve continues until the new equilibrium point E_1 is reached with the price at £1 a kilogram, where supply equals demand at 3500 kilograms a week and hence there is no tendency for the price to alter.

Assignments

10.2 The total demand for a certain commodity in three different areas, A, B and C, is as follows:

Price per unit (p)	A (000)	B (000)	C (000)
5	50	40	10
4	70	65	15
3	100	75	25
2	110	100	40
1	150	100	50

On graph paper:
  (a) Construct a simple curve to illustrate total market demand. Label it 'D'.
  (b) Sketch a supply curve which results in a market price of 3p per unit. Label it 'S'.
  (c) Show a new equilibrium which may result after a severe fall in the incomes of all consumers. (AEB 1975)

10.3 'An increase in demand will result in an increase in price and an increase in price will lead to a decrease in quantity demanded.' Explain this statement. (Includes revision.) (CAFC 1975)

10.4 In the long run, producers can adjust their fixed factors, new firms can enter the industry, and existing firms can leave it. What effect will these changes have on the supply curve for this chapter's example of beef prices and quantities?

10.5 Trace the likely effects on the price of petrol in Britain of:
  (a) a ban by Middle East states on all exports of oil to Europe;
  (b) the removal of VAT from motor-cars;
  (c) the development of an efficient, electrically-powered car. (Adapted from AEB 1971)

Elasticity of demand

Price and quantity demanded
We have seen demand as the number of units of a commodity demanded at a particular price in a given period. The strength of the relationship between price and the quantity demanded – the extent to which it decreases as the price rises, or increases as the price falls – is measured by the *elasticity of demand*.

Elasticity of demand
The idea of differing responses to changes in price is shown in Figure 10.3. Elasticity of demand is a measure of the responsiveness of quantity demanded to changes in price, and is defined as: the proportionate change in a quantity demanded, divided by the proportionate change in price, both of these usually measured as percentages:

$$\text{elasticity of demand} = \frac{\% \text{ change in quantity demanded}}{\% \text{ change in price}}$$

(Because price and quantity demanded move in opposite directions, this formula gives a negative value. Conventionally, therefore, the value is multiplied by minus-one to give a positive value – see Figure 10.3.) On this calculation the elasticity of

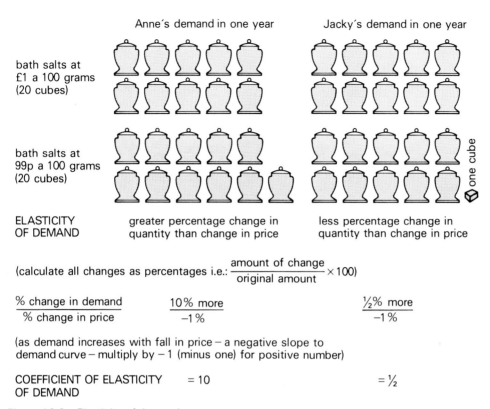

Figure 10.3 Elasticity of demand.

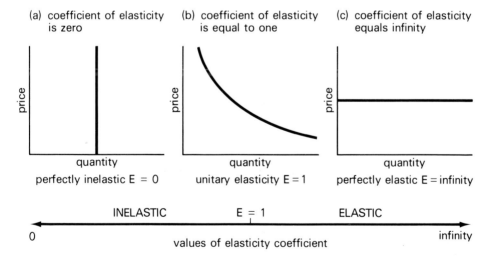

Figure 10.4 Particular cases in elasticity of demand.

demand in one of the examples in Figure 10.3 is 10 (10% ÷ 1%) a figure greater than one (> 1). Note how the percentage changes are calculated in Figure 10.3.

The value of elasticity of demand is sometimes called the *elasticity coefficient*, and may have any value from zero to infinity. Where the percentage change in quantity demanded is less than the percentage change for price, this coefficient is less than one. This shows that demand has changed proportionately less than price. Demand for such a product is therefore called *inelastic*. Where the percentage (or proportionate) change in the quantity demanded is greater than the proportionate change in price, the coefficient exceeds one, and this demand is said to be *elastic*. Look again at Figure 10.3.

Particular cases of elasticity of demand
A coefficient of elasticity equal to zero shows that the quantity demanded remains unchanged whatever the price (see Figure 10.4a) and is known as *perfectly inelastic demand*. Such demand 'curves' are vertical lines.

When the coefficient of elasticity is infinity, a small increase in price leads to demand falling away to nothing (see Figure 10.4c) and is known as *perfectly elastic demand*, shown as a horizontal line.

The percentage change in demand may be the same as the percentage change in price, giving a coefficient of elasticity equal to one, and known as *unitary elasticity*. A demand curve where elasticity is always equal to one is a rectangular hyperbola (see Figure 10.4b).

While there may be no product with a perfectly inelastic demand at every price – there must be a price beyond which any good becomes too highly priced for any one or group to buy – the understanding of this and other special cases helps in analysing demand. For example, a good's elasticity of demand may 'tend towards zero' or 'towards infinity' and will vary from point to point along most demand curves. Before looking further at elasticity of demand, the following Assignments will enable you to grasp the principles of this concept.

Assignments

10.6 The following figures are extracted from a schedule of demand and supply:

Price (p)	Quantity demanded per week	Quantity supplied per week
30	1200	900
40	1000	1000
50	800	1200

Using any method you wish, calculate the elasticity of demand when price rises from 40p to 50p. (Part of AEB 1973)

10.7 Given the following demand schedule for carrots:

Price per kilogram (p)	Quantity demande in kilograms
20	1000
15	5000
10	10 000
5	15 000
3	20 000

Calculate the elasticity of demand for carrots when their price decreases from 15p to 10p per kilogram.

10.8 Using the information in the table with Figures 9.1 and 9.6, pages 121 and 129, plot a graph to show the effect on the price of beef and the quantity demanded and supplied resulting from a decrease in the price of cattle feed. Explain your answer.

What determines elasticity of demand

Availability of substitutes
When there are adequate substitutes available for a good, a rise in its price leads customers to buy an alternative. Demand for it is, therefore, likely to be elastic because consumers will now buy the relatively cheaper substitute. Tea or coffee, beef or lamb, small cars or motorcycles, each may have an elastic demand because adequate substitutes exist in the alternative goods.

On the other hand some goods have few or even no adequate substitutes. Glass, petrol and the specially made tool for a moulded plastic toy have no substitutes in certain uses. Glass equipment and only glass can be used for some experiments, you cannot drive a petrol-engined car without petrol, and only one particular tool can be used to make the toy. So demand is inelastic – if you are driving to the coast in that car, you must buy petrol regardless of its price.

Degree of necessity
Goods and services essential to everyday life – food, soap and water – tend to be bought regardless of their price, by most consumers. Therefore demand for these necessities is inelastic.

However people can take or leave luxury goods as they wish. Therefore demand for luxuries is elastic, a small change in price causing a large change in the quantity demanded. But what may be luxuries today, can become necessities for the next generation. In this way the luxury of a wireless in the 1930s became the necessity of a radio in the 1970s. Maybe colour TVs in 1977 are becoming essentials, or will be so in the future.

The good in question
The demand for food covers a wide range of commodities. Yet, while food in general is a necessity and inelastic in demand, a particular type of food may have adequate

substitutes. A particular food is therefore in elastic demand. Cheese has elastic demand with acceptable substitutes – perhaps cooked meats or jam – being available. This illustrates how the definition of the 'good in question' is important in determining its elasticity. Are you analysing the demand for all food? . . . or a type of food? . . . or a brand of a particular type of food?

Habit

Those hooked on cigarettes or other habit-forming goods often cannot break themselves of the craving. Demand for these goods tends, therefore, to change little with price increases. As the Chancellor of the Exchequer knows only too well, the demand for such habit-forming goods is inelastic.

Price relative to income

When a commodity takes only a small proportion of consumers' incomes a large percentage increase in its price has little effect on demand. The increase in the price of matches from 3p to 4p a box is a $33\frac{1}{3}\%$ rise but has little effect on the demand for matches.

Where, however, the commodity takes a large slice of consumers' incomes, any increase in price tends to have a marked effect on demand. A small percentage increase in house prices may therefore cause a large percentage fall in demand – an elastic demand.

Durable goods

When an article has a relatively long useful life – sewing machines, furniture, and similar durables – demand for these tends to be elastic. When prices rise, users are likely to keep durable goods they have, rather than replace them at the moment. But when prices fall, demand may increase substantially. Instead of making do with the old three-piece suite, if a new one is offered in a sale at the right price, you might well buy it despite the fact that the old one could perhaps have been used for a few more years.

Elasticity of demand and total expenditure

Buyers' expenditure is the sellers' revenue

The total amount spent by customers on a good, their total outlay, is the sum received as revenue by producers of that good. A price change therefore has an effect on a producer's revenue and this is influenced by the elasticity of demand for his product.

Any producer thinking of altering his product's price needs to know its elasticity of demand in order to estimate the likely effect on his revenue of any price change. A carpet manufacturer, thinking of raising his prices, must consider what effect this will have on the demand for his carpets. If demand elasticity is unitary, any price increase is exactly offset by a fall in demand – his revenue is unaltered (see Figure 10.5). But if demand is elastic, a rise in price will decrease consumers' total expenditure – the producer's revenue. On a 10% rise in the carpets' prices, demand falls by a greater percentage. However a fall in the carpets' price by 10% when demand is elastic will lead to a greater percentage increase in the quantity demanded and

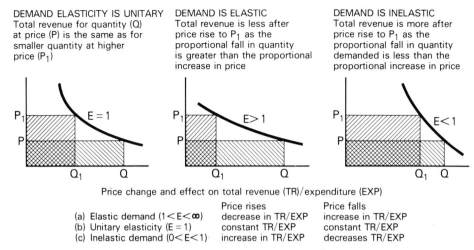

	DEMAND ELASTICITY IS UNITARY	DEMAND IS ELASTIC	DEMAND IS INELASTIC

DEMAND ELASTICITY IS UNITARY
Total revenue for quantity (Q) at price (P) is the same as for smaller quantity at higher price (P$_1$)

DEMAND IS ELASTIC
Total revenue is less after price rise to P$_1$ as the proportional fall in quantity is greater than the proportional increase in price

DEMAND IS INELASTIC
Total revenue is more after price rise to P$_1$ as the proportional fall in quantity demanded is less than the proportional increase in price

Price change and effect on total revenue (TR)/expenditure (EXP)

	Price rises	Price falls
(a) Elastic demand (1<E<∞)	decrease in TR/EXP	increase in TR/EXP
(b) Unitary elasticity (E = 1)	constant TR/EXP	constant TR/EXP
(c) Inelastic demand (0<E<1)	increase in TR/EXP	decreases TR/EXP

Figure 10.5   Effects of price changes on total revenue/expenditure.

therefore his total revenue will increase. As the elasticity of demand for carpets in this case is greater than one, the percentage changes in quantities demanded are greater than the percentage changes up or down in their price.

If demand is inelastic, a rise in price increases the consumers' total expenditure – the producer's revenue – because demand decreases by a lower proportion than prices rise (see Figure 10.5). On the other hand a fall in price with inelastic demand decreases total revenue for the good's producer, because the increase in quantity demanded is less in percentage terms than the decrease in price. A summary of these relationships is shown in Figure 10.5.

Uses of elasticity of demand
Elasticity of demand is important in the analysis of many situations and problems. You have seen its importance to a producer contemplating a price change for his goods. Similarly governments need to take account of the elasticity of demand when increasing such taxes as Value Added Tax (VAT), excise duty and other indirect taxes (see page 215). For when the tax increases a price, demand can fall off to such an extent that the total revenue from the tax may be reduced. Therefore governments tax goods with inelastic demand to raise tax revenues – such as cigarettes, beer, petrol and so on. But to curtail spending by consumers, governments tax goods which have an elastic demand, in the way some non-essentials were subject to a 25% VAT in 1975/6.

Assignments

10.9 What is meant by 'elasticity of demand'? What factors affect the elasticity of demand for tinned salmon in Britain? (AEB 1973)

10.10 Explain the statement: 'The demand for bread is inelastic.' How far do you consider the statement to be accurate. (AEB 1973)

10.11 Discuss: 'The demand for petrol is inelastic, yet the demand for a particular brand of petrol is likely to be highly elastic.' Can you think of any occasions when there might be exceptions to this general statement?

10.12 If a producer decreased his price what would happen to his total revenue if the demand for his product was (*a*) elastic, (*b*) inelastic, and (*c*) unitary?

10.13* Group research: from the spending habits of the members of each group select three items that have a highly elastic demand and three which have a highly inelastic demand. Compare your group's selections with other groups' and note comments on the content of each list.

Elasticity of supply

Price and quantity supplied
How far a producer responds by increasing or decreasing the supply of a good when its price changes, is measured by the good's elasticity of supply. This is calculated on the same principles as the coefficient of elasticity of demand (see Figure 10.6).

Elasticity of supply is the proportional change in quantity supplied, divided by the proportional change in price – usually measured as percentages:

$$\text{elasticity of supply} = \frac{\% \text{ change in quantity supplied}}{\% \text{ change in price}}$$

When the coefficient of elasticity of supply is less than one (<1) the supply is inelastic. Then as prices rise there is a proportionately smaller increase in supply. If the coefficient is greater than one (>1) the supply is elastic, and a price rise gives a proportionately greater increase in supply. When the coefficient is one, this is a unitary elasticity of supply.

What determines elasticity of supply?
The way in which production costs increase with output determines the elasticity of supply for a particular good. A detailed analysis of this is outside the scope of our studies, but in broad terms: as a good's price rises, its elasticity of supply is determined by how much production can be increased, before costs rise to such an extent that further increases in output are no longer worthwhile at the new price. In the short run these additional costs of production are those of attracting additional variable factors (see Figure 10.7).

Time has an important influence on the elasticity of supply. We have seen the momentary period when the supply of a commodity is fixed and therefore perfectly inelastic. Look again at the supply curve SM in Figure 10.2 on page 135.

Producer A – price of blank cassettes rise from £1 to £1·05 each.
  Producer expands output from 400 to 500

$$\frac{\% \text{ increase in quantity supplied}}{\% \text{ increase in price}} = \frac{25\%}{5\%} = 5$$

  Therefore in this example producer A's supply is elastic.

Producer B – price of blank cassettes rise from £1 to £1·05 each.
  Producer expands production from 400 to 410

$$\frac{\% \text{ increase in quantity supplied}}{\% \text{ increase in price}} = \frac{2\frac{1}{2}\%}{5\%} = \frac{1}{2}$$

  Therefore in this example producer B's supply is inelastic.

Figure 10.6   Examples of elasticity of supply.

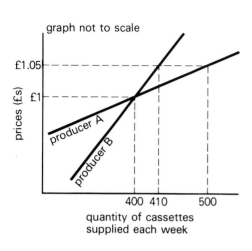

graph not to scale

£1.05

£1

prices (£s)

producer A

producer B

producer

400 410   500

quantity of cassettes
supplied each week

Both producers respond in this perfect market by expanding their supply as the price rises to £1.05p. As the price rises, 'A' expands his output to 500 cassettes, but if he made one more its *addition to his total cost* (marginal cost) would exceed £1.05 which is also the addition to his revenue from its sale (marginal revenue). Therefore he does not increase his supply beyond 500 at this price. Likewise 'B' expands his supply to the point where marginal cost equals marginal revenue, supplying 410 cassettes.

The way marginal costs increase as output expands, therefore, determines in a perfect market the elasticity of supply. Producer A's marginal costs rise more slowly than B's, enabling A to gain a greater increase in output of 100 cassettes compared to B's increase of 10 cassettes.

Since the *marginal cost* is the cost of the additional units of variable factors for producing extra cassettes, the difference between A's and B's elasticity of supply reflects the difference in the prices or marginal products of these factors.

Figure 10.7   Factor cost changes determine elasticity of supply.

For certain goods the 'short term' can cover an extensive period taking months or even years for producers to increase output and supply. With crops, the producer needs many months from sowing to harvest to increase his cereal output. Whisky distillers and rubber planters need several years to increase their output. But a manufacturer of nuts and bolts can probably increase his output by employing extra variable factors within weeks.

In the long term all factors of production can be varied and new producers can enter an industry. The elasticity of supply over these long-term periods is determined by the way long-run costs vary with output. These long-run costs include formerly fixed (in the short term) costs for buildings, land and machines now variable in the long term.

The above analyses of demand, supply and price determination are fundamental to an understanding of the way economies work, affecting each of us as buyers of goods and services, sellers of factors of production, and producers. In the next chapter we will see the practical workings of the market. But the existence of a perfectly inelastic supply in the momentary period causing an upsurge in prices, for instance, is not merely an academic toy. This and other aspects of price determination are important for all of us, real people in a complex world of supply and demand.

Assignments

10.14 The following figures are extracted from a schedule of demand and supply:

Price	Quantity demanded	Quantity supplied
£9	10 500	8 500
£10	10 000	10 000
£11	9 500	11 500

(a) Calculate the *elasticity of demand* when price rises from £10 to £11.

(b) Calculate the *elasticity of supply* when price falls from £10 to £9. (AEB 1971)

10.15 Explain and illustrate elasticity of supply. What determines the elasticity of supply of potatoes? (AEB 1972)

10.16 If there is a rapid rise in the price of tea by 25% indicate the probable effects on (a) the price of coffee, (b) the supply of tea, and (c) the price of chocolate bars. (Includes revision.) (L 1973)

10.17 The following is a hypothetical demand schedule for FA Cup Final tickets:

Price (£:p)	Quantity demanded (000s)
50	150
1.00	120
1.50	90
2.00	60
2.50	30
3.00	20
4.00	10

If the equilibrium price is £2 a ticket, draw a supply and demand diagram to illustrate how it was determined. What quantity is supplied at the equilibrium price? Comment on the shape of the supply curve.

10.18* Discuss: is the time required to increase the output of any good in part set by the limited availability and time required to increase production from agriculture and/or mineral deposits (the primary and extractive industries)?

10.19* If you have the opportunity, visit a fruit and vegetable market any morning and note one crop that is in season. Record the prices for this on six to eight stalls. Go back at the end of the same market day and note the prices now charged on these stalls. How can you account for (a) any difference between morning and late afternoon prices, and (b) any differences on either visit in the good's price on different stalls.

Suggested further reading

Harvey, Chapter 8
Harbury, Chapter 4
Paish and Culyer, Chapter 19
R Turvey, *Demand and Supply* (George Allen & Unwin, 1971)

Chapter 11
Monopoly

So far you have followed the interaction of demand and supply in competitive markets. In practice, however, there are different market structures. Sometimes there may be many buyers and sellers as in the perfectly competitive markets, but often there are situations with few sellers or producers.

Competition in practice

Competition
In a perfect market no single producer/seller can influence prices, for there are many producers selling identical goods, and many customers. Each producer is a price *taker*, facing prices set by the interaction of supply and demand forces. This price, determined where these are in balance, will not alter whatever a single producer does. If he raises prices he loses all of his customers to other sellers; if he lowers prices more customers will come to buy and there will be insufficient goods to meet the increased demand. There is therefore no incentive for him to reduce prices below the market level for a good.

Producer-sellers in these perfectly competitive markets must therefore accept the market price. They are 'price takers', for the price is set by conditions outside their control. They must decide how much of the good they will produce and offer for sale at this price.

This concept of a perfect market was our starting-point for the study of more complicated market structures. Practical examples of perfect markets occur for some farm products produced and consumed worldwide. These commodity markets (commodity in the farming sense) are often perfectly competitive because many hundreds of thousands of farmer producers grow identical types and grades of wheat, for example, to supply millions of consumers. Yet each farmer grows only a tiny portion of the whole crops – in 1971 there were 137 293 farmers growing wheat on over 19 million acres in Canada alone. Each farmer has to accept the market price set by the interaction of demand and supply for this crop.

The wheat farmer is faced by a horizontal demand curve at the market price (look again at Figure 10.4 on page 137). This is an example of a perfectly elastic demand. He receives the market price – call it P ($£$s a tonne) – however much he sells. Since the *market* price P is constant, whenever he increases his sales each additional unit sold adds P to his total revenue. This addition to total revenue on increasing sales by one unit is the *marginal revenue*. In perfectly competitive markets this is constant and equal to the market price. If the farmer increases his price above the market price, the demand for his wheat will fall to nothing. In this case of perfectly elastic demand, his customers will go and buy an identical product from his competitors.

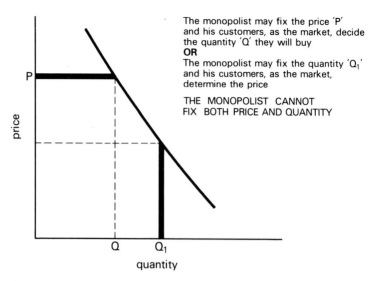

The monopolist may fix the price 'P' and his customers, as the market, decide the quantity 'Q' they will buy
OR
The monopolist may fix the quantity 'Q₁' and his customers, as the market, determine the price

THE MONOPOLIST CANNOT FIX BOTH PRICE AND QUANTITY

Figure 11.1   A monopolist's demand curve.

Monopoly

When the number of producer-sellers is small, the market structure is not perfectly competitive. Such imperfect markets may have only a few sellers, the situation of *oligopoly*, or two sellers – a *duopoly*. When there is only one seller, this is a *monopoly*.

A producer with a monopoly can raise his prices and, unlike the 'perfect competitor', still keep some customers. Although a number of them may cease to buy after a price increase, just how many continue to buy from the monopoly producer depends on what substitute or alternative goods are available, a point we shall come back to. Not only must alternatives be available but also customers, or rather ex-customers, of the monopoly producer must be willing and *able* to use them. For example, the home owner with electric central heating cannot readily use gas although this becomes relatively cheaper when electricity charges rise.

Figure 11.1 shows the demand curve faced by a producer with a monopoly – a monopolist. He may *either* fix the price and let the market, his customers, decide what quantity they want to buy, *or* he may fix the quantity he sells adjusting the price until this supply is taken up by customers. But he cannot control *both* price and quantity. The monopoly producer of reproduction prints from an engraving may decide to sell these at £5 each, then the number of collectors wanting to buy a copy will determine the monopolist's sales. Alternatively, he may decide to reproduce 100 copies. The price he can get for each of these will be that at which collectors are willing to buy these 100.

We have seen that marginal revenue is constant in perfectly competitive markets. In contrast, a monopolist's marginal revenue decreases with his output – as he moves down 'his' demand curve. Our producer of prints had a total revenue of £400 when selling 100 units at £4 each. Had he made and sold 101 prints, the price at which he could sell this quantity would be (say) £3.99 each, giving him a total revenue of £402.99 (£3.99 × 101). His marginal revenue at this level of sales is therefore £2.99 (£402.99 − £400). As the sales are increased to the level of 102 prints, the price falls to (say) £3.98 each, giving a marginal revenue of £2.97 (£405.96 − £402.99) and continues to fall in this way as the monopolist's sales are increased further.

As the price rises for the monopolist's product – the only glue that keeps true loves together – the quantity demanded decreases only slightly.

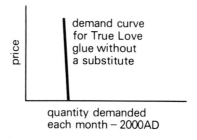

The True Love glue's producer loses some monopoly power when the Eternal Adhesive for Lovers comes on the market. Now demand for True Love glue has become more elastic as consumers may now choose the adhesive when the glue's price rises

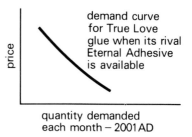

Figure 11.2   The inelastic demand for a monopolist's product with no adequate substitutes and effect of rival product.

The degree of monopoly

We have seen the extremes of perfect competition and monopoly; between these lie varying degrees of monopoly. Any producer who is able to increase his price without losing all his customers – facing a downward-sloping demand curve – possesses some degree of monopoly. So the publisher of a photographic magazine who can increase his price without losing all his customer-readers – because some enthusiasts will pay the higher price – possesses a degree of monopoly.

Monopoly power

The degree of monopoly power a producer enjoys is the extent to which he may increase prices without losing customers. Look again at Figure 10.4, page 137; the more inelastic the demand, then the fewer the customers lost when a price is raised by a certain amount. So one measure of a producer's monopoly power is the elasticity of demand for his product. The more inelastic the demand the greater his degree of monopoly power, the more elastic the demand the weaker his monopoly power.

The availability of substitutes for a commodity is important as we have seen (page 139) in establishing its elasticity of a demand. Therefore when a producer's output has no close substitutes, there will be a relatively small decrease in demand if the price of the commodity is raised. To the extent that this applies to any good, the degree of its producer's monopoly depends on the availability of adequate substitutes for this commodity (see Figure 11.2). A definition of a monopolist is therefore: one who is the sole producer of a commodity for which there is no close substitute.

Aspects of monopoly power

We have seen a monopolist as a producer able to increase prices without losing all his customers. This power *may* enable him to earn abnormally large profits in the short run; abnormally large, that is, to the *normal profit* necessary for him to continue in business. This is an example of the 'economic rent' referred to on page 37. But these excess profits may only be maintained in the short run, for other things being equal other producers will in the long run bring together the necessary factors of production – including the fixed inputs like plant and machinery – to produce a close substitute. This substitute for the monopolist's goods weakens his monopoly power as some customers are likely to buy the new alternative at any given price. In addition, his ability to retain customers on increasing his price is weakened, for the greater availability of substitutes tends to make the demand for *his* product more elastic. The inventor of the 'original safety-pin', for example, might have made supernormal profits for no one else made such a fastener. But within a year, perhaps less, other pin manufacturers no doubt brought out competing versions with 'the improved safety-pin', and the 'ultra safe safety-pin', perhaps, and the 'zip pin'. All these weakened the monopoly power of the producer of the 'original safety-pin'. He found he could sell fewer at any given price because new producers entering the industry seeking supernormal profits had tended to push prices down. The total demand was now shared among more producers (causing a leftward shift in the demand curve for his product). In addition, the demand for the 'original safety-pin' had become more elastic because of the availability of close substitutes.

When a monopolist can prevent others from producing a substitute to compete with his output, he may prolong the period over which he earns abnormal or supernormal profits from its sale. This is another aspect of monopoly power, for the longer a firm can earn profits from a monopoly the greater its monopoly power. Monopoly power therefore has two aspects: the ability to earn abnormally large profits; and the ability to do so for prolonged periods. The extent of a monopolist's success in doing these things shows the degree of his monopoly power. To what extent can he earn abnormal profits by restricting output? How long can he maintain this favourable situation of monopoly profits?

Barriers to entry

Monopolists can keep other producers out of their industries by several means. These are all barriers or restrictions on the entry of competitors.

Common among the barriers are legal ones, often – if not always – established with good reason. The law prevents unqualified people practising as doctors of medicine, lawyers and school teachers in the UK. The firm or individual with a patent is protected against competition for up to sixteen years. Only this firm or individual may produce the patented goods or license others to make them, allowing the patentee to recover the cost of developing and perfecting the idea. In 1968 over 60 000 patent applications were submitted in the UK, of these about 85% have since been granted.

Mention has been made of the reasons why governments run certain industries as monopolies. These are operated with legal barriers preventing the entry of competitors and have some special features which we shall come back to in a moment.

An historic legal barrier to entry into a market were the Royal Charters, and in 1976 the Nottingham Corporation holding Charters from AD 1200 as the only people entitled literally to organise a town market considered preventing other organisers running a Sunday market near the town.

A monopolist's abnormal profits may give him the ability to keep out competitors.

In practice many monopolies in the UK arose mainly as *scale monopolies*, from situations where there is room for only one producer in an industry to exploit economies of scale. Potential rivals are kept out of the industry because they are unlikely to get economies of scale from production, owing to the high capital outlay required, and could therefore only produce the good at a higher cost. The generation of electricity is one example already mentioned; providing a railway system is another.

Monopoly in factor markets
There are monopolies in the supply of certain factors of production. The vineyard owner growing grapes in a particular valley may have such natural advantages of soil and climate that no one else can produce wine of the taste he gets from his vintage. Some trade unions have a monopoly in the supply of labour of particular types or trades, and so a producer requiring their skills is forced to employ union men or women.

Mention has been made on page 120 of monopsony situations, where there is only one buyer for a product. This might be the only factory in a town employing skilled labour, or a single producer buying the output from suppliers of a component. The market situation of a single buyer and a single seller (a monopsonist and monopolist) is known as *bilateral monopoly*. Before looking at the implications of monopolies the following Assignments should help to establish the concepts of competition and monopoly.

Assignments

11.1 What do you understand by monopoly and why do governments attempt to control them?

11.2 'A monopolist can charge whatever price he likes.' Discuss. (IWMC 1971)

11.3 What do you understand by supernormal profits? How might a monopolist retain these in the long run?

11.4 Use the data in the following table:

Price per unit (£)	Quantity demanded per week (000)	Total revenue (£000)	Marginal revenue (£000)
10	1		
9	2		8
8		24	
7			4

To calculate: (i) marginal revenue when demand is 3000 units per week; and (ii) total revenue when the price per unit is £7. (AEB 1973)

11.5 The following information concerns the output and revenue of a firm in which the price of the unit produced (£3) does not change with variations in output.

Number of men employed	Total number of units produced per week
10	100
11	115
12	128
13	138

Calculate:
   (a) total weekly revenue when 11 men are employed;
   (b) marginal physical product when 12 men are employed;
   (c) marginal revenue when 13 men are employed.
(Includes revision.) (AEB 1971)

11.6* Discuss: 'If monopoly is the optimum form of organisation in an industry it is desirable to have it run by the state.'

Cartels and restrictive practices

Forms of cartel
Although taking many forms, a cartel is an organisation formed by several firms and/or occasionally by individuals, to exercise a degree of monopoly power. Members of a cartel would normally be in competition, but by joining together to market their products, they hope to get higher profits than they otherwise might. A form of cartel once common in the building and civil engineering industry arranged the members affairs so that tenders – offers for work at stated prices – were rigged. The customer then received offers far above a competitive price or no offers at all from all but the selected member of the cartel. This firm would put in a price, tender for the work, at a figure agreed by the cartel. In the absence of any similar offer, the firm then got the job. There was, in effect, one price offered for the job and this a price at which more than normal profits might be made.

Another form of cartel has all members firms selling their output to a single marketing company – an agent acting for the cartel. With this method the agent becomes the only supplier of the member firms' products, and they do not compete among themselves but expect more than normal profits. The total profit made by the selling agent is then shared out among members of the cartel.

Most governments have laws against many practices considered to be unfair methods of trading. These we will come back to in a moment, but one of the most undesirable groups of producers were those in secret cartels. The members of the cartel lead their customers to believe that they are trading as competitors in a fair market.

Other restrictive practices
Firms do not have to join together in a cartel to rig a market and create the appearance of competition without its competitive restraints. They may make some arrangement formally or informally to limit their output or to fix prices. At one time

in several industries in the UK firms came to common agreements, so that their collective effort in each industry resulted in some degree of monopoly power. Acting as one body they then prevented the working of competitive forces within their industry. However since 1948 and more strongly since 1956 there have been laws in the UK against this practice as explained later, although such arrangements are still legal in some countries.

A number of restrictive practices have been investigated by the Monopolies Commission in the UK. These included: firms in the calico printing industry who set up an organisation to limit capacity (investigated in 1949); the cement manufac-turers' price fixing agreement (investigated in 1961); and the Glaxo and Cow and Gate companies' geographical division of the infant food market between them (investigated in 1967).

Another way for a producer to restrict competition is to supply a dealer on the understanding that this retailer does not sell any competing products. Or a group of producers may supply only dealers whom they recognise as suitable outlets for the trade. Both these restraints on the supply of goods to retailers in general prevent anyone other than the recognised dealer or dealers selling the goods. This restriction stops other retailers selling these goods at more favourable prices. Typical of these *sole supply* agreements were the arrangements of some lamp bulb manufacturers examined by the Monopolies Commission. These firms had an association whose members would only supply a wholesaler dealing exclusively with them.

Is monopoly harmful?
We have to dismiss from the economic consideration of this question any personal prejudices against the big corporations, the Goliaths faced by the small customer, for whether the monopolist is a well-intentioned state or an unscrupulous producer, the economic principles are little altered.

The economic case *against* monopoly argues that it is undesirable, because, all things being equal, the existence of monopoly leads to a higher price and lower output in an industry than when it is perfectly competitive. The monopolist wants to get the most profit that he or she can – as does the perfect competitor. But the monopolist does this by restricting output to increase prices above the 'perfectly competitive' level. Barriers to entry allow the monopolist to continue earning mon-opoly profits in the long term without competition from rivals.

A further argument against monopoly is the lack of incentive for a monopolist to develop new products or methods. As he is enjoying monopoly profits he does not wish to change things.

The most telling argument, perhaps, against monopoly is its effects in limiting the range of choice open to consumers. Instead of having several competing products to choose from, customers must take or leave what the monopolist offers – a lack of variety possibly leading to dull uniformity in products.

The economic case *for* monopolies involves some concepts (see Figure 11.3) which we have seen in earlier chapters. The first of these considerations is the economies of scale, giving the benefits of large-scale production at reduced costs. In such cases, the bringing together of all production for certain goods under a monopoly control can lead to greater output at lower prices from the economies of scale. The mon-opolist may be encouraged to innovate improved methods and products, as he has to

Monopoly main Pros and Cons

PROS	CONS
Economies of scale in a monopolist's production can lead to greater output and lower prices.	Output will be restricted and prices raised when a perfectly competitive industry becomes monopolised.
	Barriers to the entry of rival producers into a monopolised industry, enable a monopolist to exploit his position, so that in the long run there are no new competitors in this industry, competing away his super normal profits.
To keep ahead of possible rivals, a monopolist innovates new products.	There is no incentive to develop new products as the monopolist is already earning abnormally high profits.
As monopolist's products earn abnormal profits, he is encouraged by this to bring out new products knowing profits will not be competed away.	
A monopolist can provide variety, for having satisfied the main demand for his product, he may only increase his output with goods having more specialised appeal.	The monopolist as the only producer in an industry limits consumers' range of choice to his product.

Figure 11.3   The pros and cons of monopoly.

keep ahead of potential rivals to maintain his monopoly – a contrary argument to the anti-monopoly view of innovations.

From their monopoly profits, monopolists have the funds to carry out innovations and developments. They also have the incentive to bring in innovations as monopoly profits for these are unlikely to be attacked (competed away) by rivals. Patents, you will remember, allow their holders to be shielded against competition for similar reasons for innovation can be highly expensive. RCA spent US\$165 000 000 developing colour TV before receiving any return.

Monopolies may also increase rather than restrict variety where the consumer with special tastes might otherwise not be catered for. This evening the BBC and the Independent Broadcasting main channels might both show popular comedy programmes at 8 o'clock; each, perhaps, getting 45% of the potential viewers. But the BBC control a second channel on which they can show a programme of minority interest, to get the maximum share of viewers by attracting the remaining 10%. If there were a third Authority, it would show a comedy programme with the hope of getting one third of the 90% watching comedy, making no addition to viewers' choice if they do not wish to see comedy.

UK governments' Monopoly Policy

As there are economic arguments both for and against monopoly – more innovation, less innovation, for example – British policy has been pragmatic. The Government has tended to consider whether or not a particular monopoly operates against the public interest. While there are few absolute monopolies, as we have seen, the principle adopted in deciding whether or not any one of these suppliers has a monopoly is therefore set at a control of 25% of the market. If a firm has 25% of the

UK legislation on monopolies, restrictive practices and fair trading — position in 1976

Fair Trading Act 1973
Established the Office of Fair Trading, a government agency headed by the Director General of Fair Trading, to protect consumers from unfair practices and to improve competition. The Director has wide powers to investigate trade matters and brings cases of apparent monopoly before the Monopolies and Mergers Commission. His Office also registers 'restrictive practice agreements' — see below.

Monopolies and Mergers (Enquiry and Control) Act 1965 and related legislation of 1948 to 1973
Under this legislation the Monopolies and Mergers Commission investigate cases brought to it by the Director General of Fair Trading. When a firm has 25% of the total sales of a good or service, or a merger might lead to this, the Commission investigates. They also investigate mergers where the value of assets taken over exceeds £5-million, and newspaper mergers. These activities cover local as well as national monopolies, including those that may arise with Nationalised Industries and trade unions.

On an adverse report from the Commission, the government can dissolve a monopoly or prevent a merger. The Director General of Fair Trading may also when appropriate require price lists to be published or other steps be taken whether or not the Commission has made enquiries.

In making their reports the Commission considers, among other things: (a) the effect of the monopoly on the efficient use of resources; (b) the progressive increase in industrial efficiency; and (c) development of new markets. Governments have not considered all monopolies to be harmful.

Restrictive Trade Practices Act 1968 and earlier legislation of 1956
Established procedures for the Restrictive Practices court, whose decisions must be obeyed as it is a Court of Law. Restrictive practices have been considered by governments to be generally harmful to the public interest. Therefore all agreements must be registered which restrict prices, quantities, descriptions of goods, terms of sale, persons, places, and other conditions of trading. The Director General of Fair Trading as registrar of these agreements, brings them before the Court who may allow an agreement to continue for a number of reasons, including cases where: special skills are needed in the use of the goods so the agreement protects the public; its removal would cause serious unemployment or reduce exports or cause price increases. Where such an agreement contravenes an international treaty, the Dept of Trade may make an order for the parties to modify the agreement's terms.

Resale Price Maintenance Act (1964)
The Act prohibits in general the practice of retail price maintenance under which a manufacturer sells only to retailers who agree to trade at a *retail price fixed by the manufacturer* for his goods. Such agreements are, however, permitted provided they are registered and approved through the Restrictive Practices Court. Grounds for allowing a Resale Price Maintenance (RPM) agreement to stand are that without it: (a) there could be a substantial decrease in the quality and variety of goods; (b) a reduction in the number of retail outlets; (c) an eventual increase in retail prices; (d) danger to health; and (e) reduction in before-and-after-sale service. There is also a general consideration of the 'public interest' (see below).

In 1964 the government considered RPM incompatible with competition keeping down costs and prices.

Figure 11.4   UK legislation on monopoly and restrictive practices.

sales of a product, then its operations are considered as *potentially* against the public interest. But looking at Figure 11.4 we see that the legislation is wide ranging and no doubt will alter in the future.

European Economic Community Monopoly Policy
Two articles in the Treaty of Rome, Nos. 85 and 86, regulate monopolies, mergers and restrictive practices in the Community. The European Commission is responsible for enforcing these regulations and investigating any apparent breaches in the rules. The policy – like that in the UK – is neutral taking neither a complete stand against all monopolies nor encouraging them.

The regulations were not fully established at the time of writing in 1976, but those dealing with restrictive practices are the most developed at this time. They prevent any agreement between firms and/or individuals fixing prices or sharing markets to prevent competition in the Community. The regulations apply to any such agreement restricting or destroying competition within two or more member countries. (Within each country, governments have their own legislation as we have seen with UK monopoly policy.) There are exceptions to these regulations against restrictive practices, through provisions not unlike the 'gateway clause' in UK legislation. This allows firms to operate with a degree of monopoly where the arrangement in the Commission's view will improve production or distribution or promote progress in an industry. Each agreement is considered on its merits.

In 1969 ten companies known as the 'Aniline Dye' trust were fined by the EEC for operating a common price agreement during 1964 and 1965. This is an example of EEC action against a 'consented practice' contravening the Market's anti-monopoly laws.

Assignments

11.7 What are monopolies? How does the government seek to control private monopolies? (L 1972)

11.8 List the pros and cons of monopoly and illustrate with examples.

11.9 Update Figure 11.4 at the time of your study from sources available in the local library.

11.10* Discuss: 'Monopolies inevitably restrict consumers' choice.'

11.11* Group research: each group select a patented product. What is the likely justification for granting of this patent right?

11.12* The bus fare of 30p from the village to town is increased to 50p. How may this affect the monopoly power of the village shop? List the likely consequences of such a change on the shop's pricing policy and its customers' buying habits.

11.13* Check your list of definitions, your cross-referencing of topics, and your set of newspaper cuttings are up to date with your study.

Suggested further reading

Harvey, Chapter 9
D Lee, V Anthony and A Skuse, *Monopoly* (Heinemann, 1968)
Paish and Culyer, Chapters 16 and 22
Powicke, Chapter 9
Stanlake, Chapter 15

Chapter 12
The Economy as a whole; the nation's income

We have seen something of the economic problems facing individual units – consumers, producers and industries. Now we look at these in the economy as a whole, beginning with a study of the nation's or national income.

Income, expenditure and output

What is national income?
The national income of a country is the value of goods and services produced as a result of the country's *productive* activity over a given time period, usually a year. There are three ways of measuring this *flow* of goods and services. One can add together the incomes received – the factor rewards – of people owning the factors of production used in making the commodities. Secondly one can add together the amounts spent in buying these goods and services. Or thirdly one can add together the output of the various industries producing them.

These three calculations – the income, expenditure and output methods – are only different ways of looking at the same thing (see Figure 12.1). Despite the problems of measurement, therefore, they have identical values: National Income (NI) equals National Expenditure (NE) equals National Output (NO), usually written as: $NI \equiv NE \equiv NO$.

The country of Dreamland 1980

National Income		National Expenditure		National Output	
Incomes of suppliers of factors of production		Expenditure by buyers of goods and services		Output by producers of goods and services	
	£-millions		£-millions		£-millions
Land owners' rents	20	Purchase of consumer goods & services	75	Output by farmers	30
Labour wages and salaries	60	Purchase of capital goods	25	Output by manu- facturers	40
Capital owners' interest received	11			Output from service industries	30
Entrepreneurs' profits	9				
	£100		£100		£100

This is a closed economy with no overseas interests nor imports or exports.

Figure 12.1   National Income $\equiv$ National Expenditure $\equiv$ National Output.

Theory and practice

In practice difficulties arise because allowances must be made in these calculations for various complexities of everyday economic life. These complications arise from the effects of government activities, the effect of trade with other countries, and the interdependence of producers. Nevertheless the identity $NI \equiv NE \equiv NO$ still holds.

In calculations of the United Kingdom's national income, the complexities can be summarised as arising from:

1. The part played in the economy by governments, for the state is both producer and purchaser of goods and services, while also collecting and spending taxes.

2. The UK citizens are involved in trade with the rest of the world, importing goods, etc from abroad, and exporting commodities to customers in other countries.

3. Many producers' outputs are the inputs of other producers. This interdependence is seen in the output of nut and bolt manufacturers being one of the inputs for motor-car producers.

In following through the three methods of calculating a nation's income, these complexities become clear.

The Income Method

In producing goods and services, incomes are received by the people or organisations who are the suppliers of factors of production, and their total amount is the nation's income. The wage and salary earners, employees or those who are self-employed have income as their reward for the factor of production labour. Profits of individuals and firms, along with any surpluses made by nationalised industries and public corporations, are income in this calculation. Also included is income from rents, and interest on capital.

There are, however, some forms of income that must be excluded. These *transfer earnings* are receipts or incomes which do not arise from *current* production – family allowances, old age pensions from the State and other social security benefits are examples. They do not represent payment for current production of any good or service; they are merely transfers from the income of others made for the benefit of those receiving the allowances. Such transfers are brought about by government taxing incomes and using the proceeds to pay these allowances.

If transfer income is not excluded there would be a double counting of this part of the national income, for if you receive £2000 as a reward for your part in currently producing goods and pay £600 in taxes, this £600 is a transfer of your income to a pensioner, perhaps. Your gross income of £2000 must be included in calculating national income, but if in error the pensioner's £600 were included this would be taking the '£600' in twice. Only your £2000 of income came from the current production of goods and services.

The total of incomes arising from currently produced goods and services is known as 'the total domestic income'. We will see below its relation to national income.

The Expenditure Method

A nation's income can also be calculated as the total amount paid by buyers of goods and services in a period. The expenditure may be either on goods for *consumption* or for *investment* (adding to the stock of capital). Consumption here includes all current spending on goods and services; by private individuals – consumer expenditure –

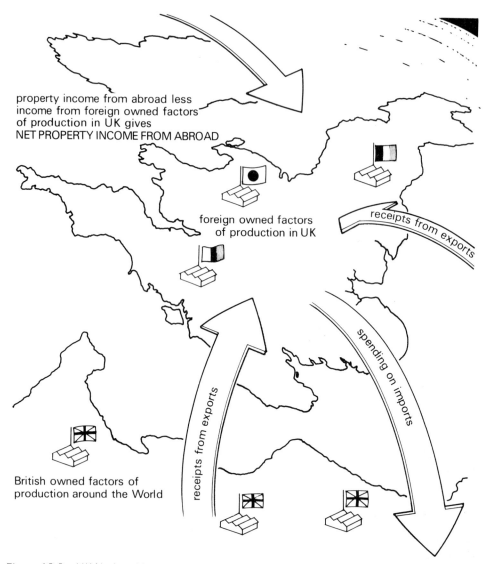

Figure 12.2   UK National Income: exports, imports and net property income from abroad.

and that of local and central government – public authority consumption.

The investment expenditure included in National Expenditure may be in fixed assets (plant and factories and houses) when it is called *fixed investment* or fixed capital formation. It may be in stocks of raw materials, work-in-progress (unfinished work in the course of production or building) and finished stocks, such investment being 'capital formation in stocks'.

Some buyers of goods and services produced in the UK are in other countries. Exports to them must therefore be included in any calculation of the total expenditure on goods and services as a measure of the nation's income. On the other hand expenditure on goods from abroad (imports) must be excluded, for these do not generate income in the UK (see Figure 12.2).

A stage in the calculation of National Income

Income aspect – 1974	£-millions		Expenditure aspect – 1974	£-millions
Gross Domestic Incomes	77 853		Gross Domestic Product at	
less: Stock appreciation	5 964		market prices	81 032
			less: Taxes on expenditure	11 351
				69 681
			add: Subsidies	2 944
	£71 889			£72 625

Since National Income is identical with National Expenditure, the National Income arrived at by the two methods should be the same figure. Differences (see text) are grouped in the *residual error*:

Gross Domestic Product at Factor Cost –	
Expenditure aspect calculation	72 625
Income aspect calculation	71 889
Residual Error	£736

This residual is added to Income Aspect and Output Aspect of National Income – see summary Figure 12.6.

Figure 12.3 Residual error.

All expenditure including exports, the total amount spent in the UK by buyers, is the *Total Final Expenditure at market prices*. From this can be subtracted the amount spent on imports; this then gives the *Gross Domestic Product (GDP) at market prices*. This is the total value of goods and services produced in the UK in terms of 'the prices at which they are purchased'. But some prices may include indirect taxes like VAT and excise duties, while others may benefit from subsidies. In order to measure the GDP in terms of the prices producers receive (factor prices), these taxes must be deducted and the subsidies added to the GDP at market prices to get the GDP at factor prices (see Figure 12.6 on page 163).

Reconciling National Income and Expenditure
Having calculated the total Domestic Income an adjustment is often needed for changes in the price of stocks. These may appreciate for if you bought ten tandems worth £60 each for resale, the five remaining unsold at the end of the first year could each be worth £80. The three left at the end of the second year could be worth £100 each. Yet nothing has been done to these bikes, they have just appreciated in value. Such stock appreciations (or depreciations when prices fall) do not reflect any production, and are therefore deducted from the total Domestic Income or added as depreciation of stock.

Even after adjusting the National Income figure for changes in stock values (see Figure 12.3) there will still be differences between this and National Expenditure, although we know that in theory that they are the same, for what we all earn as income is spent eventually either by ourselves or others on our behalf. However, many of the statistics used in calculating National Income and National Expenditure are imprecise. The result is a difference between National Income and National Expenditure (see Figure 12.3) and shown in the published figures as a *residual error*. For convenience this difference is treated in these government statistics as part of the National Income account.

Look again at Figure 12.3. After subtracting stock appreciation from total domestic incomes and allowing for residual error, you have a figure that is the Gross Domestic Product (GDP) at factor prices or cost. That is: the amount received by producers in the United Kingdom for the goods and services they produce.

Gross National Product

The Gross Domestic Product (GDP) is not the whole story of a nation's income, since individuals and organisations in the UK own investments abroad and receive income from them as interest on loans, dividends and profits. In so far as these incomes are received in the UK, they add to the nation's income. At the same time there are investors living in other countries who draw similar incomes from investments they own in the UK. Examples of these payments to and from the country are numerous but two illustrate the effect. British Petroleum in 1975 received monies from their investments overseas, while in the same year some British companies paid money to their owners abroad.

The net amount of the inflow and outflow of all these incomes is known as *the net property income from abroad*. In Britain inflows have exceeded outflows for many years – a net inflow, although some countries pay more property income abroad than they receive – a net outflow. The UK net property income from abroad must be added to the total Domestic Incomes to arrive at the income received by United Kingdom owners of factors of production (see Figure 12.2).

In calculating the nation's income in terms of National Expenditure the same net property income from abroad is added to the Gross Domestic Product at factor cost (see above). This is because net property income from abroad can be regarded as 'the net expenditure by people in other countries on output of UK-owned factors of production in these countries' – income to the UK owners of these factors (see Figure 12.2).

These adjustments – adding net property income from abroad to income and expenditure, Gross Domestic Product at factor cost – gives the *Gross National Product (GNP) at factor cost.*

Depreciation

Our calculations so far of both GDP (Gross Domestic Product) and GNP (Gross National Product) take no account of the wear and tear on capital – plant, machinery and similar producer goods. Nor have the figures made any allowance for capital equipment that is out of date and must be replaced. A calculation of this consumption of capital through depreciation and obsolescence can be made. This amount of output to replenish 'used' capital can be deducted from the Gross National Product to give the *Net National Product* or *Net National Income* (see Figure 12.4).

We have therefore calculated Net National Income in two ways – from National Income and National Expenditure – making appropriate allowances for overseas trade and income, changes in the price of stock and other adjustments. There is, however, a third method of arriving at the nation's income – National Output – and in considering this we go back to the first steps in calculating a nation's income.

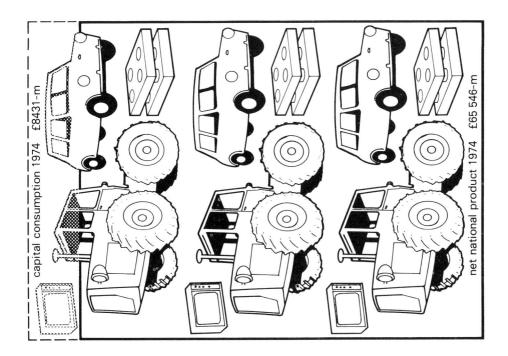

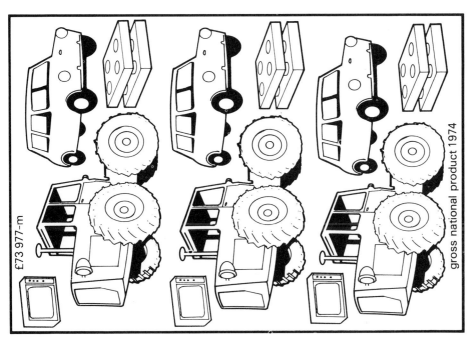

Figure 12.4   Consumption of capital.

value of output

value added

pigs raised
£80

£80

killed and cured
£120

+ £40

packaged
£160

+ £40

retailing £200

+ £40

= £200

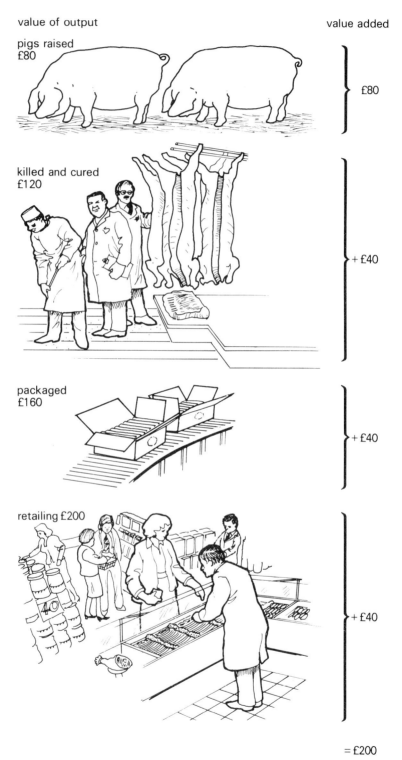

Figure 12.5   An example of added-value output calculation.

Income Aspect	£-m	Expenditure Aspect	£-m	Output Aspect*	£-m
Income from employment	52 001	Consumers' expenditure	51 670	Agriculture, forestry and fishing	2 116
Income from self-employment	7 895	Public authorities consumption	16 641	Mining & quarrying	1 021
Gross trading profits of companies	9 706	Gross fixed investment	16 247	Manufacturing	20 645
				Construction	5 645
Gross trading surplus of public corporations	2 426	Value of physical increase in stocks	1 082	Gas, electricity and water	2 255
		Exports of goods and services	22 186	Transport	4 624
Gross trading surplus of other public enterprises	119			Communication	2 024
Rent	5 706	Total final expenditure at market prices	107 826	Distributive trade	7 003
				Insurance, finance and business services	6 750
Total domestic Incomes	77 853	*less:* Imports of goods and services	26 794 –	Ownership of dwellings†	4 310
less: Stock appreciation	5 964 –			Public administration and defence	5 312
		GDP at market prices	81 032	Public health and educational services	4 854
Residual error	736	*less:* Taxes on expenditure	11 351 –	Other services	8 735
		Subsidies	2 944		
Gross Domestic Product at Factor Cost	72 625		72 625	Total	75 294
				Adjustment for financial services	3 405 –
Net property income from abroad	1 352			Residual error	736
			1 352		72 625
Gross National Product at Factor Cost	73 977		73 977		1 352
less: Capital consumption	8 431 –		8 431 –		73 977
					8 431 –
National Income	£65 546		£65 546		£65 546

* This table shows the 'value added' by producers, that is the excess of the value of their current output over the value of goods and services purchased from outside their respective industries and used in production.
† This service represents the value of owner-occupied dwellings and is calculated from rateable values less the expenditure on maintenance and repairs. The contribution is in some ways equivalent to a 'rent', for if these dwellings were let to other people than their owners a rent to the landlord would be shown in the figure for rents.

Source: *Annual abstract of statistics* (HMSO).

Figure 12.6   Summary of National Income, NE and NO for 1974.

The Output Method

This method of calculating national income adds together the output of producers in the economy. But we know that the output of many producers is the input for others. This interdependence results in the output value of most producers' goods containing in part the value of their suppliers' output. Therefore a calculation of National Output (NO) only includes the *value added* to goods by each producer (see Figure 12.5). National Output is the total of these 'added values' that each producer contributes, less the cost of any imported goods and services.

Figure 12.5 makes this clear, for if we merely added all the output values, the total sum would far exceed the value of the finished products. By only adding together the 'added values' we come to a total which is the value of the finished goods. We can add therefore either the totals of these finished goods' value or the value added in various stages contributed by producers. Having totalled the added values or the values of finished goods to arrive at the output within the United Kingdom (see Figure 12.6) the net property income from abroad is added to get the Gross National Product. This net income as we have seen is related to factors abroad but owned by people in the UK, and is the output from UK-owned factors abroad.

UK National Income

In the next chapter are some examples of the way National Income statistics are used. One such use is, however, in measuring the *growth* in the volume of output and changes in living standards. Because of their importance in this and other analyses, United Kingdom statistics of National Income have been collected regularly since 1941, and by the 1970s were published annually in the National Income and Expenditure Blue Book. A summary of the three methods of calculating National Income are shown in Figure 12.6 based on figures in the Blue Book.

Before looking at the use and occasional misuse of National Income statistics, one must understand that the UK published figures only include goods and services which are exchanged for money. Many types of production – do-it-yourself decorating, home dressmaking (not for sale), growing one's own vegetables – are not included; nor is the important and large contribution made by housewives in unpaid services running homes. A typical anomaly that can arise because unpaid work is not included in UK income statistics relates to unpaid housewives. If a housewife who has not been paid for her own work in the home takes a job, then her income of, say, £30 is included in the statistics. Should she also pay £10 a week to someone to do her housework now that she goes out, this £10 will also enter into the statistics. Yet £40 (£30 + £10) is not the true measure of the increase in production for the housework was being done before, although no value was put on it in the National Income figures. Therefore these published UK figures of National Income understate the position. However, in other countries, as we will see in the next chapter, national statistics make some allowance for these unpaid jobs, and in the UK an amount or notional value is allowed for in figures of farmers' incomes and expenditure to cover the consumption of their own produce.

Assignments

12.1 'National Income, National Expenditure and National Output are merely three different ways of looking at the same thing.' Explain this statement.

12.2 What do you understand by 'double counting'? Illustrate your answer with an example.

12.3 (*a*) Study the most recent issue of the *National Income Blue Book* and update the information in Figure 12.6.
   (*b*) Discuss the changes and/or note their significance.

12.4 Why is depreciation deducted when calculating National Income?

12.5 What allowance is made in calculating National Income for the United Kingdom's relationships with other countries?

Suggested further reading

Harbury, Chapter 6
Harvey, Chapter 19
J Harvey and M Johnson, *An Introduction to Macroeconomics* (Macmillan, 1971), Chapter 2
Stanlake, Chapter 17

Chapter 13

How well off?

Countries, like individuals, need to know how well off they are, how much income they have. This information is important for many purposes. Governments have to decide what each might fairly contribute to a common fund, perhaps for their joint defence as under the NATO pact or for other benefits as under an EEC fund. At other times the amount of aid given to poor countries can depend on how poor they are relative to the richer nations. Governments also need to know how their economies' performance compare to others, particularly when it comes to questions of increases in living standards over a period of years.

National Income statistics

Their use
In the same way that individuals base the calculation of how well off they are in terms of income, so countries base their calculations on the National Income statistics we considered in chapter 12. Look at Figure 13.1; this shows a doubling of the British National Income from £16 668 million in 1956 to £35 249 million in 1969.

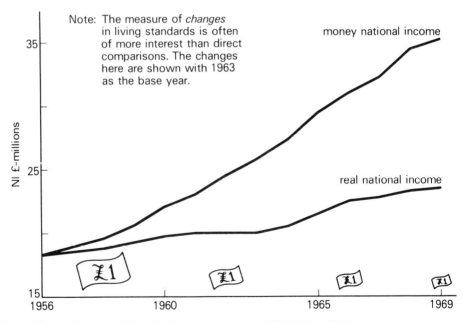

Figure 13.1   Money and Real National Incomes for UK 1956 to 1969

These figures measure the output of goods and services in £:p terms for the years 1956 and 1969. But the purchasing power of the £ varies, buying less as the prices of goods rise. Therefore, to arrive at changes in the *volume* of goods and services produced year by year, we must take account of these variations in the value of money (the price level, as we will see later).

The *Retail Price Index* measures changes in the level of prices and therefore 'the value of money' (see chapter 14). By using the Index we can make the adjustment necessary to take account of changes in the value of money (or the price level) to arrive at a table of 'real' values, that is: a table of the *volume* of goods and services produced. When the figures for 1956 and 1969 in Figure 13.1 are adjusted for these variations, the doubling of National Income represents a much less spectacular increase in the *volume* of goods and services produced. To make these calculations in a comparison of 1956 and 1969 National Income figures, we begin by considering the difference in price levels as measured by the Retail Price Index, between these two years:

In 1956 first year of this comparison
   – the RPI stood at 100
      this is called the 'base year'

In 1969 second year for comparison
   – the RPI stood at 152

The increase in prices of 52% between 1956 and 1969 clearly caused a major part of the increase in money value of the National Income between these years. But we can allow for the difference in the price levels and adjust the 1969 National Income figures to put these in terms of 1956 prices. Then we get a set of 'National Income' figures measured in terms of constant prices; that is, what the National Income would have been in 1969 if the value of money remained constant at its 1956 level. This measure in terms of money-with-a-constant-value gives a measure of *Real National Income* (see Figure 13.1).

National Income measured at current and constant prices
The distinction between *Real* and *Money* values is very important when considering National Income or individuals' incomes. It is a feature of everyday life in the 1970s, for the amount your spending money buys this year may be much less in times of rising prices than you could get for the same sum of money last year. Your real income is the goods and services you can buy with your money income, and while your money income can increase in £:p (pounds and pence) its actual purchasing power may be less than last year.

In the calculation of Real or constant-price National Income from Money National Income or current-price figures, a formula is used that for any year 'X' may be expressed as:

$$\text{Real National Income in yr X at constant prices} = \frac{\text{Money value of National Income in yr X}}{\text{Price Index in yr X}} \times 100$$

Using this formula the National Income at 1956 prices – the *Real National Income* – in Britain was £23 200 million in 1969 (£35 240 m × $\frac{100}{152}$). As we have used 1956 as the base year (prices = 100) we say '£23 200 million is the National Income for 1969 expressed in terms of 1956 prices'. Since we are dealing with the 'base year' 1956, Real National Income that year in terms of 1956 prices was £16 668 million – the same as National Income in terms of current prices of that year. Or in other words: £16 668 million × $\frac{100}{100}$.

Comparing these constant price National Income figures, the increase between 1956 and 1969 was £6530 million (£23 200 m − £16 670 m). This shows a rise of 39% in real terms, a very different increase from the 100% in money or current price terms. The graphs in Figure 13.1 compare National Income in money terms and National Income in Real Terms for the years 1956 to 1969.

Limitations in comparisons of National Income statistics
When comparing Real National Income figures calculated on a particular 'base year' we meet the problems of Index numbers to be described in detail in chapter 14. But when calculating on this basis no account is taken of changes in the composition of output nor of the quality of commodities produced. For example: a country may be preparing to defend itself in an expected war, and the extra armaments produced form part of its National Income. However these weapons make no direct contribution to the satisfaction of consumers' daily wants.

We saw that National Income statistics only include goods and services exchanged for money. Many other types of production are not included: the labour in home decorating and other d-i-y jobs and the domestic work of housewives. In addition the value and quantity of peasant families' home-grown food can be significant in some economies, where the total amount they consume themselves is substantial. In some countries, including Holland, an attempt is made to put a value on housewives' domestic work for National Income purposes. Although no cash wage is paid for doing these chores, value is *imputed* – a notional money wage is attributed to the job – and National Income statistics include these 'wages'. We also saw in chapter 12 the misleading effect in these statistics when a housewife goes out to work and pays someone to do her house cleaning.

National Income figures make no distinction between consumer goods (goods for direct consumption), and capital goods (goods produced to help produce other goods). This can lead to some problems in comparisons of National Income between countries. One country may be forgoing current consumption in order to get a greater output of capital goods for *future* increases in the output of consumer goods. Yet this investment for the future is not reflected in the consumer goods currently available.

We have detailed the three major problems encountered in comparing National Incomes: changes in composition, production or output not exchanged for money, and production of capital relative to consumer goods. While these are important in year against year comparisons in any economy, they are even more significant in comparisons between countries (see Figure 13.2).

Real Income per head of employed population
Figure 13.1 shows a rise in total British Real Income, but this does not necessarily mean that each person is better off in consuming more goods and services. The

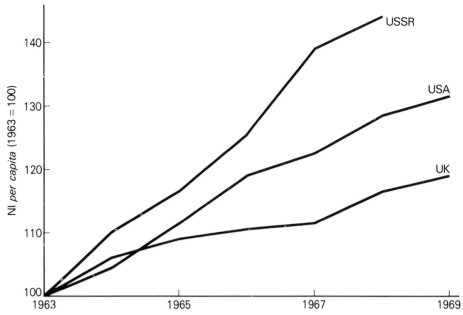

Figure 13.2   Changes in National income *per capita* in the UK, USA and USSR for 1963 to 1969.

population may have increased, as indeed it did in Britain between 1956 and 1969 with a rise of $8\frac{1}{2}\%$ to 55.53 million. The National Income then had to go round a greater number of people. We can compare the Real National Income per head or *per capita* for these two years by dividing Real National Income by figures of population size.

In Britain this figure was £417.8 (£23 200 m ÷ 55.53 million) for 1969. Many of the population are not engaged in producing goods and services, look again at Figure 3.3, page 42. Therefore a measure of production per head is calculated as National Income (or National Output) per head on the basis of the numbers at work. This gives, for example, a measure of how productive we are. In Britain in 1956 the total employed labour force was 23.75 million and by 1969 it had only risen to 24.9 million. However the Real National Income (see Figure 13.1) had risen from £16 668 million in 1956 to £23 200 million by 1969. On these figures we can calculate the Real National Income per head of the employed labour force for these years as:

$$\begin{array}{cc} 1956 & 1969 \end{array}$$

$$\frac{\overset{\text{million}}{£16\ 668}}{23.75} = £701.8 \text{ per head}$$

$$\frac{\overset{\text{million}}{£23\ 200}}{24.9} = £931.7 \text{ per head}$$

This increase from £701.8 to £931.7 per head is about 33% and provides a reasonable measure of how much more productive we became by 1969 compared with 1956. The figures also give some measure of economic progress over this period. These figures of Real NI per head of the employed labour force may also be used to make very approximate comparisons between how productive one country's employed population is on average against those in another country. But the differences between countries and between time periods reflect among other things differences in the quantity and quality of capital goods per worker.

Summary
To summarise the position before looking at more comparisons: Real National Income per head of the population is a useful measure of standards of living since it measures the volume of goods and services available per person. But if we are interested in measuring how productive we are in the UK or measuring our own progress, we should consider Real NI per head of the employed population.

The danger of averages and generalisations
We have seen the misleading results which sometimes arise from the careless use of statistics. Averages for example tell us nothing about distribution. Statistics also create pitfalls for the unwary student studying NI data, for the figures average out variations in Real NI *per capita* as between individuals. There may be great differences between a few rich and many poor people's share of a National Income. Therefore a rise in this or in Real NI per head may not mean *each* person is better off through consuming more goods and services.

The increased Real NI may have been achieved as a result of the work force putting in longer hours, or by adverse working arrangements with more shift work perhaps. These conditions can materially affect the individuals' living standards. Yet very often people ask 'how well off are we compared with *them*?' when we intend to make a comparison of living standards. This may be a comparison with how our fathers lived or how people live in other countries or some other comparison. Yet by using either Real NI per head of population or per head of the work force, no account is taken of either how this income is actually distributed, nor the conditions of work under which it was produced.

These conditions could result in the comparison of annual Real NI per head of two working populations being equal at £500, yet in one case the top few thousand may receive incomes of £5000 each and the bottom 100 000 as little as £50. In the second population, however, the distribution of incomes might be much more even. At the same time, the workers in the first population might each put in 50 hours a week, while those in the second only work 40 hours a week.

For some amusing and informative views on the dangers of statistical abuses read *How to lie with statistics* (Penguin).

Comparisons of standards of living
Bearing in mind the limitations of averages, the comparison of Real NI per head of the population provides a basis for comparisons of living standards for people in different countries. Figure 13.3 shows useful methods of making international comparisons of living standards as seen in the example for Great Britain, West Germany, Japan, USA, Ghana, India, Brazil and Saudi Arabia. However the NI figures on which these are based need several adjustments to make them comparable. Some adjustments are statistical as we have seen in the Dutch adjustment of NI for imputed income to housewives, and the UK adjustment for farmers' consumption of their own products. The hours and conditions of work in these countries also varies.

	UK	West Germany	Japan	USA	Ghana	India	Brazil	Saudi Arabia
GNP per capita 1974 US $	3 590	6 260	4 070	6 670	430	140	920	2 830
Average annual growth in per capita GNP at constant prices 1960–74 as %	2·3	3·7	4·0	2·9	−0·2	1·1	4·0	8·4
Doctors per 1000 inhabitants 1970–74	1·3	1·9	1·2	1·6	0·1	0·2	0·5	0·2
Television sets per 1000 inhabitants 1973	309	298	229	523	3	0·3	51	2*
Hospital beds per 1000 inhabitants	9	11	13	7	1	1	4	1
in years shown	1971	1973	1972	1973	1973	1968	1973	1972
Telephones per 1000 inhabitants 1974	366	302	356	657***	6	3	25	10***
Passenger cars per 1000 inhabitants 1973	244	267	133	478	4**	1	35	7*

Years other than stated: *1970, **1972 and ***1973.

Figure 13.3 International comparisons of standards of living; some monetary and non-monetary aspects.

On the mainland of Europe, for example, many countries enjoy a greater number of holidays for Saints' Days than are taken in the United Kingdom.

Next there are the differences in the types of goods making up the National Incomes of these countries, goods that may vary not only in quality but also in nature. The English like beer and sliced bread, the Yugoslavs prefer wine and coarse bread. Therefore comparisons have to be made by grouping together selected items. This is called a 'basket of goods' and is thought to represent fairly the weekly consumption by a *typical* family in each country.

There are also important problems which arise because the countries use different currencies, and revaluing one country's National Income in terms of another's currency is not entirely satisfactory. This difficulty arises because exchange rates are not determined by the relative purchasing power, broadly speaking, of any two currencies. What does affect these exchange rates is the goods and services which enter into the trade between the countries. For these reasons, when comparing living standards, comparisons between countries' currencies are often based on the prices of 'the basket of goods'. The comparison of living standards is made in terms of the number of these 'baskets' which the *per capita* income can buy in various countries.

There are also environmental differences between countries. These may include man-made pollution because production has been obtained at a high social cost, and natural phenomena particularly the weather which must be countered by using a proportion of the National Income. The heavy snows in North America, for example, can 'cost' an amount equivalent to several per cent of the United States National Income in clearing roads and keeping communications open in the winter. Elsewhere, the droughts faced by some African farmers may lead to demands on Output/Income, not present in temperate climates.

Assignments

13.1 The following information concerns an imaginary country, Noland:

	1960	1969
National Income (£m)	400	625
Index of prices	100	125

Calculate the percentage increase in Noland's National Income in real terms from 1960 to 1969. (Part only AEB 1971)

13.2 Real National Income statistics are often presented in a *per capita* form. What does this mean? What use can be made of such figures?

13.3* Group research: using the table of UK National Income figures from Figure 12.6 as updated in a previous Assignment, and other statistics, construct an index of living standards in recent years.

13.4* What difficulties are there in using National Income statistics to compare living standards between any two countries of your choice?

13.5* Discuss: why has the standard of living of the inhabitants of the United Kingdom risen over the past 25 years? (L 1972)

Suggested further reading

Edey, Peacock and Cooper, *National Income and Social Accounting* (Hutchinson)
Harvey, Chapter 19
Paish and Culyer, Chapter 4
Powicke *et al.*, Chapter 2
Stanlake, Chapter 24
Donaldson, Chapter 10

Chapter 14

Money

In everyday terms we all think of money as the stuff one buys things with – a bit of the 'ready' jingling in your pocket or 'crinkle' in your wallet. In economics money is more precisely defined and has many uses, with the origin of money stemming from the need to have something which all accept in exchange for goods.

Money – what it is and why we use it

Barter

Many primitive societies throughout history have existed by a system of barter. When one person has more goods than he or she wants to consume, this surplus may be swopped for another person's goods. The farmer with more wheat than he requires may then exchange it for meat from a herdsman or butcher. But there are important difficulties with barter.

These difficulties become acute when there is an increase in both the number and the variety of goods people want. Even in a simple society, however, there have to be two people who want to make a swop. This *double coincidence of wants* happens only when one person has a surplus of goods another wants, and the second person in turn has something the first man wants.

For this *double coincidence* to occur, X (our farmer, say) must find Y (a herdsman) who is not only willing to take X's goods but also has goods X wants in exchange – a herdsman wanting wheat and willing to give meat for it. Many people might want what X has to offer but none may want Y's goods. There may be difficulties in our farmer getting in touch with the herdsman (or X communicating with Y) supposing that they each wanted the other's goods, for X might live in the south of England and Y in the north of Scotland.

Some goods just cannot be divided into small units. You may have a working elephant but want a tasty sauce; but you will have a job to find anyone with sauce who wants to exchange it for an elephant. The man with the sauce may want to barter it for a motor-car and the motor-car owner might be willing to do a deal. He gets sauce for his motor-car and then might barter the sauce for your elephant. The chain of deals is getting complicated.

In primitive economies with only (say) fish, meat and rice to barter, such a chain of deals may not be too difficult to set up with a series of 'double coincidences of wants'. But there is no way you can split up your working elephant to barter it against small or small amounts of goods, unless you accept much less than the animal's value to you. Nor can you reasonably expect to swop it with several people for a combination of small goods – bottles of sauce and chopsticks, perhaps.

In a barter system you also need to hold a variety of goods to meet the different demands of those with goods you want. The primitive man may hold fish, meat and rice to exchange with a potter wanting meat, a smith wanting fish and the witch-doctor wanting rice. In today's society this would mean storing the wide range of goods your ironmonger, the garage mechanic, the medical practitioner, the school-teacher and the local barber may want; a variety of goods impractical to store. They may also lose their value while being stored, for even cattle and rice cannot be kept overlong and we have seen that many modern food products have a short shelf life.

Another snag with barter is that there is no standard unit to measure the relative value of different goods. How many bottles of sauce was that elephant worth? Or how many tonnes of rice might you expect for it? Is it worth as much as this or that motor-car? The parties to each deal have to make up their own minds without the convenience of comparisons with other goods. Maybe you know that your neighbour swopped his elephant for two tonnes of rice, but perhaps nobody has swopped one for sauce before.

Figure 14.1 summarises the difficulties of barter. Despite these, some states have brought off successful barter deals. In the 1930s the Germans reportedly swopped whaling ships with the Norwegians in exchange for whale oil. This in turn the Germans swopped with a British company for margarine.

'Money'
The difficulties of barter led early man to the use of a generally acceptable good which everyone would take in exchange for his or her goods. So your elephant might be exchanged with someone who wants it and is willing to give you some of this good – cowry shells or sharks teeth, perhaps, accepted by everyone in exchange for other goods. These shells or teeth or whatever are accepted by all in exchange for goods, and are therefore a form of money (see Figure 14.2).

In Germany during the months immediately after World War II, cigarettes were

The problems of *barter* – need for double-coincidence and opportunity to set this up; some goods will not divide nor can they be swopped for a combination of goods; need to store a variety of goods; deterioration in storage; and what is the relative value of one good to another?

Figure 14.1   The difficulties of barter.

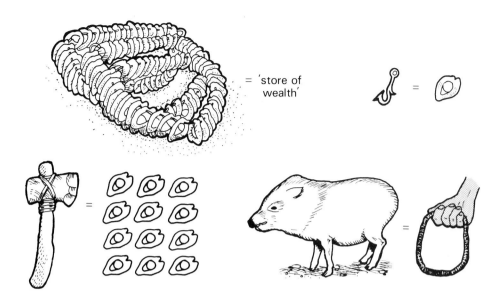

= 'store of wealth'

Figure 14.2   A cowry shell 'economy'.

used as 'money', the Dogan tribe in the Sudan use guinea-pig like animals. But in sophisticated societies with a high degree of specialisation a more practical form of money is essential, for without it this degree of labour specialisation would not be possible. Workers need paying in money, not in kind which would entail the problems above. With the money received as wages they can then each buy a different variety of goods to satisfy their wants.

The substance used as money is chosen largely as a matter of custom. Remember that the important feature of money is its acceptance by everyone in exchange for goods and services. Cattle, cowry shells and sharks teeth, however, are not very satisfactory as they do not have a standard quality or size. Cattle may deteriorate when kept, they cannot be used for small payments and they are difficult to move around. Because of each beast's different quality, there are difficulties when anyone offers a poorer one in exchange for goods they want. Precious metals, however, have been accepted as 'money' from early times, to overcome some of these difficulties. They can be stored and do not deteriorate and may be exchanged in small quantities from a larger block or ingot.

Early coins and notes
Metal can also be minted into coins of a standard size and quality, with values related to their weights in precious metal. In the 12th century BC a golden talent was twice the weight and therefore almost certainly twice the value of the gold half-talent used by the early Greeks. Such standard weights and sizes, denominations of coin, allow them to be counted easily, whereas precious metal in other forms like gold bars has to be weighed to check the quantity and assayed. Small quantities of metal coins may be carried about, but as this makes them potentially easy to steal, any large quantity had – and has – to be kept in a safe place.

By the mid-17th century, goldsmiths storing these precious metal coins were giving the depositors paper receipts for the coins stored. In time these receipts came to be accepted as equivalent to the precious coins they represented, for the notes were promises to pay so much coin when presented to the banker. Then the merchant X gave Y one of these receipts, rather than draw out the coin from its safe storage and pay Y. Y in turn found it convenient to pass on this receipt to Z in exchange for goods. Soon these and other receipt notes became money since they were accepted by everyone in exchange for other goods and services. While the precious metal coins stayed in the goldsmith–banker's safe, at any time a note holder could present this to the banker who would redeem his promise by exchanging the note for coins (see Figure 14.3).

Modern paper money has its origins in these early notes promising to pay precious metal coins, as we will see in the fourth part of this chapter. But notes as paper money no longer represent quite so simple a 'promise to pay' precious metal.

Legal tender
Paper money is not wanted in exchange for goods and services for itself for it is only printing on paper. Yet as it is generally accepted it is a form of money. Those holding it can be confident that *they* can exchange it for goods and services, even though the notes cannot any longer be exchanged for precious metal to the value printed on the note.

People in a State are bound to accept payment in each denomination of the currency up to the amount specified. In the United Kingdom in 1976 the total amount of each denomination of note and coin you were bound to accept in payment was: bronze coins for amounts up to 20p; 'silver' coins with values up to and including 10p for amounts up to £5; 50p pieces up to £10; and notes up to any amount.

No law was needed, however, to make cigarettes acceptable as 'money' in Germany during the summer of 1945. Similarly gold is widely accepted in payment for goods and services all over the world.

Assignments

14.1 Outline with suitable examples the difficulties of barter.

14.2 What is money and why do we use it?

14.3* Discuss: what four possible items might you and your friends use as 'money' if notes and coin were no longer available? In noting the conclusions from this discussion explain your choices.

The functions of money
Money serves four purposes or useful functions. It is a medium of exchange, a measure of value, a standard of deferred payment and a store of wealth.

Money as a medium of exchange
The function of money as a medium of exchange overcomes all the difficulties of a barter system. We have seen how it enables workers in a society with a high degree of division of labour to have money for wages rather than goods – labour is paid its reward in money. Workers accept this money not for any value in itself but because

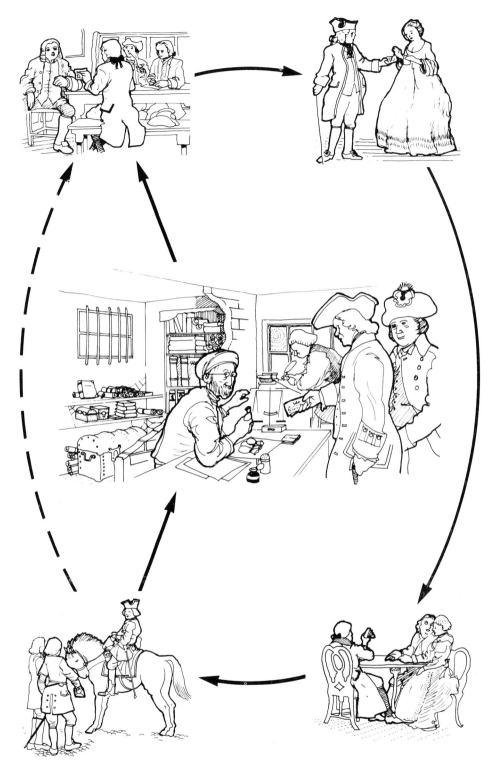

Figure 14.3   A goldsmith's note circulation.

they know it is acceptable to others in exchange for desired goods and services.

You can receive money in large quantities and then break this down for small transactions. You can take money in exchange for your goods, knowing that this will be accepted by those willing to supply you with the goods and services that you want.

Money as a measure of value and a unit of account
Money is a useful means by which to measure the value of goods, especially when they cannot be easily compared. Rather than trying to decide how many bottles of sauce, or motor-cars, your elephant should be exchanged for, it is easier to compare their money prices.

Prices and values in terms of money are also the basis of all financial records – invoice prices, ledger accounts and profit and loss accounts to name a few everyday accounting records. At the same time, more sophisticated statistics and accounting procedures like budget forecasts would be impractical without money as the unit of account in their calculation.

Money as a standard of deferred payment
Debts and loans are transacted in units of money. The loans described on page 106 are only feasible when the lender can be assured that repayment by the borrower will be in a form acceptable in a year, perhaps, from the date of the loan. Whether the repayment is deferred for this or any other period, the lender wants to be repaid the loan and interest in a form which will be accepted by others in exchange for goods and services.

Money is useful in this way as a standard now (in the present) which will also be the medium of exchange in the foreseeable future. Therefore it is used as the unit for measuring loans and similar deferred payments. In the last section of this chapter we will see that there are a number of institutions – banks, building societies and insurance companies among them – whose business depends on the existence of money, especially in its function as a standard of deferred payment.

Money as a store of value or wealth
Money is a useful way to store any surplus of income over your current requirements. It does not physically deteriorate in store like cattle whether you keep it in a bank or under the mattress, although its purchasing power may decrease as prices rise, as we will see in more detail in chapter 17.

As a medium of exchange money may be used to buy goods or services, so any store of money – in cash or bank accounts – is a fluid form of holding assets or wealth: it may be (too?) easily spent on this or that. An individual's wealth is the stock of assets he or she possesses including houses, motor-cars, furniture, stocks and shares and cash. These various forms of asset have varying degrees of liquidity. The most liquid is cash itself – money. As the most *liquid asset* money can quickly and easily be exchanged for goods or services. Should wealth be kept in other assets – cars, houses, shares, etc – these are less liquid for they have to be sold to get money before you may buy something else.

More than notes and coin
So far in this chapter the origins of money have been traced through precious metal coins, then as paper notes backed by promises to pay precious metal, and today's

paper money without such backing. But today the majority of coins are made of non-precious metals worthless than their face value. The 10p piece minted in 1975 was of $\frac{3}{4}$ copper and $\frac{1}{4}$ nickel worth a few pence, although the silver florins minted in the decade after World War II contain 50% silver, and are now worth a lot more than their 10p face value. These silver coins are likely to disappear from circulation despite laws against defacing or melting down any British coin. Dishonest citizens may melt down the silver coins to get more for them than their face value, and no doubt small quantities go abroad where there is no law against melting down British coins.

Money as the currency of an economy may – and in the British economy does – have no intrinsic value. In theory anyone might provide a form of money, generally acceptable, although in practice the law prevents all but the Bank of England in England and Wales from issuing bank notes (paper money). The situation in Scotland is slightly different as we will see later. But the British and many others use cheques as a form of 'money'. The cheque you sign is in simple terms a request to your bank to pay money from your account to the person you name or to his or her bank account. This is a convenient and safe way to pay money for it is easy to carry around and can be in a form that is useless to a thief. Although cheques are not legal tender, for others are not obliged to take them in payment, they are nevertheless widely accepted in exchange for goods and services and therefore a form of 'money'.

The introduction of cheque cards has extended the use of cheques, for card holders may buy up to £30 worth of goods in most shops, supermarkets and other places of business, paying by cheque. This is accepted because the retailer is guaranteed payment by the card holder's bank, provided his or her card number is written on the back of the cheque and the seller follows a few rules.

The essence of the cheque card is the confidence that it gives those accepting cheques from its holder: that the cheque like money is a medium (or good) that can be exchanged for any other good or service which the recipient may want. Since these are difficult ideas to grasp the following Assignments are designed to clarify them.

Assignments

14.4 What is meant by the statement: 'Money is a medium of exchange'? How far do you consider this to be a satisfactory definition of money? (AEB 1973)

14.5 Discuss: for what purposes do people demand money, that is: choose to hold their assets in liquid form as money? Note the conclusions of this discussion and/or explain your answer.

14.6 What effect do rising prices (inflation) have on savings and savers?

14.7 As a builder you offer to put up a new garage *next* year for £1000. What precautions could you take in a period of inflation when making this offer?

The value of money

Purchasing power
The value of any good or service is the amount of other goods that will be given in exchange for it. So when an economist speaks of the value of money, he or she means

'the current amount of goods and services a unit of money will buy'. This concept was introduced in chapter 13; look back at Figure 13.1, page 166. We saw that the amount of goods one can buy for say £1 will fall if *prices rise*; or increase if *prices fall*. In short: the value of money is inversely related to the level of prices.

Changes in the value of money
A change in the value of a unit of money may therefore be measured by the changes in the quantities of goods it will buy. But which goods should be used in making this calculation? Individual men and women have different combinations of things they want to buy. The artist is interested in the price of paints, canvas and brushes; if any of these increase in price then to him the value of his money has fallen. But these price changes have no effect on the value of money to people who are not interested in painting. A rise in the price of luxuries – caviar and silk ties – may represent a decrease in the value of money to a millionaire but do not affect Joe Average.

Some prices in practice may increase while others fall or increase more slowly, so any attempt to measure the change of prices in general must be made by taking a representative selection of goods. But these must be relevant to the study, for there is no point in taking caviar into the selection when analysing the effect of price changes for the average family. Nor for that matter would you include artists' oil paints. The selection can change depending on the purpose of the study or analysis. If it is intended to give some indication of the changes in money's value as it affects the standard of living of the average family, then a selection of typical goods which the average family buys make up a theoretical basket of goods on which to base the calculations. (Remember: chapter 13?) The extent to which these prices increase or decrease will measure the fall or rise in the value of the average family's money. For the family as consumers, the prices of the goods in this basket will be those that they in the shops – retail prices.

As we saw in chapter 13, consumers' living standards can be measured by their real incomes – what they can buy from their limited money – and are influenced by the price of the goods in their 'basket'. This is an important reason for measuring the level of retail prices. At other times one may need to know the changes in price levels of raw materials or of producer or other types of goods.

Index numbers
Before looking at the measurement of changes in the value of money, we now need to understand in more detail the *Index Numbers* used in chapter 13. The starting-point is what is called the *base year*, the one from which all other Index Numbers in a series are calculated. Mathematically an Index Number is a figure illustrating the values taken by any variable. For this study an Index Number can be used to compare the price at one date (the base year) with that at another – used in the following example for a change from one year to another. If the price of a pint of milk was $6\frac{1}{2}$p in 1974 as the base year, then this price is taken as 100%. By 1976 the price of $8\frac{1}{2}$p a pint is then 131% of the 1974 price ($\frac{8\frac{1}{4}}{6\frac{1}{4}} \times 100$). Therefore the Index Number in 1976 for milk at '1974 prices' is 131. This number can be used like any Index Number to build a table (see Figure 14.4).

Constructing tables of Index Numbers needs care not only in doing the relatively simple mathematics but also in the selection of goods as we have seen. Pensioners buy different goods from those bought by newlyweds, the well-off buy different

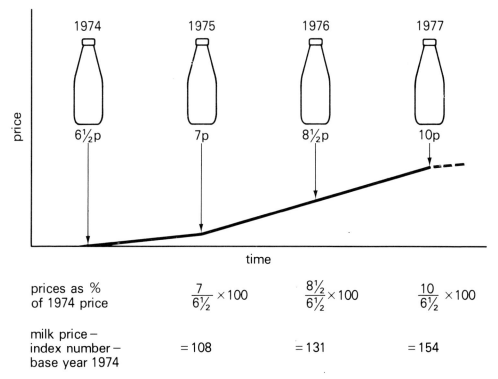

prices as % of 1974 price	$\frac{7}{6\frac{1}{2}} \times 100$	$\frac{8\frac{1}{2}}{6\frac{1}{2}} \times 100$	$\frac{10}{6\frac{1}{2}} \times 100$
milk price – index number – base year 1974	= 108	= 131	= 154

Figure 14.4 A simple table of index numbers.

goods and services from those bought by the less fortunate. These patterns of expenditure – the way people spend their limited incomes – were markedly different between families. The *Family Expenditure Survey* for 1973 showed that households with incomes between £10 and £15 a week spent on average about a third of their incomes on food, whereas those with incomes between £80 and £100 a week spent on average only 15% of their incomes on food. Therefore any basket of goods to be representative of these contrasting families' expenditures must contain different goods. And so the Index Numbers for 'prices in general' must be calculated on the pattern of expenditure – the 'basket' – for the average family's income and family size (parents and children).

Weighting for importance
Once the selection of goods and services has been made for this or that income level, you can work out an Index Number for the price change of each item. However not all goods are bought in the same quantities, so some allowance must be made for this in calculating one Index Number representing *all* price changes in this 'basket' (see Figure 14.5).

If the Index Numbers for each item in this diagram were merely added together we could average them to 225, but this is meaningless because each item is not of equal importance to the families. They spend much less of their income on salt than they spend on meat. Even a fourfold increase in salt prices would then only have a

(a)	Unit Prices 1975 (b)	Unit Prices 1976 (c)	Prices Index 1976 as a % of 1975 (d)	Weights (e)	Weighted relative change (d) × (e) (f)
Bread	14p	21p	150	60	9 000
Meat	60p	75p	125	35	4 375
Salt	10p	40p	400	5	2 000
					15 375

$$\text{The index number for this selection of goods} = \frac{15\,375}{100}$$

$$= 153\tfrac{3}{4}$$

Figure 14.5   Weighting of quantities in index numbers.

small effect on the family's real income. But a doubling of bread prices would be a far more significant price change affecting the family's real income, substantially reducing the value of their money. This change in bread prices has a greater importance or 'weight' than that for salt in the selection of goods shown in Figure 14.5. To allow for this in calculating a single Index Number representing the change of prices in this basket of goods, account is taken of the proportion of the family's income spent on each item. They spent 60% on bread, 35% on meat and 5% on salt – a monotonous diet but simplified illustration. After calculating the price index for individual goods (column d), the weightings in column e are applied to give weighted totals in column f for each good. The grand total of these divided by 100 (the total weighting) gives the Index Number for goods selected, and represents the increase in prices for the family buying them, that is: a fall in the value of *their* money.

In applying this weighting technique to a wider range of goods in a study of price index figures for a 'basket', there are difficulties in making satisfactory comparisons. Even a typical family's pattern of expenditure alters from year to year, especially when real incomes rise, for they will then probably buy more luxuries. In practice no simple allowance can be easily made for such changes, and an index of prices in later years is still based on the goods selected for the 'basket' in the base year – what was in the 'basket' in the base year remains the basis for later comparisons of price levels against it. In recent years, however, the weights used in compiling the UK Retail Price Index described below have been revised each year.

There are other changes as the years go by for which the figures cannot be readily adjusted. These are described in Figure 14.6 which shows the basket of goods in the base year still being used in comparisons against later years although several changes may have taken place. The weights for different items in the 'basket' may have changed – with fewer cinema visits, perhaps but more take-away meals bought. The size of the typical family may have changed from mum and dad with two children in the base year, to the parents and three children in a later year. The quality of what they buy may have changed – fatty meat in the base year to lean meat in a later period. There may be completely new products – black-and-white TV in the base

Some elements of index numbers in a notional comparison of money's value for families with incomes between £75 and £100 between the years AD 2200 and 2225

	Base year	1st Comparison	2nd Comparison
Elements in the calculations	AD2200	Base yr + 2 AD 2202	Base yr + 25 AD 2225
Average family size	2 parents 2 children	2 parents 1 child	1½ parents 1 child
Some items from the 'basket': Foods –			
beef, price per kilogram	£3·02	£4·20	see below
eggs, price for 10	£1·04	£1·71	£1·60
Weighting for –			
beef as % of total weekly expenditure	5·2%	4·3%	no longer eaten
eggs as % of total weekly expenditure	0·5%	0·6%	0·8%
Electricity (adjusted for weighting) at £ per week	£10·00	£8·50	£4·05
Contribution to community environment services – an innovation of AD 2219			£2·20

Notes:
1 Average family sizes are not the same from year to year and by AD 2225 might well be different to anything 20th Century economists could imagine.
2 The complete fall off in beef consumption between AD 2200 and AD 2225 arose when protein concentrates replaced animal meats in the diet of these families.
3 The innovation of controlled environments (rain to order, sunshine when required, etc) changes the pattern of electricity consumption with presumably different ways for these families to live in their surroundings.
4 The index numbers for AD 2202 and AD 2225 as compiled on the basis of the basket and weights of the year 2200 (as the base year) are 98 and 175 respectively. But these index numbers must be treated with caution, because of different items and weightings in these three years resulting from changes like those described above.

Figure 14.6   Some problems of index numbers.

year 'basket' may have been replaced in these families' homes by video–tape operated colour TVs. But none of these can be covered by a price index comparisons to a given base year.

Choice of base year and of prices

There are arguments for saying that no year is a 'normal' year, but the base year should not be abnormal – one of wartime or great national disaster. What is needed is a typical year so that future comparisons with it can be sensibly made.

The retail prices chosen for an index may themselves cause some problems. Should those collecting them for the Retail Price Index use ordinary retail prices, or these prices less cash discounts and perhaps less the value of trading stamps? In the UK prices for cash transactions are used, as we will see in a moment. Some other decisions made in meeting these difficulties can be seen in the following comments on the UK Retail Price Index. But alterations in actual conditions from those of the base year make any Price Index Number for a 'basket' of goods only an indication of the change in prices from the base year. The further one moves from the base year in the analysis or calculation of the price index, the less reliable this figure becomes.

The UK Retail Price Index

The Retail Price Index is published monthly in the United Kingdom and compiled by the Department of Employment in 1977, and by its predecessors since 1904. The early indices included only food prices, but from 1914 they included items like clothing and rent and became known as the 'cost of living index'. An official inquiry in 1904 had established the typical family's pattern of expenditure and this was used for the basket of goods on which the index was based until after World War II. By then the 1904 selection of goods including domestic gas mantles was badly out of date and did not compare with goods being bought by the average family in the late 1940s. The Cost of Living Advisory Committee was therefore set up in 1947, and an 'Interim Index of Prices' compiled. After a few years this was replaced by an Index of Retail Prices in 1956 with a basket and weights based on an inquiry into expenditure in 1953–4.

Since 1957 a continuous inquiry into the goods and services bought by families – their pattern of expenditure – has been made through the *Family Expenditure Survey*, conducted by the Government Social Survey department incorporated in the Office of Population Censuses and Surveys. This pattern, shown in Figure 14.7, includes expenditure on goods and services but does not include some items that are in most family and households' spending – life insurances premiums, subs to trade unions, betting and other items that vary greatly between different families or cannot be easily measured. The prices for goods and services in this basket are *not all* collected every month, although the figure for the Retail Price Index is published monthly.

The weighting for different patterns of expenditure, prior to 1974, was based on the average proportion of expenditure on the selected goods (or 'basket') over the three previous years. Since 1974 the weighting has been based on the average patterns of expenditure over the previous twelve months. Certain classes of families are also excluded for purposes of this weighting. In 1977 those excluded were: households where the head of the family had a gross income of £90 or more a week; and those with at least 75% of their income from state pensions and allowances.

The information used in calculating the Retail Price Index covers wage-earners and medium salary earners, about 90% of the households in the UK and therefore gives a measure of *the value of money to them*. Special indices of retail prices are also published: for '1 person' and '2 person' pensioner households (two quarterly indices), and for low-income households with three or more children. Government departments also compile price indices for particular types of goods purchased by various groups in the economy. These include: prices considerably affected by imported goods' costs; prices of goods mainly manufactured in the UK – divided into those from home-produced raw materials and those from imported raw materials; prices for goods and services mainly produced by nationalised industries; and an index of how certain prices change over the year – seasonally. You can follow through examples of these in the Assignments below.

Collecting prices for UK Retail Price Index

The prices used are those charged for cash transactions in a variety of shops, and in towns with different-sized populations situated in different parts of the country.

Some typical adjustments made to these cash prices as averaged for various types of shop and town include quality allowances. Old and new potatoes' prices are adjusted for differences in their qualities. The price of beer is included, but since beer has different strengths, a separate adjustment is made to allow for these differences. With clothing, retailers are asked to give the price of the same type of garment each time they give a price for the index. If the quality of the garment changes, however, the retailer records this and appropriate allowances are made by those compiling the index to account as far as possible for the true change in prices.

General Index of Retail Prices
Average 1970 = 100
(all items)

1948	42·6	1958	66·2	1968	89·2
1949	43·8	1959	66·5	1969	94·0
1950	45·2	1960	67·2	1970	100·0
1951	49·3	1961	69·5	1971	109·4
1952	53·8	1962	72·5	1972	117·2
1953	55·4	1963	73·9	1973	128·0
1954	56·5	1964	76·3	1974	148·5
1955	59·0	1965	80·0	1975	184·1
1956	61·9	1966	83·1		
1957	64·2	1967	85·2		

Source: *Economic trends – annual supplement 1975*

Figure 14.7   Price index in the UK 1948 to 1975 (for graph see Figure 17.3 on page 249).

The Retail Price Index (RPI) and associated indices are calculated on prices for a selected day in each month – usually the Tuesday nearest the 15th of the month. About five weeks later the RPI figure is published in the Monthly Digest of Statistics and the Department of Employment Gazette. This Price Index is not a completely satisfactory measure of the standard of living nor of the cost of living, but is a measure of price changes and the fluctuations in the value of money for *the typical family* being considered.

Assignments

14.8 Show how an index of prices is constructed, and discuss in your answer-notes its usefulness in documenting price changes. Illustrate your answer with examples from the Retail Price Index.

14.9 On taking your first job (or on promotion) what might you expect as your gross money income? What type of deductions are likely to be made? Distinguish between your likely gross and net incomes in both real and money terms.

14.10 Consult the Retail Price Index in the *Department of Employment Gazette* (or equivalent publication at time of your study). Plot a graph for the values for each of the last twelve months recorded. How representative is this graph of the changes in the value of money to you – your money?

14.11* Group research: compile a 'basket' of ten different items most frequently bought by members of your group. Work out the weighting (according to members' average proportion of expenditure). Prepare a price index for this basket over the next college term. Use this index to measure changes in your *real* income each month. Compare each group's table of index numbers with the Retail Price Index.

Money and financial institutions

Money markets
Money can be bought and sold in the same way as fruit or any other goods. But as we saw the medium – the coin, the note, the cheque – has no intrinsic value. What is being offered in this market are *'promises to pay'* acceptable to all who deal in money. So if Tom gives an IOU (I-owe-you note) for £10 to John in exchange for a cash loan of £10, John may keep the IOU and later get paid by Tom. But John could also sell to Sheila this IOU – Tom's promise to pay £10. But she may doubt if Tom's promise is as good as it should be, since Tom is always wandering and once stole a pig; so she may have trouble collecting the money that he has promised to pay. She therefore might not be prepared to give John the £10 face value of Tom's IOU, instead offering only £6 for it. This over-simplifies money market deals, but shows the different values people put on promises-to-pay. John thought Tom's promise worth the £10 he lent him; Sheila thought it worth only £6.

Looking later at the deals and transactions of money markets, we will find that a promise-to-pay will have no more value than what someone else will pay for it. But the currency of the state has a face value and is the unit of account all must accept. Nevertheless its *value* too can change, as we have seen, in purchasing power as prices change; each unit of money buys more or fewer goods and so is worth more or less in real terms.

In money markets, there are broadly two types of 'good': the currency and government securities as promises often to pay cash at a future date; *and* other people's or organisations' promises-to-pay, measured in units of the currency. Before getting into the realms of high finance, however, you will find that the mechanics of these money markets provide a simple approach to its mysteries, although the whole existence of such markets depends on *confidence* – the acceptance that promises-to-pay will be kept.

The Money and Capital Markets in the United Kingdom
Figure 8.3 on page 107 shows the sources of business and other finance from the money and capital markets. We saw that the institutions in these markets provide money for short- and long-term investment in industry and commerce. But this is

only part of their function and they are only some of the institutions making up the whole money market. Those institutions mentioned in chapter 8 – Commercial Banks, Pension Funds, Investment Trusts, Unit Trusts, Finance for Industry Ltd, and the Stock Exchange – are part of the Money and Capital Markets. Other institutions – Discount Houses, Acceptance Houses and Building Societies among them – also make up these markets. Their functions are described later but each group of institutions is not only made up of interdependent firms, but the groups themselves are highly interdependent on each other. At the centre is the Bank of England with a controlling influence over the entire Money Market (see Figure 14.8).

We have seen the commercial banks as lenders of money (page 105). They have other functions which make their part in the Money Market of particular interest, and once these banking functions have been understood, there are also parallels which help to explain the working of other Money Market institutions.

Origins of commercial banks
We saw earlier in this chapter how promises to pay precious metal became notes accepted as money. In 17th-century England this happened when merchants left their gold coin, gold plate and other surplus liquid assets with goldsmiths for safe keeping. The goldsmiths' and some silversmiths' receipts became money, accepted by merchants in payment for goods or settlement of debts.

The merchant holding a goldsmith's receipt would sign his own name on the back of this note, endorsing it, before passing it to another merchant in payment for goods or a debt. The new holder of the receipt could then take it to the goldsmith and get gold; or himself use it to buy goods, endorsing it in turn with his name and passing on the goldsmith's promise to pay back or redeem the note with gold.

Goldsmiths found that some merchants preferred a note that was made out as a promise to pay gold to whomever held this receipt – payable to bearer. The merchants could pass these notes from one to another in payment for a good without any need to endorse them, and at any time exchange them for gold at the goldsmith's shop. However, these 'pay to bearer receipts' – like modern currency notes – had to be looked after as they could be stolen and the thief could present them to an unsuspecting goldsmith. In the close-knit merchant communities this was not quite as risky a prospect as today, for any unusual holder of a bearer-receipt would probably be questioned by the goldsmith before he paid what was due on the note.

The next step was for goldsmiths to issue receipts not for any particular sum of gold left with them, but in convenient units of money – £1, £5 and so on – in bearer receipts. Anyone presenting the goldsmith with one of these notes could then get gold or gold coin to the amount of its face value – £5, or £10 or whatever. Some goldsmith-bankers even issued forms to customers, so that they could write in the amounts to be paid to others – a system of cheques.

Early note issues
The £5, £10 and other denominations of bearer-receipts were each backed by gold in the goldsmith's safe or strongroom. However the goldsmiths found that no mer-

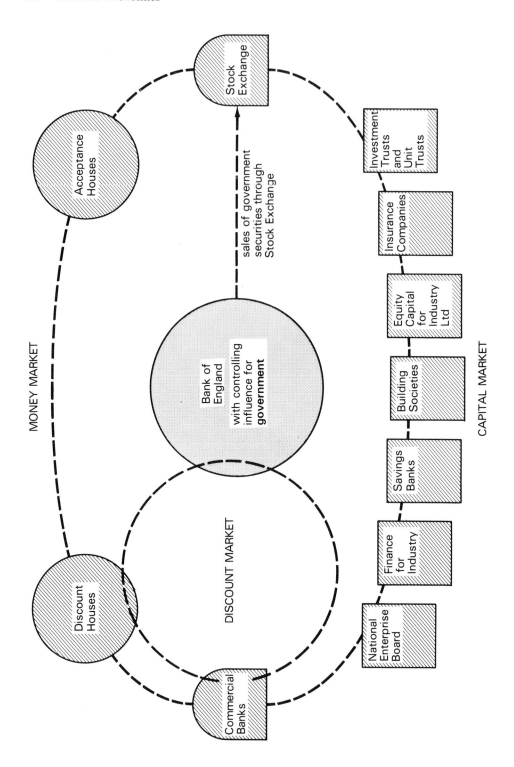

Figure 14.8   Institutions in the money and capital markets.

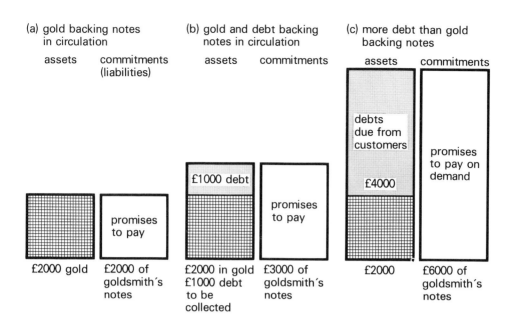

Figure 14.9   A goldsmith–banker's creation of credit-money.

chant was likely to want all his gold at once, and certainly not *all* the customers at any one time required gold for small day-to-day transactions. Nearly all major transactions were settled by merchants passing the goldsmith's receipts to each other, so probably a large proportion of the gold never moved from the safe. What was used was often soon replaced by new amounts of gold left (deposited) by other merchants with the goldsmiths.

Goldsmiths came to realise that if they only needed a small amount of their gold for day-to-day transactions, they might lend 'money' by issuing notes to merchants who wanted to borrow. These notes with the goldsmith's name on them were accepted by all merchants as being no different from his other notes backed by gold, although now (see Figure 14.9) the total amount of all the notes he had issued was not backed by gold. In part it was backed by debts he had to collect. The goldsmith had become a 'banker' in effect creating money – as notes people were willing to accept in payment for goods or debts. The extent to which he might successfully do this was only limited by the amount of gold needed to meet his cusumers' daily 'cash' requirements.

The goldsmith–banker could lend a merchant £100 to refit a ship, giving the merchant £100 in notes which he wrote out or at least signed as promises to pay gold if and when the notes were returned to him. If the goldsmith had £1000 of gold in his safe, knowing this was sufficient to meet customers' daily requirements, then he might lend out ten times this amount and still satisfy any merchants wanting to exchange (redeem) the notes for gold. The merchant refitting his ship would pay the goldsmith–banker interest on his £100 and so there was every incentive for the banker to lend all that he prudently could. But by lending too much relative to the gold he had in the safe, he might not have enough gold or coin to pay even the few who wanted to get cash for notes. If this happened and news of it got about, every note holder would lose confidence in the bank; they would all want paying at once which would produce a 'run on the bank'. Unable to collect in the debts due, or collect them quickly enough, from the man refitting his ship and others, the banker would be out of business. For although in the long run he might collect the debts and in turn pay the note holders, this is not what they wanted. They wanted instant cash or gold for the notes when presented to the goldsmith–banker. If they could not get it, confidence in the goldsmith's notes was lost, and they became worthless.

Bank reserves

In modern commercial banking little if any gold is held, but reserves – taking the place of the gold in the goldsmith's safe – are in notes and coin, as we will see later. However, the rules of sound banking apply unchanged with the passing of the centuries. The banker must have adequate reserves to meet his customers daily needs for cash and be able to honour his other commitments.

If he lends more than he prudently should on the liquid reserves he has, or lends money foolishly to customers who cannot repay him on time, he risks losing his customers' confidence and going out of business. In the early 1970s many so-called 'fringe banks' in the UK got into this position, and came to grief. They had lent money *long-term* to property companies and received *short-term* deposits from customers. Without adequate reserves, some of these banks could not repay the deposits when required, for they were unable to collect the loans they had made. Even selling the properties taken over in place of the loans would not eventually have produced the cash needed because property values fell. To avoid a disastrous loss of confidence in the UK Money Market, the Bank of England stepped in and arranged for the depositors to be paid out. The fringe banks concerned were then put under different managements and a 'life-boat' fund created to see them through the time of difficulty.

Origins of the Bank of England

The Bank of England has watched over depositors' and others' interests for many years, protecting people's confidence in the Money Market as a whole. Although today the Bank of England is a government agency, this was not the case until 1946, when it was nationalised. Before then it was a joint-stock banking company. But as bankers to the Government the Bank of England has had a special position in the Money Market since it was first created.

In 1694 a number of goldsmiths formed a company to finance William III's war with Louis XIV of France, on the understanding that no other bank could become a joint-stock company with owners enjoying limited liability. Over the following centuries a series of Acts of Parliament regulated the company's position as the Bank of England. In 1708 an Act prohibited any banking partnerships with more than six partners from issuing notes, giving the Bank a monopoly among large banks who might issue notes in England.

However during the 18th and early 19th centuries, many small country banks with less than six partners – who could still issue notes – imprudently issued more notes than their reserves could support and went bust. Subsequently the ban on joint-stock banks was lifted, and the issuing of notes by all banks was permitted. The new joint-stock banks (and banking partnerships with more than six partners issuing notes) were still not allowed to open offices within 65 miles of London, probably a day's journey to and from the capital at that time. The Bank of England was also permitted by the same act of 1826 to open offices in Birmingham, Bristol, Hull, Leeds, Liverpool, Manchester, Newcastle and Plymouth. Seven years later (1833) the joint-stock banks were given the right to operate in London but not to issue notes. A further limit was placed on issuing notes, when in 1844 an Act prevented any newly formed banks doing this and took steps to restrict the issues by existing banks. From that date a bank in England and Wales lost the right to issue notes if it stopped payment (could not honour its notes), amalgamated with others or became a joint-stock company.

Since 1946 the Bank of England has been nationalised, although even before then its role in the economy as the agent implementing government monetary policy was important. In a moment we will come back to the Bank's position in the Money Market of the 1970s. The issue of notes, however, is now confined in the UK to the Bank of England, although a few banks in Scotland and Northern Ireland have a limited right to issue notes. (Such note issues must be backed by Bank of England notes held by these banks.)

The cheque system

To follow the chronological history of banking, the development that followed the issue of notes was the use of cheques. From the time the goldsmiths were issuing notes as receipts which could be exchanged for gold, they were also acting on their merchant customers' written instructions to pay sums to others. Mention was made of this cheque system on page 179. Cheques have a number of advantages for they may be made out for exact amounts, and are easier and safer to carry than notes and coin. From the early goldsmith's point of view the order from a merchant transferring money to another customer of the goldsmith's meant no more than book entries. The merchant asking for money to be transferred from his deposit would have this deducted from the money due on his account – the record of gold or other deposits the goldsmith–banker held for him. The recipient would have it added to his deposit – credited to his account as money due to him from the bank.

When commercial banks were no longer allowed to issue notes, they extended the use of the cheque system. For although cheques are not always as readily accepted in payment by individuals or firms as are a banker's note, they are nevertheless a form of money. If the banks could pass these cheques between each other, then an order – a cheque – on your banker to pay your grocer's bill could be passed by the grocer through his bank to your bank. This needed simplifying for thousands of different cheques on even a few banks were – and are – a lot of paperwork and book entries. Yet all you and your grocer's banks needed to do was debit (deduct from what they owed on) your account and credit the grocer's, although each account was with a different bank.

The 'clearing system' (see Figure 14.10) made this arrangement feasible, as bankers met to 'settle only the differences'. So your cheque along with thousands of others might total £10 500 due from your bank to your grocer's bank. But this bank in turn might have to pay your bank £9800 on its cheques which your bank holds. By your bank making a single payment of £700 (£10 500–£9800) the difference is settled (that is: paid) and the bundles of cheques can be exchanged. At first bankers met in coffee houses to make these settlements, but in 1773 a 'Clearing House' was

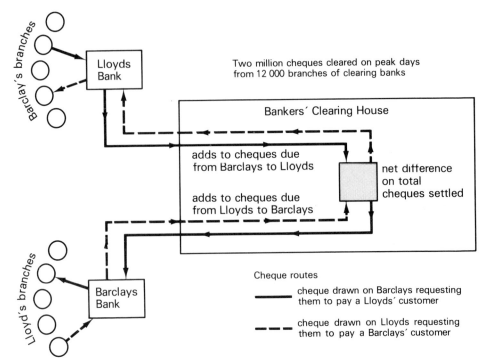

Figure 14.10   Examples of the cheque clearing system.

set up by some banks to settle the differences on accumulated totals of each day's cheques and this operates today. The differences are now settled through the clearing banks' accounts with the Bank of England for among other things the Bank of England is the bankers' bank. The members of the Clearing House are known as 'Clearing Banks' and apart from a few small banks consist of the 'big four' banks (see page 199) and the Co-operative Bank. However not every bank is a member of the Clearing House and therefore some have themselves to use a 'clearing bank' to clear cheques.

Advantages of the cheque system
In addition to the convenience for the customer, cheques enable a bank to continue lending a greater amount of money than is covered by cash deposits the bank holds. The bank may allow a borrower to draw cheques up to an agreed amount, a parallel to the goldsmith's issuing of notes to the merchant wanting to refit his ship.

The cheque system works so satisfactorily that in the 20th century it has become the most important means of settling debts and other transactions. Important, that is, since the total value of cheques cleared *each day* was about £6500 million in the UK alone during 1974.

Assignments

14.12 'Our money comprises notes and coin. These are issued by the Bank of England, and the supply of money is therefore under its control.' Explain why this statement is inadequate. (L 1971)
(Leave space in your notes here for additions after further reading in this chapter.)

14.13 Compile a calendar of key events in the history of commercial banking.

14.14* Group research: set up a system of IOUs for trading within the class. Settle individually between each pair of members at the end of the week. The following week pass all IOU-notes through a central group, each member 'settling' his or her net debt, or receiving their amounts due, from the central group. (No cash need pass, the whole exercise being one of record only!)

14.15* 'The capital market serves the needs of industry and commerce, governments, and local authorities.' Outline the main elements within the capital market which undertake these functions. (L 1972)

14.16* Money and capital markets are examples of markets that are not specifically located in particular areas. Next time you are in a town or city centre, take note of how many branches of financial institutions you come across. Note whether they are in the money or capital markets, and their likely interrelationships.

Modern banking

Bank services
Banking has developed through the centuries, with the cheque system as only one of the many services banks perform today. In the UK and in most other countries their formation and activities are regulated by a number of laws to help prevent abuses of the banking system since these institutions can have considerable influence on the smooth running of an economy. Almost all banks offer their customers a complete banking service – holding money on the customer's account, providing cheque facilities, advising on financial matters, arranging loans, making payments in foreign currencies, issuing travellers cheques, issuing 'cash cards' and credit cards, among other services. They may also act as trustees and look after the affairs (estates) of deceased customers. (See Assignment 14.21 below.)

Bills of Exchange
Typical of the special functions performed by banks is the discounting of commercial bills, although Discount Houses are the specialists in these transactions. You will remember Tom's IOU which Sheila bought from John (page 186); this was a crude example of discounting 'paper'. In money markets all manner of documents representing legal commitments to pay money are loosely described as 'paper'. In commerce (see Figure 14.11) a trader or firm can sell goods and send the buyer a bill of exchange. This is drawn up in a form the buyer signs to acknowledge that he (or she) owes the money, and showing when this should be paid. By signing the bill the buyer accepts his legal commitment to pay the debt. On trade bills this payment may be due at any time in the future – usually three months from the date the buyer of the goods signed the bill. There are many points of law relating to bills of exchange, outside the scope of this book, but they help to protect the financial interests of traders and others who carry out transactions with these bills.

The seller of the goods receives back the bill accepted by the buyer. This the seller can then hold until the date for payment is due – till the bill matures. Or he may use the bill to settle a debt he owes if the creditor will take it. But if he wants cash now, he can *sell the bill*. A Discount House will buy it, but at less than the sum due on maturity, for they must be recompensed for being out of this sum until the bill matures. (Although they are *not* making a loan against the bill's value, the effect

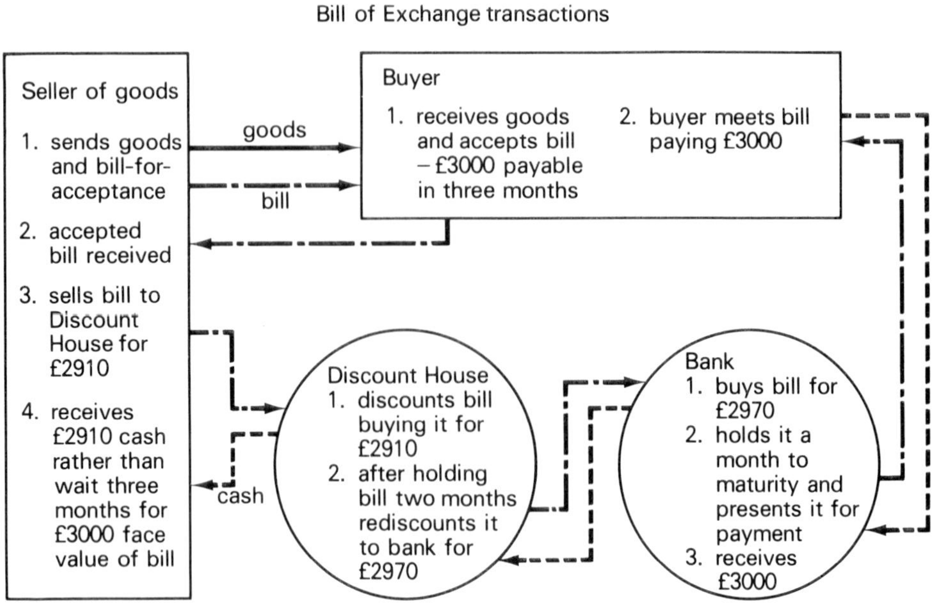

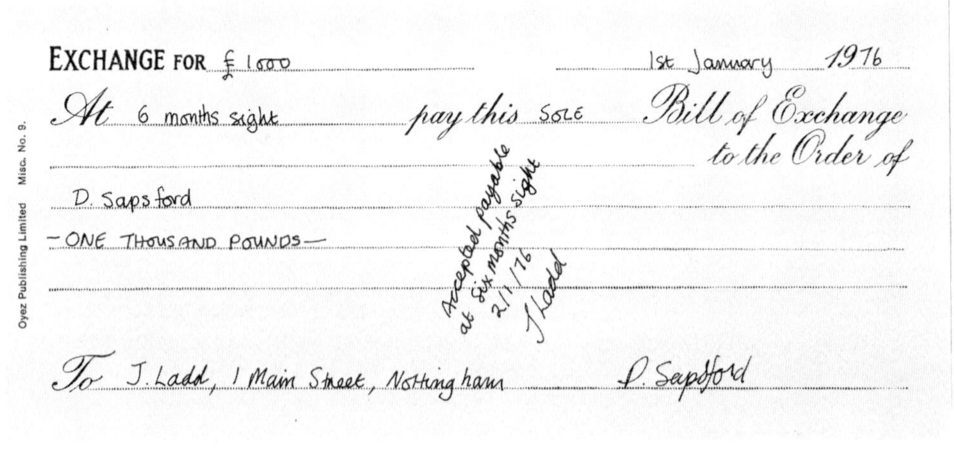

Bill of Exchange transactions

Figure 14.11   Specimen bill of exchange and transactions on discounting and rediscounting.

financially is similar and so they are said to be 'out of this money'.) The amount the seller receives depends on the time the bill has to run to maturity and on the financial standing of the acceptor. If the bill is 'first class' with little risk of the acceptor defaulting, then the discount house will calculate the bill's current value at an appropriate rate of interest, say 12% a year. A £1000 bill with three months to run to maturity will then have a discounted or current value of £970. In paying today £970 for the bill, which three months later will be worth £1000 on the bill's maturity, the discount house will earn £30 (£1000 − £970).

This type of arithmetic, 'discounting', is used in many other financial calculations as we often need to know the *present value* of a sum to be received in the future. A

discounting, or applying 'backwards interest', for sums to be received in the future at different dates – payments under an agreement, perhaps – can give their present values for use in comparisons of various sorts.

Discount Houses and banks may increase their interest rates for discounting bills if there is any doubt over the acceptor's willingness to pay or ability to meet the bills. This unwillingness may arise because the original goods turn out to be of poorer or different quality than expected, or perhaps because of some error in their documentation on being shipped, leading to the acceptor delaying payment.

Acceptance

If the buyer or firm accepting the bill is of good financial standing with a reputation for paying commitments on time, the seller of the original goods will have no trouble discounting the bill. Other buyers of goods accepting bills may not be such good risks or may be unknown to the Discount House.

The seller of goods holding a potentially risky bill may get the help of an *Acceptance House*. These institutions – often departments of the Merchant Banks described below – have agents around the world and can check the financial standing of a bill's acceptor. When satisfied, the Acceptance House will itself accept the bill, charging a fee to its holder. The House undertakes to pay the bill should the original acceptor fail to do so on time. With an Acceptance House's signature on the bill, the holder can then discount it more easily and at a cheaper rate of interest.

Treasury Bills

The Government regularly issue Treasury Bills that are not unlike commercial bills of exchange – although as government 'paper' they do not need accepting. These Treasury Bills are government commitments to pay cash at a future date, usually three months (91 days) and are sold to the Money Market by the Government to raise funds for short terms. The Discount Houses, banks and other institutions bid for the lots offered, their price being determined by the demand for and supply of Treasury Bills. The difference between their face value and the bid price – the discount – has been important in determining the *Minimum Lending Rate* described later. The use of Treasury Bills has greatly increased over the years as a method of government borrowing for the short term. We will come back to this later in chapter 15.

Discount Houses

These Houses originally discounted commercial bills but these are used less in the mid-20th century than in the 19th, having been replaced by cheques and other forms of bank transfers. Discount Houses in the 1970s therefore deal mainly in Treasury Bills. Although commercial banks could take up all the Treasury Bills the Government offers, there is an agreement between the eleven Discount Houses and the banks allowing a proportion of these bills to go to the Discount Houses. Working in very large sums – a turnover of £100 million a day is not unusual in a Discount House – they make a very small percentage of the bills' value in their deals.

They not only buy commercial and Treasury Bills but also sell them, perhaps holding a three-month bill for a month and then re-selling (re-discounting) it to a bank or other institution. The commercial banks lend large sums of money to Discount Houses, a relationship described later.

Merchant Banks

We have seen how Merchant Banks offer a service as Acceptance Houses, but the decline in the use of commercial bills has led to a reduction in this type of activity.

There is no legal definition of a Merchant Bank but many are old-established institutions often founded on the activities of banking families, like the Rothschilds. The senior members of these firms have a wide reputation for their sound financial advice to large and small customers, but their help is particularly sought as *Issuing Houses* – when a company wants to raise fresh capital, or has a complex financial deal in buying or selling its products. The banks have many overseas connections, established agents or branches with knowledge of local conditions, money markets and economies.

These banks also provide many ordinary banking services but are famous for their services to international trade. They sometimes also join in consortiums of banks to raise large sums of money for smaller governments and for major projects. Not all merchant banks are of a size, however, to take such large financial risks. Indeed some have been unable to meet their obligations in the ordinary course of business as we saw on page 190. The Government, therefore, proposed new legislation in the 1976 White Paper 'The Licensing and Supervision of Deposit Taking Institutions'. This proposed law will require all deposit-taking institutions (loosely described as finance houses) to hold a licence from the Bank of England unless they are recognised banks. The 'recognised banks' not needing a licence will be those of established repute like the clearing banks.

Savings Banks

These were established for working people, and opened in the evenings and on Saturdays, originally to encourage small savers to put by a few shillings each week.

Typical of Savings Banks are the Trustee and Post Office Savings Banks, offering many although sometimes not all the services of modern commercial banking. They pay interest on the amount left in deposit accounts. But there can be restrictions on the total amount that can be held on deposit or withdrawn at one time. The National Savings Bank in 1976 allowed a maximum of £10 000 on any customer's account, and limited withdrawals to £20 at any one time on demand. Since the mid-1970s some Savings Banks have been providing a cheque service for customers, but traditionally their customers paid in and withdrew most sums in cash.

Savings Banks use the money they receive from depositors mainly to buy government securities, or lend it in other ways to government and other public bodies.

National Giro

Set up in 1968, the National Giro operates through some 21 000 Post Office branches, and has reduced the number of cash transactions being used in paying household bills and rents. Giro payments and customer accounts have many similarities to those of clearing banks. All the records of Giro transactions pass through the National Giro Centre at Bootle (Merseyside) where details of customers' accounts are kept on a computer. This system of transfers is generally quicker than the cheque clearing system. There is also an advantage for customers as Post Offices have longer business hours than banks.

Giro customers with suitable references can have cheque cards, personal loans and limited overdrafts for short periods. Account holders have a cheque book for paying those who do not have Giro accounts. In 1976 6p was charged for recording these *girocheques*, but no charge was made for depositing cash, and paying other Giro account holders by transfer or standing order (regular payments made, say, monthly). Post-paid envelopes for sending instructions to the Giro Centre are virtually free to account holders. Cash may be drawn from Post Offices, in amounts up to £30 every other business day without prior notice.

Giro has taken some years to become established, but by 1976 was handling 200 million transactions a year. Included in these were rents collected through Giro from about a million homes for over 120 Local Authorities. Over £5000 million a year was being paid in by businesses. There are advantages to the Post Office when these cash deposits are made at its branches, for it needs large amounts of cash to pay out pensions and other allowances.

Money Shops

A number of hire-purchase and other companies opened street shops in the 1960s to provide personal loans and some other banking services. They tended to attract customers who wanted to borrow for purposes for which the commercial banks would generally not be willing to advance loans. For if the purpose of the loan was buying furniture, for example, this would not sell for its original price should the borrower default. In view of such risks, the money shops charged suitably high interest rates.

Building Societies

Building societies specialise in providing money for buying homes. The borrower takes out a mortgage pledging his or her house against the money advanced towards the purchase price, and repaying this loan with interest over a long period – often twenty-five years.

The money lent has been collected in deposits from savers who are paid a lower rate of interest than the society receives from its borrowers. The difference between these two interest rates – received from mortgagees and paid to depositors – give a society the funds to cover its running expenses. Building societies do not operate for profit. Their 'shareholders', like depositors, receive a fixed rate of interest. They receive slightly higher interest than a society's depositors, since should the society be dissolved, depositors are paid out before shareholder members. Interest is paid with special income tax arrangements so that these shareholders and depositors receive an already taxed income.

The societies hold surplus cash on occasions for an upsurge in the supply of mortgage funds might lead to house price increases as more people attempt to buy them. Such surplus funds are used to buy government securities. At other times the Government have lent money to the societies when otherwise interest rates charged to mortgagees would have risen.

Commercial Banks

The Commercial Banks provide the public with a full banking service as described on page 193. With some millions of customers, the four major Commercial Banks – Barclays, Lloyds, Midland and National Westminster Banks – offer a wide service to

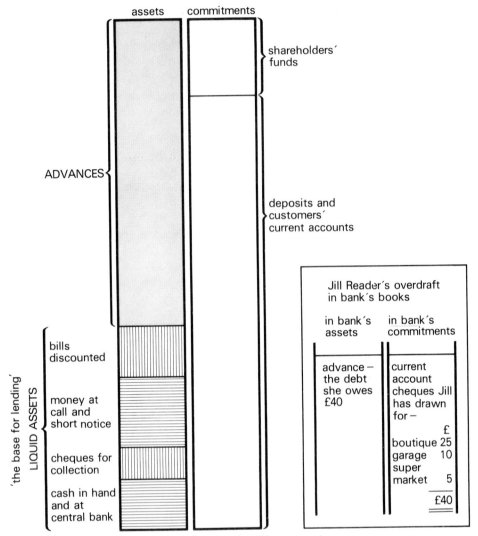

Figure 14.12   Commercial bank lending – a simplified example.

the public. Any financially responsible person can open a bank account; that is: anyone who in the banker's view is not likely to abuse the bank's cheque or other facilities.

One of the Commercial Banks' functions is to create 'money' in the form of credit in the cheque system described earlier. These overdraft and other loans to customers are only in part backed by liquid assets (Figure 14.12). The significant feature of this is the way that banks – like the goldsmiths of earlier days – create credit as money generally accepted by traders and others in day to day transactions. Although the personal 'promise to pay' by a customer of the bank would not be generally accepted as money without a reputable bank's backing, the bank is the *catalyst of confidence*. If you tried to pay your local record shop, the hire-purchase on your moped and the college book shop with chits of paper saying '*Sapsford and Ladd, Authors and Financiers promise to pay . . .*' then you would hardly be surprised when these traders refused to take such apparently worthless paper. But a promise to pay by a reputable banker is generally as good as cash.

This confidence in a banker's promise has been built up in most cases by banks taking care over a long period to have only customers who do not abuse the system, and the banks' own reputation for sound money management.

In the United Kingdom over the years the smaller Commercial Banks have merged and amalgamated, so that in the 1970s, there are relatively few, with four large banking companies having the major share of commercial banking: The Midland, Lloyds, National Westminster and Barclays – known colloquially as the 'big four'. Each has a network of branches throughout the country – a great convenience to a customer; and through their size gain the economies of scale. This size also enhances the confidence people have in a bank's ability to meet its commitments.

As limited companies these banks aim to earn profits for their shareholders, and face the same dilemma as the early bankers in maintaining adequate reserves while lending out as much as they prudently can. Look again at Figures 14.9 and 14.12. The Commercial Banks hold liquid assets as money available for customers' day to day transactions. The liquid assets are in the form of cash in the banks' safes and 'money' in other forms easily and quickly converted into cash. We will come back to the importance of these reserves but first an explanation of commercial banking transactions makes their role in the economy easier to follow.

Commercial Banking

Customers with money surplus to their current requirements may lodge it with a bank. In paying this money – cash and cheques – into their accounts, these customers lend it to the bank. They may pay it into a 'current account' and expect to get it out on demand, or it may be paid into a deposit account when the customer can only get it back by first giving a week's or a month's notice. Whether the deposit is 'weekly' or 'monthly' or for some other term is agreed between the customer and the bank as the minimum notice the customer should give in withdrawing money from deposit. The bank pay interest on this money on deposit, which may be higher the longer the term.

Banks do not usually pay interest on current accounts for these monies may be withdrawn on demand, and in administering an account there are the expenses of keeping records, premises and so on. The banks may charge for these services, after allowing for the interest the average amount in the account *might* have earned. This imputed interest, an implied but not actually paid interest, can offset part or all of a bank's expenses in looking after an account. Therefore no charge may be made for your current account if an agreed minimum average amount is kept in it. But no interest is paid out by the bank should the minimum be exceeded, except at the Co-operative Bank which pays interest on current accounts.

Banks lend money at higher interest rates than they pay to depositors in order to cover their expenses and make a contribution to their profits.

The methods of making bank loans were explained in chapter 8, page 105, and we have seen the dilemma between seeking profits and the need for liquidity. So in addition to taking care over those they accept as customers and those granted loans, the banks take steps to lessen the risks of a possible run on their liquid resources. Bankers are cautious of the purposes for which they lend, and arrange for these various loans to be repaid by customers on dates that ensure a steady flow of repayments day by day. In this way they apportion their loans to customers for suitable periods. In addition, their holding of Treasury Bills, for example, may be arranged to have some maturing this week, some next, and so on. The banks also lend money for only comparatively short periods and make sure they have adequate security – a customer's life insurance policy, perhaps – against any loans. Such security or *collateral*, as it is called, will usually be reasonably easily sold and likely to bring in sufficient funds to pay off the loan should the borrower default.

Bank assets
The loans to customers, their customers' overdrafts and Treasury Bills are among the clearing banks' assets. A study of these helps to show the way various types of financial institutions are linked. The London Clearing Banks (the big four and some smaller Commercial Banks) give details of their assets to the Bank of England who publish a summary of these (see Figure 14.13) every quarter. This shows the pattern of these banks' lending and their other assets, under headings in order of their liquidity. The 'cash in hand and at the Bank of England' is the most liquid with 'other assets' and 'special deposits' the least liquid in this list. The less liquid an asset, the less quickly it can be turned into cash, and generally speaking the greater the return or profit from it.

The details in Figure 14.13 describe each asset and the following points are of particular note:

1. Cash in hand and at the Bank of England – these are notes and coins in the safes or on the banks' own current accounts with the Bank of England (virtually as good as cash) and must meet the banks' daily cash needs for their customers. Banking experience suggested that cash equal to a twelfth of the deposits might be needed for the depositors' daily requirements. As the most liquid of assets, these items earn no interest for they are not being used. But from time to time governments have required banks to hold a particular sum – for example, the pre-1971 mandatory 8% cash ratio – in cash or on current account with the Bank of England – as we will see later.

2. Balances at other banks – these are amounts due as claims on other banks for cheques not yet settled through the Clearing House, and other balances with non-clearing banks. The balances earn no income as they are soon to be cash reserves after settlement and so are highly liquid.

3. Money on call or short notice – these very short-term loans can be easily 'called in' and include amounts lent but immediately repayable should the bank ask for repayment. They are mainly loans to Discount Houses who have used this money to discount bills; as the loans are on short notice they are fairly liquid, earning the banks relatively low interest.

4. Bills discounted – these Treasury and Commercial Bills are those the banks have bought and/or discounted. Some will mature each day or week as mentioned earlier, but on average the bills held by the banks have about six weeks to run to maturity. They are therefore less liquid than money on call and earn a slightly higher rate of interest.

Cash, money on call or short notice, money with the Bank of England, short-term loans and discounted bills make up the 'liquid assets' of banks. These assets can all

London Clearing Banks' assets 15th January 1975

	£-millions	Assets included in Reserve Asset Ratio
Coin, notes and balances with Bank of England	976	balance with B of E
Balances with other U.K. banks	4 153	
Money at call and short notice	1 304	all
Bills discounted		
Treasury bills	400	all
Other bills	726	all
Investment in government stocks	1 260	stocks for redemption
Loans to local authorities	118	within 1 year
Advances	16 393	
Certificates of deposit	444	
Other assets	440	
Acceptances	147	
Special deposits	554	
	£26 915	

Note: the main items are described in the text, other items include: *Loans to Local Authorities* – a form of advances; *certificates of deposit* – not unlike Bills of Exchange being drawn on a bank *by the bank itself; acceptances* – amounts due on bills

Controls on banks' liquidity

(a) 12½% reserve asset ratio – used after Sept. 1971 and comprising assets listed above. Total deposits = 8 ×reserve assets. Therefore any change in reserve assets is multiplied eight times to give the change in total deposits.

(b) 8% cash ratio – used prior to Sept. 1971 and comprised of cash in safes and tills and balance with Bank of England. Total deposits = 12½× cash assets

(c) 28% liquidity ratio – used prior to Sept. 1971 and comprised of cash-ratio items and other quickly realised assets. Total deposits = 3 4/7 × liquid assets

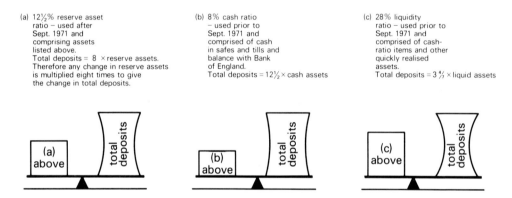

Figure 14.13   A simplified schedule of the London Clearing Bank's assets.

be turned into cash quickly and so do not earn much interest. By controlling the amount of these, just as they may control the amount of cash banks hold, a government can limit the amount of credit-money banks may create in relation to their assets (see page 206).

5. *Investments* – these assets are government stocks (securities) and loans to Local Authorities, with the majority of the stocks having less than five years to run to maturity. These stocks may also be sold at any time and with this attribute are fairly liquid.

6. *Advances* – these longer term (although not necessarily long-term) loans are made to individuals, firms and state enterprises. The advances are made to farmers buying seed and repaying the loan after their harvest, to manufacturers for working

capital (see page 44), to individuals with personal loans to buy cars or for other purposes, and overdrafts for all or any of these purposes. From advances the banks earn higher interest rates as the loans may be outstanding for months rather than days or weeks and are not liquid assets. At the same time, the customer who is not a good risk may be charged even more than the usual rate for an advance.

7. *Other assets* – these include the banks' buildings, fixtures and other fixed assets. Also under this heading are the amounts some banks have invested in ownership or part ownership of hire-purchase and credit-card issuing companies. These operate as separate entities but are controlled by the banks as owners (although not all HP and credit-card companies are owned by banks).

8. *Special deposits (if any)* – these are sums placed with the Bank of England from time to time as part of the Government's mechanism for controlling the supply of money, a feature described in more detail later.

Credit-Money
Look again at Figure 14.12. The Commercial Banks' function in providing credit – something their customers can spend on goods and services – has an influence on the economy. If the banks create a lot of credit, the demand for goods and services will tend to rise and vice versa. For these and other reasons the Government aims to control the supply of credit-money.

We must not forget that the amount of credit-money is limited not only by regulations through the extent of a bank's 'reserve assets', but also by sound banking practice – the amount a bank holds in cash and liquid assets regardless of any government regulations. And whenever a loan is given – an asset created in the bank's books – there is a corresponding liability to honour the commitment of the deposit credited to the customer. In other words: the total assets of a bank including its claims against those who have borrowed from it must equal its liabilities to depositors and what is 'due' to its owners (the shareholders' investment in a limited liability banking company).

Assignments

14.17 'The arrangement of a commercial bank's assets represents a compromise between liquidity and profitability.' Explain this statement.

14.18 How do commercial banks 'create' money? (AEB 1975)

14.19 What is a current account with a commercial bank? What advantages does it have for the user? (AEB 1975)

14.20* Using IOUs as 'bills of exchange' set up a series of transactions involving a discount house, an acceptance house, and a commercial bank. Draw a flow diagram of the journey of these 'bills' to show how they might be passed in a series of transactions between these institutions.

14.21* What are the main services banks provide for their customers? How are these services paid for? (L 1972)
(You may use this Assignment for group research on facilities offered by local branches of up to four different banks.)

The Central Bank

The Bank of England's role
In the United Kingdom the Bank of England is the Central Bank. Some of its history
has been mentioned, but as an agency of the Government, even before it was
nationalised in 1946, the Bank has acted as a controlling influence on the money
market for two centuries and more. The Bank manages the monetary system in
accordance with government policies (see Figure 14.14).

Broadly speaking, government monetary policies are concerned with influencing
the supply and availability of money and its price (that is: interest rates as the price
for credit). This supply or stock is made up – again broadly speaking – of two forms
of money, notes-and-coins and bank deposits (credit-money). During the first quarter of 1975 the supply was £37 422 million of which £5448 million was notes-and-
coin in circulation, and £31 974 million was bank deposits.

The availability and price of money can influence the level of activity in the
economy. If consumers and entrepreneurs can get credit easily and cheaply, their
demand for goods and services will tend to increase. So a reduction of hire-purchase
interest rates or the minimum deposit required on cars, for example, will tend to
increase the demand for them. The same effect occurs when interest rates (the price
of borrowing to finance the purchase of capital equipment for instance) fall, and
entrepreneurs tend to invest in more machines and other capital goods – that is: at
the lower price they demand more. On the other hand an increase in the interest
rates and decrease in the availability of credit tends to lead to a reduction in
consumers' and producers' demand for goods and services.

The Bank of England as the agency bringing about such changes in the supply of
money and interest rates implements governments' monetary policies. As the sole
issuer of notes-and-coin, it is able to control this part of the supply of money; to
control the whole supply it must also control bank deposits (credit-money).

The Bank of England's function as the Central Bank can be divided for study
purposes into two parts. The following paragraphs show first these separate functions and then some of the means used to bring about government monetary objectives in the economy.

Central Bank's non-government accounts
The Bank has no facilities for the general public to open accounts and does not
compete with the Commercial Banks for private business. However, a small number
of accounts are maintained for individuals, firms and corporate bodies. Some of these
are of very long standing and others of more recent origin involving close business
association with the Bank. As bankers to the Commercial Banks, the Bank of
England provides them with notes-and-coin from current accounts. These accounts
may be used by the banks as any customer uses an account, and in the case of
clearing banks are used to settle differences on clearing cheques.

If a Commercial Bank is short of liquid assets for its customers' immediate
requirements, it calls in money at call with Discount Houses. They may in the last
resort go to the Bank of England to replace these funds as we will see in a moment.
As the Bank does not want any commercial house or bank to delay on meeting its
commitments, for fear this may weaken confidence not only in that house or bank
but in the whole Money Market, the Bank of England will provide the Discount

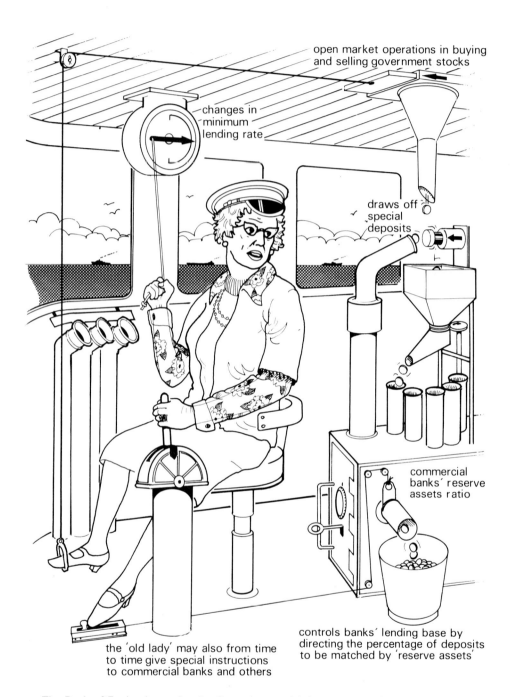

The Bank of England acts for the Government with instruments of monetary policy

Figure 14.14   The Bank of England – the 'old' lady of Threadneedle Street.

House with the cash required. However as *'lender of last resort'* the Bank of England is also acting for the Government as explained below.

There are a number of British institutions – the Church Commissioners, among them – with accounts at the Bank of England. Some foreign banks also have accounts there. For all these customers the Bank of England acts as adviser and provides all the other services which a customer expects from his banker.

The Central Bank – bankers to the Government

The Bank of England, as the Central Bank, advises on and arranges loans for government activities. Although the bulk of government funds comes from taxes, some is borrowed in various ways including, as we have seen, by the sale of government securities and Treasury Bills. Government borrowing is administered by the Bank. It also lends money to government departments from the 'Ways and Means Account' when for any short period the Government's expenditure exceeds its collections from taxes and borrowings.

Issue of Notes-and-Coin

As the only bank issuing notes in England and Wales, the Bank controls the number of notes in circulation. The Bank, in conjunction with the Royal Mint, also controls the amount of coins in circulation. Since 1931 the notes have not been backed by gold, but are backed by government securities as part of the National Debt. At one time part was backed by gold; the note issue *not backed by gold* was called the Fiduciary Issue, but this now applies to the whole note issue.

Lender of last resort

We saw that when Commercial Banks are short of cash, they call in money from Discount Houses (the money at call or short notice). A Discount House, however, may not have the cash required, having discounted bills, and be forced to borrow from the Bank of England as *lender of last resort* in rediscounting first-class bills. The Commercial Banks are then able to collect these funds in turn from the Discount Houses. On these occasions the Bank of England charges a higher discount rate than that current in the discount market, so the Houses make a loss on rediscounting these bills. This has the effect of making Discount Houses increase the rate they charge for subsequently discounting bills. The demand for their services then tends to decrease and consequently they borrow less money at call from the banks.

The penal rate charged by the Bank of England was at one time called the *Bank Rate*, but after the changes in 1971 has been known as the *Minimum Lending Rate* (MLR). It is about $\frac{1}{2}\%$ above the average rate paid on Treasury Bills.

Managing the Exchange Equalisation Account

The Bank of England may from time to time use the stocks of foreign currencies it holds on the Exchange Equalisation Account to buy and sell sterling. The Bank enters the foreign exchange markets to stabilise the price of sterling in terms of other currencies. Sterling may be bought and sold on foreign exchange markets around the world, where its price is basically determined by the interaction of demand and supply forces.

Instruments of monetary policy
There are a number of ways the Government may decide – with the Bank's advice or otherwise – to act in the Money Market and other spheres of the economy. These methods have varied over the years, with some distinct changes on the introduction of 'competition and credit control' in 1971. Government actions in the Money Market are often also linked to non-banking regulations – the term or period to repayment of HP loans, for example.

The characteristics of several methods (or instruments) used in this way by governments are set out below in showing how these may and have influenced the monetary system (see also Figure 14.14). At the time of your studies these instruments may only be used in part or have been superseded by other methods, so Assignment 14.22, may be important.

Controls on banks' liquidity
Government regulations can set the amount of liquid assets banks must hold as the lending base backing credit-money. *Before 1971* by agreement with the Bank of England, banks held at least the equivalent of 8% of their deposits in 'cash' (notes, coin and balances with the Bank of England) as the *cash ratio* in the backing for loans. But this alone was not a sufficient control of the banks' liquidity. So a further amount equal to 20% of deposits also had to be held in quickly realised (liquid) assets, giving a *liquidity ratio* of 28% (8% + 20%). Under the pre-1971 system this liquidity ratio gave the Government an influence over the extent of credit-money Commercial Banks could create from the deposits they received.

After September 1971 the use of 'cash ratio' and 'liquidity ratio' was dropped, but regulating the amount of liquid assets banks must hold as a lending base was continued, since these regulations are also safeguards for the public against imprudent banking. Since 1971 the banks had at least to hold a *reserve asset ratio* of certain specified liquid assets equivalent to $12\frac{1}{2}\%$ of their liability to depositors (see Figure 14.13). The assets comprising the 'reserve asset ratio' included balances on *current* account with the Bank of England, money on call, Treasury and other bills, and government securities due for redemption (to be repaid) within a year. They did *not* include cash in safes and tills, nor balances with other UK banks.

The intention in making the changes in September 1971 was to 'achieve more flexible but still effective arrangements . . . operating on the banks' resources rather than by directly guiding their lending' to quote the then Chancellor of the Exchequer. The authorities felt that the restrictions to competition in the pre-1971 controls should be replaced by a reserve asset ratio applying across the whole of the banking system.

Special deposits
A Commercial Bank's liquidity base (see Figure 14.12) can be cut by drawing off some of its liquid assets into the Bank of England. This was first carried out in 1960 and is made in the form of Special Deposits. The Treasury, whose main task is to manage the economy to achieve the economic objectives laid down by government ministers and approved by Parliament, may instruct banks to make these Special Deposits from time to time. The sums are transferred to the Bank of England and calculated as a percentage of each bank's deposits – 4% in August 1973, and 3% in September 1975, are examples. The Special Deposits are frozen, as it were, in the

Bank of England and cannot be used by the banks to back credit-money (customers' accounts). Although interest is paid on them, the date they will be returned to the banks is unknown until the Government changes its policy. Therefore Special Deposits are not liquid in the Commercial Banks' assets.

Special instructions to banks
Guidance from the Bank of England is given from time to time on the priority for Commercial Banks' lending. For example, exporters may get loans in preference to others when the country needs increased exports. At other times the banks might be told not to lend money for the purchase of consumer goods, or there might be an upper limit (a ceiling) on the total amount banks may lend for certain purposes at any one time.

In July 1976, for example, a notice was issued to the banks and Finance Houses taking deposits. This emphasised the need for priority in lending for working capital and fixed investment by manufacturing industry, and for the expansion of exports and savings of imports.

Although the Bank has power to issue directives, strictly speaking these have not been given at any time up to mid-1976.

Minimum lending rate
Before 1971 the Bank of England as 'lender of last resort' could increase or lower the interest rate – the Bank Rate – charged to Discount Houses forced to borrow when short of liquid assets. This is called 'forced into the Bank'. Although none of the Discount Houses might actually be 'in the Bank', the mere fact that the Bank Rate was published provided a guide to all interest rates. The Commercial Banks therefore set the rates of interest they would pay depositors at some 2% under Bank Rate, and charged about 2% over this rate for loans. In turn these bank interest rates affected all interest rates including charges for hire-purchase. The HP companies had loans from the banks; so as the bank interest charges rose these traders increased *their* charges for interest, which tended to decrease their customers' demand for such credit, and in consequence the demand for the goods it might help to buy.

After 1971 the Commercial Banks were expected to arrive at interest rates (both paid and charged) without reference to the Bank of England's *minimum lending rate*. The theory of this approach was that market forces – the interest rate offered high enough to attract deposits, the interest charged low enough for customers to take loans – would lead to each bank arriving at their own *base rate*. From this a bank might settle a base-rate-less-2%, say, to pay depositors and plus 2% to charge on loans.

In practice the 'minimum lending rate' has tended to influence all interest rates much as the Bank Rate did. Commercial Banks' interest rates tend to keep in step, with each bank, in response to competition, paying about the same rate for deposits, and also charging for loans higher but similar rates to each other's.

Open market operations
The holder of government security (or stock) draws interest usually each half year. When the stock matures (not unlike a bill of exchange maturing) the holder is repaid. He or she will receive the face value of the stock or a sum related to it. At any one time there are various types of government stocks, known as British Funds, held by

the public and institutions. These stocks pay different interest rates and run for various periods – *short-dated* having up to five years to run, *medium-dated* with five to fifteen, *long-dated* with over fifteen years, and a few 'undated'. These stocks may be bought and sold on the Stock Exchange. After being issued in two parts in 1969 and 1971 the $8\frac{3}{4}\%$ Treasury Loan 1997 due to be redeemed in 1997 was worth about £68 (per £100 of face value) in June 1976. The Government itself may enter the market to buy or sell such stock, for there is no need for the Government to wait until redemption dates before buying back a stock or part of it (see Figure 14.15).

By buying stocks the Government increases the banks' balances with the Bank of England, giving the Commercial Banks and others more liquid assets and so increasing the base for the banks' lending. Or by selling stocks the Government can reduce the banks' balances with the Bank of England. This in turn reduces the Commercial Banks' lending base of *cash*. Before 1971, as we saw, the cash assets had to equal at least 8% of deposits. So less cash by whichever control meant less credit-money created – lending being reduced by *12 times* the cash reduction. In practice, however, a reduction of cash was almost immediately replaced by calling in money 'at call and short notice' mainly from the Discount Houses. These loans formed part of the liquidity ratio of 28% mentioned above. Therefore the leverage (see Figure 14.13, page 201) was less than the 1-to-12 implied by the cash ratio. After 1971 the $12\frac{1}{2}\%$ reserve asset ratio has given a leverage on a decrease of these equal to 1-to-8 (see Figure 14.13).

Full circle
By the 1970s the monetary system has become a maze of note issues, deposits, credit-money and government regulations. But despite these complexities, we have seen the simple principles involved. Money is any 'good' generally accepted in payment for other goods or settlement of debts – whether this is cowry shells or the cheque a government takes in selling securities to a bank.

Assignments

14.22 Describe the ways in which the Bank of England can control and influence commercial banks. (L 1971)
(This updates details of Figure 14.14 at the time of your study.)

14.23 What is a central bank? Why is it necessary for a central bank to regulate the activities of the commercial banks? (L 1972)

14.24 (a) List the main assets of a typical commercial bank.
  (b) Explain what is meant by the eligible reserve asset ratio and its significance to a bank's ability to create credit.
  (c) What are special deposits? In what circumstances and why would they be used? (JMB 1975 – includes revision)

14.25 Define each of the following terms as used in economics and, with the aid of examples, show their interrelationship: (a) market; (b) specialisation; (c) money. (L 1973 – includes revision)

14.26* Explain the difference between: (a) a central bank; (b) commercial banks; (c) savings banks. What is their usual interrelationship? (L 1973)

14.27* Describe the function of the following: (a) an insurance broker; (b) a building

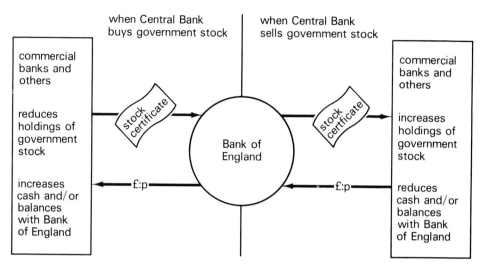

Figure 14.15   Government open market operations.

society; (c) an employment exchange (update title if necessary); (d) the National Savings Committee. (Adapted from AEB 1975 – includes revision)
Two of the above require research in local library for appropriate definitions.

Suggested further reading

Donaldson, Chapter 2
Harvey, Chapters 20 and 21
Harvey and Johnson, Chapter 9
Paish and Culyer, Chapters 30, 31 and 32
Powicke, Chapter 12
Stanlake, Chapters 22 and 23

Chapter 15
Government finance

The part played or not played by governments in an economy is very important whether they command in a *Doforall* society or leave individuals to make their own economic decisions in a *Maxforus* society of chapter 1. Having made a study of government monetary policy in the last chapter, in this chapter we will examine the spending and tax raising activities of governments – the *fiscal* policies.

Government revenues

Sources
During the 1970s about half the total expenditure in the British economy is public spending (at the direction of central and local government) as we will see later in this chapter. About two-thirds of this is paid out of taxes (see Figure 15.1); the remainder comes from six other sources. These are:
1. Social Security (National Insurance) contributions from employers and employees
2. trading surpluses on publicly-owned corporations and agencies
3. council house and other rents
4. interest and dividends received
5. borrowing
6. lotteries.
The first four of these are self-explanatory but included as 'trading surpluses' are net incomes from the Post Office, the charges for National Health prescriptions, dental treatment, local authority charges for use of swimming baths etc.

National Debt
We have seen something of government borrowing through Treasury Bills and the sale of government securities which are part of the National Debt (see Figure 15.2). This is divided into two main components: the short term or floating debt; and capital expenditure or long-term debt. The former consists of Treasury Bills and loans from the 'Ways and Means Account' (see page 205). The repayment of long-term debts for roads, schools and other capital expenditure is spread over a number of years. But the major part of the National Debt was incurred in the two World Wars of this century.

Taxation objectives
Taxes have been raised by rulers of various nations and states since Biblical times. In more recent centuries taxes have been raised to pay for those goods and services

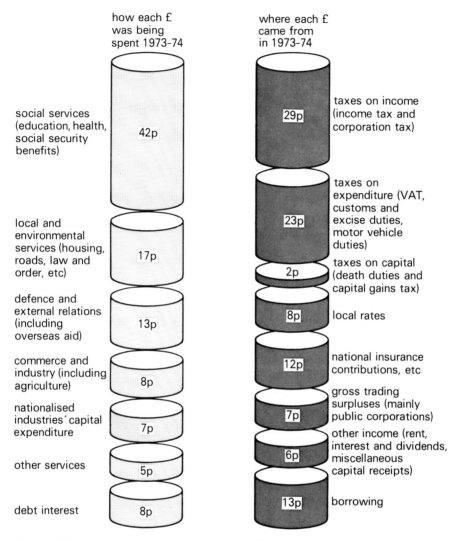

how each £
was being
spent 1973-74

where each £
came from
in 1973-74

social services
(education, health,
social security
benefits)
42p

taxes on income
(income tax and
corporation tax)
29p

local and
environmental
services (housing,
roads, law and
order, etc)
17p

taxes on
expenditure (VAT,
customs and
excise duties,
motor vehicle
duties)
23p

defence and
external relations
(including
overseas aid)
13p

taxes on capital
(death duties and
capital gains tax)
2p

local rates
8p

commerce and
industry (including
agriculture)
8p

national insurance
contributions, etc
12p

nationalised
industries' capital
expenditure
7p

gross trading
surpluses (mainly
public corporations)
7p

other services
5p

other income (rent,
interest and dividends,
miscellaneous
capital receipts)
6p

debt interest
8p

borrowing
13p

Figure 15.1   Government expenditure and where the money came from (estimates 1973/4). Source: *Treasury Broadsheet.*

which the community needs and that private producers are unwilling to produce or to produce at prices the majority can pay. In the UK justice, defence and medicine are examples. Through taxation, the costs are met by the community and not by individuals.

Since World War II to a greater extent than before 1939, British governments have also used taxation to influence other aspects of the workings of the economy. Consumption and employment levels, production and investment, and to some extent the distribution of incomes in the community are all influenced by taxes from time to time.

Before looking at the way taxes are raised and money borrowed, we need to understand some important principles.

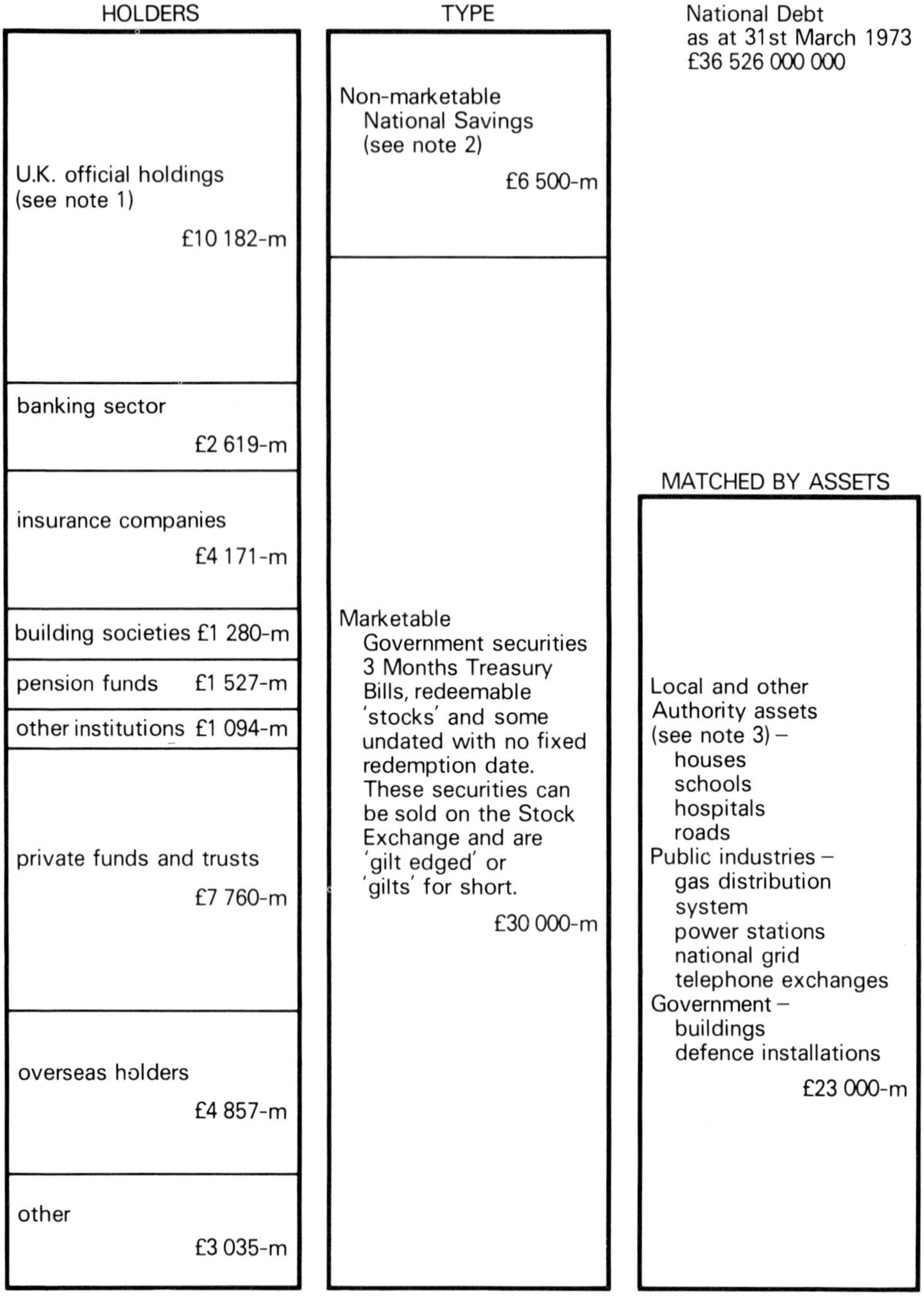

HOLDERS	TYPE	National Debt as at 31st March 1973 £36 526 000 000

U.K. official holdings (see note 1)

£10 182-m

Non-marketable National Savings (see note 2)

£6 500-m

banking sector

£2 619-m

insurance companies

£4 171-m

MATCHED BY ASSETS

building societies £1 280-m

pension funds   £1 527-m

other institutions £1 094-m

Marketable Government securities 3 Months Treasury Bills, redeemable 'stocks' and some undated with no fixed redemption date. These securities can be sold on the Stock Exchange and are 'gilt edged' or 'gilts' for short.

£30 000-m

Local and other Authority assets (see note 3) –
  houses
  schools
  hospitals
  roads
Public industries –
  gas distribution
  system
  power stations
  national grid
  telephone exchanges
Government –
  buildings
  defence installations

£23 000-m

private funds and trusts

£7 760-m

overseas holders

£4 857-m

other

£3 035-m

Notes:
1. U.K. official holdings are amounts held by government departments – £4700-m invested for the National Insurance fund, Trustee Savings banks, etc; *nearly £3800-m held by Bank of England backing note issue;* £1100-m also held by Bank of England; and £600-m by other government bodies
2. Non-marketable portion mainly National Savings in bonds etc. the original buyer must hold or redeem – over one sixth of total
3. Money lent to Local Authorities and Nationalised Industries for building houses etc.

Source: *Bank of England* – figures are of government and government guaranteed securities only

Figure 15.2   The National Debt.

'Principles of taxation'
Adam Smith set out in *The Wealth of Nations* some guiding principles for taxation which can be summarised as follows:

1. Ability to pay – individuals should be asked to make equal sacrifices. Today this is taken to cover sacrifices according to family circumstances and ability to pay taxes. An unequal sacrifice occurs when a poll tax, a charge of so much a head, is raised. A man with an income of £1000 a year pays the same amount as one with £5000. Nor is tax at a straight percentage of income necessarily any fairer. For when tax is 30%, although the £1000 a year man pays £300 and the £5000 a year man pays £1500, the man with the small income gives up relatively far more. The things he has to give up to pay this tax may involve him in a greater sacrifice, than that made by the richer man paying his tax.

This is an example of a *proportional tax*, one which takes a constant percentage of income regardless of income levels. *Regressive taxes* take a greater proportion of lower incomes however, and include many taxes charged on expenditure such as indirect taxes like television licences which cost a greater proportion of the poor man's income than the man with £5000 a year. Other taxes may, however, be *progressive* taking a higher proportion of incomes as these increase.

2. Certainty – tax-payers should clearly and easily understand how much they will have to pay, and when.

3. A tax should be easily paid and collected – like the system of Pay-As-You-Earn (PAYE) for income tax on wages and salaries which has the advantage of straightforward regular payment and collection.

4. Economy in collection – a tax should be cheap to collect otherwise it will to some extent be self-defeating. In the fiscal year 1974–75 the Inland Revenue spent the equivalent of 1·75% of the net amount received in gathering £14 235·8 million of Inland Revenue duties including income tax. (The treasury's year runs to 5 April.)

Structure and type
Taxes in the UK during the 1970s have mainly been of three types – on incomes, on capital and on expenditure. The characteristics of each of these are shown in Figures 15.3–15.5. The taxes on income are paid whether this is earned or 'unearned' as interest or dividends, and charged on individuals, firms and state run industries. A number of allowances are given to tax-payers so that these taxes are not paid on their total incomes. The allowances take account of family circumstances and investments in machinery and so on made by businesses. In 1975/6 the basic rate for Income Tax on individuals was 35% of their income (after allowances) up to £4500, and at progressively higher rates after this.

Wage and salary earners paid Income Tax under PAYE and the self-employed pay by two instalments – tax on incomes of 1975/6 being paid by them in January and July 1977.

Corporation Tax is paid by limited companies on their 'incomes' as profit after certain allowances for capital and other expenditure. The rate in 1976 was 52%.

As *direct taxes* (Figure 15.3) chargeable on incomes or profits, both Income Tax and Corporation Tax cannot be avoided by those with incomes, and are paid direct to the Government. (The prudent arrangement of your affairs to legally lessen your tax liability is called avoidance. Evasion of tax is when this is not paid fraudulently and therefore illegal.)

DIRECT TAXES

Income Tax

Paid on the taxable incomes of all residents in the UK (with few exceptions that included officials of foreign governments in 1976). Income for this tax includes wages, salaries, fees, bonuses, the cash value of some 'perks', pensions, dividends and interest on loans etc. It also included any such income these residents earned from abroad. Husbands' and wives' incomes were usually added together in calculating this tax in 1975/6 but this arrangement was under review.

Allowances deducted from the total income before calculating the tax for 1975/6 included: for single person's allowance £675; for a married man's allowance £955; for children, varying with age on 6 April 1975 – under 11 £240, aged 11 to 16 £275; over 16 but in full time school or other training £305. Additional allowances were also given to single parent families, to those with dependent close relatives, the blind, and the elderly (those born before 6 April 1911, in calculating 1975/6 tax). There was also some relief for amounts paid in annual premiums for Life Insurance and pension contributions.

Certain income was not taxable – the first £40 of interest on National Savings Bank, Trustee and some other government approved savings. Building Society interest was not taxed in the normal way, and taxpayers paying on the basic rate (see below) had no tax to pay on interest from a Society, but those with over £4500 of taxable income had a special adjustment for Building Society interest. These are only two examples of the many special features of income tax that affect taxpayers.

A simple example of Income Tax payable in 1975/6

	£
John Bee's total income	2000
Less: Personal Allowance as a single man	675
Taxable income	1325
Tax payable at basic rate of 35%	£463·75

Rates of Income Tax in 1975/6 were: 35% – the **Basic Rate** – paid on the first £4500 of taxable income; 40% on the next £500; and rising in steps on succeeding amounts (45% on the next £1000, 50% on the next, and so on) until the rate reached 83% on each £1000 or part thereof over £20 000.

Capital Gains Tax (CGT)

CGT is paid by UK residents who receive any gain on the disposal of such assets as land, buildings, machinery, shares and leases. The definitions of 'assets' and 'disposal' for this purpose are comprehensive. Disposal covers the sale, transfer and gift of an asset.

Gains on the disposal of the following, however, were exempt from CGT in 1975/6: private residences (taxpayers' homes); household and personal goods worth less than £1000 for an item or 'set' of items; animals and boats as 'wasting assets'; private cars; Savings Certificates and certain other Government savings bonds etc; gifts each worth under £100; life insurance policies; and compensation for injury. Nor was CGT payable in 1975/6 when the total value of assets a taxpayer disposed of that year was worth less than £500.

Losses on the disposal of assets are deducted in calculating the net capital gains for CGT, which in 1975/6 was a flat 30%. However a taxpayer with less than £5000 of taxable gains that year could pay less than 30%, under special provisions in the legislation.

Capital Transfer Tax (CTT)

Paid on gifts during a donor's lifetime and/or occurring on his or her death. These transfers may be in cash, property, company shares, or in any form that has a value. The tax is paid on the amount by which the value of a donor's estate is reduced by the gift. (This is not necessarily the same as the increase in the recipient's estate on receiving the gift.)

The tax was paid in 1975/6 on a series of steps or bands of the *accumulated* total of gifts by a donor, the rate increasing for each band, but with a lower series of rates for gifts during a donor's lifetime from the rate payable on his or her death. The effect of this can be seen in the following examples:

A gift of £5000 by someone who had already given away £15 000 gave rise to 5% CTT on the £5000, that is £250 tax in 1975, when the donor was alive.

Had the £5000 been given on the death of the donor that year, and his previous gifts been £15 000, then the tax would have been at 10% — £500 CTT.

Although the rates at death are double those for gifts by the living in the lower tax bands, the highest rate on gifts during a lifetime or on death are 75% for amounts over £2-million. The tax has to be paid in addition to the gift, the recipients paying £250 and £500 respectively in our example, out of the £5000 gift.

Exemptions from CTT in 1975 included: transfers between husbands and wives; first £100 000 of gifts to charity and some other charitable gifts; the first £1000 each year of any donor's gifts; gifts up to £100 for each single donee no matter how many; and the first £15 000 of gifts by any donor accumulated over his/her lifetime and on death.

Corporation Tax (CT)

All UK companies are liable to pay Corporation Tax if they are resident in the UK. It is not paid by partnerships as every partner is liable for Income Tax on his/her share of the partnership profits. The tax is also paid by non-resident companies (those based abroad) if they trade through a branch or agency in the UK. Corporations exempt from CT included: Local Authorities; Building Societies; Life Assurance Companies; co-operatives; and charities. The tax is charged on all profits *and capital gains* arising in what was called 'the accounting period' which might differ from the Income Tax (fiscal) year which ends on 5 April. The rate of CT (around 50% in the 1970s) is set by the Finance Acts, the laws passed enacting such Budget proposals as are approved by Parliament.

To calculate the profits liable to CT, a company's profits as shown in its Profit & Loss Account, are adjusted for various items allowed or disallowed in calculating Corporation Tax. For example: there are Capital Allowances in respect of buildings, machinery and other fixed assets' depreciation. These allowances usually differ from the sums allowed for depreciation in the company's accounts. There are also special provisions for calculating profits for CT when a company is controlled by a small group of shareholders. These regulations prevent individuals using companies to accumulate untaxed income.

The tax is paid 9 months after the end of the accounting period.

INDIRECT TAXES

Value Added Tax — see Figure 15.4

Wines, spirits, beers and ciders — taxes on these drinks are usually calculated by volume according to the alcohol content of the drink. The rate of tax may vary according to the type of drink, and sometimes according to its country of origin.

Cigarettes and tobacco taxes may be charged according to the weight of tobacco used or on the volume of tobacco in a particular pack or cigarette.

Petrol, diesel and heating oils — the tax may vary according to the strength and expected use of fuels, with higher rates on high octane petrol for cars. A lower rate is usually charged on diesel fuel which is mainly used in commercial vehicles, and low rates on fuel used in farm tractors and for heating oils.

Motor vehicle road taxes are generally charged at a single sum for all private cars regardless of size, a smaller sum being charged for motor-cycles and less still for mopeds. But over the years a variety of rates have been used, often related to the engine size in private cars. Commercial vehicles may be taxed at a single sum each year for smaller vans and higher rates — varying according to weight or other measures of size — for lorries, passenger transport vehicles etc. Farm tractors and mobile cranes have often been taxed at specially low rates.

Customs duties — these may be charged at so-much a unit imported (e.g. £5 per radio) but are usually levied at prescribed rates on the weight or volume of an imported commodity. On occasions a commodity may include only a proportion of a taxable good and its importer charged accordingly. When there is a tax on sugar, for example, the importer of soft drinks has to pay customs duty on the sugar content of these drinks.

General — the Customs & Excise in the UK (or their equivalent in other countries) issue from time to time a list of all duties, and the Excise charges for licences to carry on various trades. For example, licences are required to sell postage stamps, to sell beer and spirits, to operate a gambling club and operate a dance hall.

Figure 15.3   The structure of direct and indirect taxes.

Example of Value Added Tax (VAT) on making and selling 5 chairs

	Total paid at each stage incl. 8% VAT	Tax paid in purchase price	Tax collected on sales	Difference paid to Customs
Chair maker buys imported timber for £125 + VAT	£135	£10	£16	£6
Retailer buys these chairs for £200 + VAT	£216	£16	£28	£12
Customer buys them for £350 + VAT	£378	£28		

The producer/retailer at each stage in effect pays VAT on the *value added* by his work on the goods he bought (see Figure 12.5 for other examples of value-added). Note how the chair maker collects tax from the retailer, and the retailer collects it from the final customer. The retailer has paid tax to the chair maker, and the chair maker has paid tax to the importer of timber (who in turn pays the VAT he collects over to the Customs & Excise). At each stage the difference between *tax collected* and *tax paid* equals the VAT at 8% on the value of the work done: as the chair maker added £75 to the £125 of timber for a sales price of £200 for the chairs, he pays £6 (8% of £75) to the Customs and Excise.

Special Cases of Value Added Tax
Zero Rated individuals and businesses do not pay VAT but can reclaim VAT on any goods and services they buy that included this tax in their price. Included in this category are sales of food, books, *all exports*, coal, electricity and work of the construction industry.
Exempt services, trades and businesses, with *no rating*, are outside the VAT system, do not pay VAT nor can they recover any VAT paid on goods and services they buy. In this category are transactions in education, insurance, postal services, betting, finance, health, burials and cremations, interest on loans and land sales.
Small businesses with sales in any year under £5000 do not pay VAT (but may recover VAT that they have paid in the price of goods and services purchased, provided the business is registered for VAT).

Figure 15.4   VAT including 'zero' and 'no' rating.

Tax on capital when it changes hands in certain circumstances (see Figure 15.3) is called Capital Transfer Tax. This is a direct tax charged when any sizeable gift is made from one person to another in life or on death. It has replaced Death Duties at one time paid on any sizeable value of goods and property (an estate) passing to others on the death of the owner.

A Capital Gains Tax is charged on the profits less losses made on the *sale* of any capital assets. These gains are charged at a percentage on taxable gains. But gains from owner-occupied house sales, private motor-cars, and other goods sold for less than £1000 (in 1976) are exempt (see Figure 15.3). Capital Gains Tax is a direct tax.

The taxes on expenditure – Value Added Tax, Customs and Excise duties on spirits and tobacco are examples – add to the price of goods or services. (See Figure 15.3 for details.) These are *indirect taxes* in effect collected by sellers of these goods, for payment to the Government. They may be avoided by not buying the taxed goods. Typical is Value Added Tax (VAT) which replaced earlier taxes on expenditure such as Purchase Tax. It is charged as a percentage of the value added in each stage of production for most goods (see Figure 15.4). (We saw this concept of *value-added* in the study of National Income in chapter 12.) The rates have varied from time to time with a 'standard rate' of 8% in the summer of 1976 and a higher rate on less essential goods – washing machines, hi-fi's, and some other durables – at $12\frac{1}{2}\%$.

One effect of adding an indirect tax to the price of goods was seen in 1975, when a VAT rate of 25% on less essential goods contributed to a steep fall in the demand for

DIRECT TAXES

Advantages	Disadvantages
A progressive rate can achieve an equality of sacrifice.	Disincentive to overtime and harder work or taking responsibility, for extra pay after tax is insufficient compensation. (But some may work harder to get more take-home pay despite tax.)
Can be calculated to take account of different family circumstances – allowances for children, etc.	Disincentive to work for family's future due to Capital Transfer and possibly similar taxes.
Easily charged and collected for bulk of cases through Pay-As-You-Earn (PAYE) which is difficult to evade.	Tax on interest discourages personal and other saving.
A government can often estimate the yield in advance.	May reduce the amount available for re-investment when taken from business profits.

INDIRECT TAXES

Advantages	Disadvantages
Can discourage consumption of harmful goods like cigarettes.	Does not take account of personal circumstances or income.
When charges on luxuries gives the taxpayer the choice of paying or not paying them.	As flat-rate taxes they are regressive.
Can to some extent regulate consumer spending by influencing prices.	Influence price levels.
Can be altered quickly and easily – 'overnight' changes of rate.	Can only be applied to goods with inelastic demand, when used to raise revenue. Can also lead to marked fluctuations in demand when applied to goods in elastic demand, e.g.: VAT on boats, cameras and TVs.

Figure 15.5   Advantages and disadvantages of direct and indirect taxes.

these, with some consequent unemployment. Indirect taxes are regressive as they fall harder on the poor than the rich when buying taxed goods.

Local Authority Rates and Taxes
Rates are a tax paid on the 'assessed' value of property, an estimated annual value equivalent to its rent based on certain criteria. Paid directly to the local authority, they cannot be avoided by property owners nor by occupiers. Rates are also charged on shops and other business premises including factories.

There are arguments for changing the system of local Rates with their regressive effect on poorer households, especially when homes with two or three wage/salary earners pay the same Rates as the single person owning a similar home. The detailed implications of local Rates and alternative methods of raising revenue towards Local Authority spending are set out in the Layfield Committee's report 'Local Government Finance Committee of Enquiry'. The Layfield Committee pointed out that any system of local government finance should be based on *accountability*, so that amounts expended are subject to democratic control, and should be fair between areas. (They explained that areas with relatively wealthy communities tend to become richer as rateable values rise.)

One proposal is to raise a Local Income Tax as well as Rates; another is to assess farming land to the full Rate, although in the mid-1970s there are special reliefs from Rates for owners or occupiers of agricultural land.

At the time of your studies check the current practice in the UK. We will come back in a moment to the implication of local taxes contributing to the cost of community expenditure. The Layfield Committee's report is only one of a series of government committee reports brought out from time to time on current topics of interest to economics students. Although the detail in some may be too intricate for your level of study, their conclusions are a source of exam questions.

Direct or indirect taxes?
The arguments for and against these forms of taxation are set out in Figure 15.5.

Assignments

15.1 What are the advantages of income tax and value added tax to (*a*) wage-earners, (*b*) pensioners, and (*c*) the government? (Adapted from L 1972)

15.2 Explain, with appropriate examples, the advantages and disadvantages of raising revenue by (*a*) direct taxation, and (*b*) indirect taxation. (L 1972)

15.3 Distinguish carefully between income tax, customs duties, and local rates as different forms of taxation indicating their relative advantages and disadvantages. (L 1973)

15.4 What are (or *were* at the time of your study) local rates and how are (or were) they levied? Do you consider them to be a 'good tax'? Justify your views.

15.5 List the indirect taxes in force at the time of your study. Select four taxed items. Is the tax imposed on these items (*a*) to raise revenue, or (*b*) to decrease consumption? Explain your answer and amplify your list with notes of explanation.

15.6* Discuss: how might revenue be raised to meet local authority expenditure? What effect do the choices made have on poor and better off communities?

Government expenditure

The purse strings
The economy – with the problem of scarce resources to meet unlimited wants – can seldom provide all the resources a government at local and national level might want to deploy. However, the broad division in spending revenue – as these powers stood in 1976 in the UK – by those who held the purse strings are shown in Figure 15.6. Local Authorities were responsible for providing education and other community services like refuse disposal. The Central Government was responsible for national defence and such other matters as affect all communities in the country.

With the size and objectives of the public sector, the scarce resources should be allocated by a government to the best advantage in achieving objectives. So govern-

UK Public Sector Spending 1974–5

	£-millions	%
Central Government – including a number of services through local outlets (e.g. social security and unemployment services)	27 000	61
Public Corporations – including water and area health authorities' expenditure	4 000	9
Local Government	13 200	30
	£44 200	100

The relative proportions between the three parts of the public sector did not vary greatly during the mid-1970s, but the division is more complicated than this simple summary suggests. For local government, as Local Authorities, received the bulk of their income from central government. These Authorities were and are also bound (as are public corporations) by Parliamentary decisions which often tend to put the national interest before the preferences of local communities.

Rate Support Grant (RSG)
The major part of the funds Local Authorities receive from central government are in the form of a RSG towards the costs of their day-to-day operations. Much of this revenue expenditure is wages paid to teachers, social workers, engineers, dustmen, clerks and other council employees. When Parliament has decided the total amount of the Rate Support Grant it is shared between Local Authorities on a basis that takes account of three major factors. An Authority's *need* when, for example, there are more than the average number of children to educate in its area. Areas where less than the usual amount of Rates may be collected, because of the low value of property in the area, receive special consideration. And the RSG to a particular area is calculated to meet the 'domestic rate relief' given to owners of private dwellings who pay lower rates than industrial premises.

The central government in the mid-1970s imposed responsibilities on local government and recommended minimum standards for some services. Such legislation and guidance relied on the voluntary co-operation of Local Authorities, as did other steps to keep down local government spending. But from 1976–7 there were pre-determined *cash limits* to the amounts of extra RSG an Authority might receive when its employees' wages and other costs increased. (Before this date the RSG was increased during a year to cover such increased costs.)

Specific and supplementary grants
These are given by central government towards the cost of specific services – running the local buses, perhaps. As these grants are earmarked for a particular service or operation they cannot be used for other activities.

Loans from Central Government
Local Authorities build houses and flats to rent, by far the largest part of their Capital Expenditure (the funds invested long-term in the community's fixed capital assets). They also build schools, roads and other public works like swimming baths. Much of the cost of this work is financed by loans raised from the public, although the terms of these may on occasions be set within limits ordered by central government. Central government also provides loans for certain of these long-term – Capital – projects.

Figure 15.6   Who holds the purse strings.

ments need to plan their expenditure: they may estimate how many homes will be needed and allocate resources to build these; they project future changes in the structure of the population as we saw in chapter 2. As these spending plans in the mid-1970s affect about a half of the UK total output, they are still important, whether made by Local or Central Authorities.

Local Government expenditure

Local authorities control about one-third of the total public expenditure in the UK. In 1976/7 there was considerable discussion on the extent of Local Authorities' control of expenditure. The following comments, therefore, describe the situation in the mid-1970s.

The Local Authorities are responsible for education, fire services, refuse collection, refuse disposal, sewage, maintenance of roads, old people's welfare and other local needs – as shown in Figure 15.7. There are also area Water Authorities who collect water rates and arrange the distribution, purification and many associated features of water supplies.

The elected representatives in Local Government are in theory and often in practice closer to their community's problems than those in Central Government. In other words: local councillors could be expected to know more about a delay in emptying dustbins, than the Member of Parliament for the area. However the choices open to a Local Authority may be restricted by limits that the Central Governments set on the amounts that can be spent on particular services.

Central Government expenditure

A summary of the British Government's estimated expenditure (and revenue) in 1973/4 is shown in Figure 15.1 on page 211. The Central Government is responsible for: defence; costs of carrying out foreign policies, overseas aid; social security benefits like pensions and child allowances; national health services; interest on the National Debt; deficits on trading by state enterprises; food subsidies; and some of the other public expenditure shared in part with Local Authorities.

There are points of detail in this division of responsibility that need not concern us here. Therefore the following five headings of public expenditure cover some items paid in part by both Central and Local Governments (see also Figure 15.1 and Figure 15.7).

1. To provide social and economic security – this takes the major portion of money spent by government and includes all those payments made to achieve a minimum standard of life for all. In this category are payments for education, health services, social 'benefits' (unemployment pay, supplementary benefit, etc), family allowances, old age pensions, family income supplements, sickness benefit, housing grants and other subsidies.

2. Local environment and allied services – the cost of maintaining law and order through the police and the courts, fire services, maintenance of roads, provision of housing, consumer protection services, and all those public services which enable the community to go about its day-to-day affairs without fear of economic or other bullies.

3. Defence and external relations – included here are the costs of defending the country or being prepared to do so, including payments connected with the North

CURRENT ACCOUNT

Expenditure	£-millions	%	Revenue	£-millions	%
Education	3 301	36	Rates	2 737	30
Environment (other than housing)	738	8	Trading surplus	91	1
Roads and Public Lighting	404	4	Rent for:		
Police	632	7	Dwellings	1 095	12
National Health Service	65	1	Other premises	456	5
School meals and milk	267	3	Interest etc	274	3
Scholarships and grants	228	3	Government grants:		
Personal social services	588	6	Non-specific	3 832	42
General administration	203	1	Earmarked	640	7
Housing subsidies	126	1			
Other expenditure	724	9			
Interest on debts:					
Loans other than central govn.	1 200	13			
Central government loans	649	8			
	£9 125	100		£9 125	100

CAPITAL ACCOUNT

Expenditure	£-millions	%	Revenue	£-millions	%
Housing	1 649	41	Current surplus	678	17
Environment (other than housing)	356	9	Capital grants	238	6
Education	473	12	Loans:		
Net lending	481	12	from central government	1 156	29
Roads and public lighting	340	8	other	1 914	48
Capital grants	248	6			
Other expenditure	439	12			
	£3 986	100		£3 986	100

Figure 15.7 Local authority income and expenditure 1974. Source: *Central Statistical Office.*

Atlantic Treaty Organisation (NATO) and other foreign policy commitments like overseas aid.

4. Commerce and industry – payments are made from time to time to assist industry – for example in regional policies, chapter 6 – and to protect employment where market forces otherwise might cause hardship. Included here also are payments to farmers and other support for agriculture. These payments to commerce and industry are intended to counter the adverse effects of market forces, as when the Leyland Company and Rolls Royce might have succumbed if they had not been financially aided from public spending.

5. Other payments – these include the interest on the National Debt (£2284 million) in 1973/4, equal to about $3\frac{1}{2}\%$ of the GNP, being the amounts paid on Treasury Bills and other government securities for money borrowed over the years.

Also under this heading are payments to enable state enterprises to buy capital goods
such as steel mills.

Budget concepts
The idea of any budget in the general sense is to forecast what you may expect to
happen in the future, as the result of what you *may* receive and spend in the coming
period. You may work out a projected budget income for yourself at £5 a week for
the next six months, a total budget income of £130. Having decided this allows you
to pay £1 a month on HP for a hi-fi, everything goes fine until you have to give up
your paper-round or some other event cuts your income. Having a budget you can
then reconsider what you must do; without it you will be guessing. For the budget
shows *all* you expect to receive and how you intend to spend it. A change of income
should then be matched by a cut in your outgoings listed in the budget – your
reminder of what is in prospect financially.

Governments must budget in a similar way, although on more sophisticated principles. Otherwise the effects of a decision one day cannot be seen in the light of its
effects on the overall plans for the future.

The Budget
In chapter 17 we will see something of the problems of unemployment and inflation
in the UK economy. In recent years attempts to solve these two problems have
dominated government policies. However there are four main objectives, taken with
the over-riding needs of the people to feed themselves and resist aggressors, in the
economic policies of UK and other governments:

1. To achieve economic growth – improving the standards of living by increasing the
output per head of the population (but remember the reservations mentioned on
page 170).

2. To achieve full employment – minimising the number of people out of work.

3. To achieve a stability of price level – maintaining the value of money.

4. To achieve external balance – balancing the amounts paid to foreign countries
with the amount received.

The relationship between each of the four objectives – known as 'trade offs' – are
complex.

There is general agreement that all four objectives are difficult to achieve at the
same time. Therefore governments have to compromise in deciding the extent to
which policies lean further towards one objective at the expense of one or more of the
others.

One of the main ways governments implement their chosen policy is through the
budget. The Government's position has often been compared to a housewife's making ends meet; and until the 1940s the Government's actions in the economy were
largely, if not entirely, confined to balancing its expenditure against its revenue.
Since that decade, however, the extent of government participation in the economy –
its spending being about half of the total UK expenditure in the 1970s – has led
economists and others to realise that any one year's expenditure need not be covered
by revenue, provided the Government can borrow the difference.

The Budget therefore is no longer used mainly to balance government income
against its expenditure, but as a means of implementing policies to achieve the
objectives mentioned above. A government might then spend more than it receives

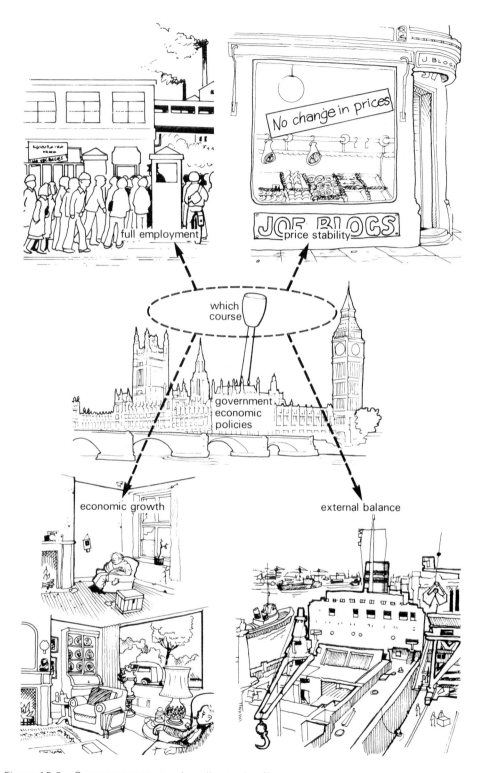

Figure 15.8   Government economic policy trade offs.

in taxes one year, making up the difference by borrowing and, as this spending exceeds taxes it will increase the amount of income individuals have to spend and therefore the level of demand for goods and services (see Figure 15.8). In this case it may come from a cut in taxes or through increased government expenditure on projects like new roads and other public works.

The decisions and the way they are implemented in steering the economy need a delicate touch to avoid too much or too little action, too soon or too late. An analogy has been drawn comparing 'steering the economy (with) driving a car with all but the back window blacked out, and having brakes and steering that take a long time to come into effect'. Only with hindsight can one see the full effect of government economic policies, and these often take months and perhaps even years to come into effect.

The Chancellor of the Exchequer presents a Budget to the House of Commons every year, usually in early April; but he may produce additional Budgets at other times. When presenting the annual Budget, the Chancellor reviews the economy putting forward judgements on its likely course and the policies – taxation, subsidies and so on – proposed to modify any unacceptable features in the way the economy is moving.

Assignments

15.7 How do local authorities raise revenues at the time of your study? Check copies of local authority's finance committee minutes in your local library.

15.8 Suppose that in your first job you earn £40 per week. What deductions will be made by the government from your wage before you receive it? Account for these deductions and indicate the purpose to which the money is put. (Adapted from AEB 1974)

15.9 Update the tax allowance details shown in Figure 15.3. Calculate how much tax you would be likely to pay on the wages in Assignment 15.8 above. What difference will be made to the amount of tax you pay (a) on getting married and (b) on buying a house?

15.10 What are the economic objectives of the most recent Budget at the time of your study? Note these from the newspaper reports (in library) of the Chancellor of the Exchequer's Budget speech. Take two or more of these and describe how they were to be achieved.

15.11 (a) Distinguish clearly between direct and indirect taxes, giving examples of each. (b) What are the main objectives of public expenditure on education? (L 1971 – includes revision)

15.12* Discuss: 'Economic rent can be taxed without affecting the allocation of resources.'

Suggested further reading

Harvey, Chapter 22
Powicke, Chapter 11
Stanlake, Chapter 30

Chapter 16
International trade and payments

The United Kingdom economy has many links with other countries as part of the world economy. In this chapter the fundamental principles of the world economy's trade and payments are shown with their many parallels to the studies made in earlier chapters.

The basis of international trade

International division of labour
Two related features of importance within a country's economy apply equally to the world economy. Both were described in chapter 4: the specialisation or division of labour leading to greater output from given factors of production; and the principle of comparative advantage, with each worker (or country) concentrating on production of the good for which he (or it) has the comparative advantage, to achieve the greater output from specialisation.

Countries may specialise for much the same reasons as regions specialise as we saw in chapter 6, because of natural and/or acquired advantages. This specialisation by a country should be arranged according to the principle of comparative cost for the maximum benefit from a given amount of the world's resources. This is the principle of comparative advantage as applied to countries (see Figure 16.1).

International specialisation
A country may have both natural advantages (factor endowments) and acquired advantages in the production of particular goods and services. However the borders between countries, the boundaries of their domains, may have been arbitrarily drawn without regard to factor endowments in particular territories. The American–Canadian border which runs for over a thousand kilometres along the 49th parallel of latitude typifies this, since it takes no account of mineral deposits north or south of this line. Throughout history, however, wars have been fought over – and borders influenced by – natural resources.

The advantage of such natural resources is unevenly distributed. Areas such as the Middle East, Texas and the British North Sea are endowed with oil and gas deposits, while India among other states has no known commercial oil deposits. Although a close substitute may be produced synthetically, the cost in terms of the factors of production employed is usually far greater than the cost of the natural equivalent. Some cannot be made artificially. Others may be acceptable alternatives like synthetic rubber but still have limited uses by comparison with the natural products.

The advantages of climate are perhaps obvious but not always fully understood.

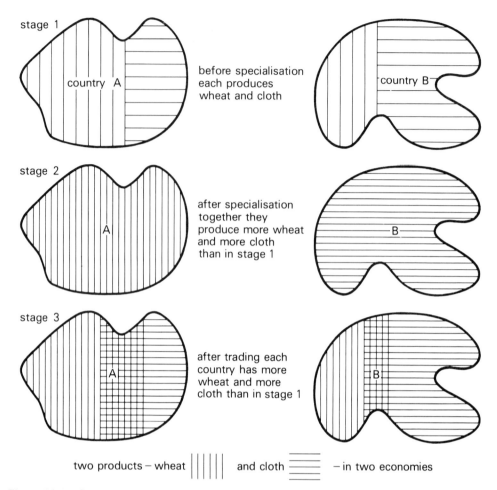

stage 1

country A

before specialisation
each produces
wheat and cloth

country B

stage 2

A

after specialisation
together they
produce more wheat
and more cloth
than in stage 1

B

stage 3

A

after trading each
country has more
wheat and more
cloth than in stage 1

B

two products – wheat   and cloth   – in two economies

Figure 16.1   Specialisation and trade between simple economies.

For each 1° centigrade that the annual average temperature falls there is a month cut off the growing season for grain in temperate climates. In the north of England hot-house tomatoes can be grown but are costly to produce (with oil or other heating, greenhouse glass, and other factors required) by comparison with outdoor tomato crops of the Channel Islands.

To reap the benefits of such advantages countries may specialise and apply the principles of comparative cost advantage. The *Maxforus* society of chapter 1 might produce wine and the *Doforall* society grow wheat. But some form of exchange would be necessary for man cannot live on either wine or wheat alone. The two countries might barter wine for wheat but we saw the disadvantages of barter in practice (page 174). International specialisation by countries, therefore, requires trade or exchange between them, so that each can obtain the goods it requires from the others. This is *international trade*.

Countries must engage in international trade if they are to get those goods which they cannot or are unwilling to produce because they would involve too great a sacrifice of scarce resources, or they cannot themselves produce in sufficient quantity to meet the demand at home. The British have no natural deposits of chrome ore and so must import it if they are to produce some types of hardened steel or chrome-plated car components. Although bananas can be grown in the UK these – like the tomatoes mentioned above – demand a great sacrifice of resources. They are therefore imported from the West Indies among other places with tropical climates suited to the bananas' cultivation. Despite home production of motor-cars, some different models are imported while some domestically produced cars are exported. In all these cases in Britain, as in any other country entering international trade, decisions are based on opportunity costs (see chapter 1). The use of scarce resources by a country to produce goods for exchange with another country means that the exporting country must forego some production for domestic use.

Figures 16.2, 16.3 and 16.4 show the situation in two countries A and B before and after the application of the principle of comparative cost in specialisation to increase their joint output of wheat and cloth.

After specialising – one in wheat, the other in cloth production – the two countries have produced 100 more units of wheat and 120 more units of cloth, and have increased the output of their 'world'. Both countries have gained by their specialisation producing more of both goods.

Terms of Trade

What are the conditions under which the specialisation took place in the example of Figure 16.3? And what might induce a country to specialise to achieve the consequent benefits? The situation must provide some mutual advantage with each of two countries receiving goods at less factor cost than they incur producing them themselves. Country B must be able to exchange a unit of cloth against a unit of

Production by two wheat-and-cloth economies, countries A and B

	Units of resource*	Output per unit of resource	
		cloth units	wheat units
Country A	200	8	10
Country B	300	10	15

Using these resources without specialisation the countries may produce:

	Units of resource*	cloth units	wheat units
Country A	60	480	
Country A	140		1400
	200		
Country B	100	1000	
Country B	200		3000
	300		
'World' total without specialisation		1480	4400

*Resources are assumed to have perfect mobility between cloth and wheat production in this simple example.

Figure 16.2   Production in two simple economies.

Specialisation by two wheat-and-cloth economies, countries A and B, according to the principle of comparative cost

| | Output per unit of resource | |
	cloth units	wheat units
Country A	8	10
Country B	10	15
Country B's absolute advantages	2	5
	= 25%	= 50%

B's comparative cost advantage lies in wheat production, being 50% better than country A as opposed to 25% better in producing cloth:

| | Output per unit of resource | |
	cloth units	wheat units
Country A	1600	—
Country B	—	4500
'World' total after specialisation	1600	4500

Note: The principle of *comparative cost* is applied to countries' production and is an extension of the principle of comparative advantage applying to individuals.

Figure 16.3   Specialisation in two simple economies.

wheat from country A more cheaply – in terms of the factors of production used – than B can grow wheat. This rate at which one country can exchange its goods for those of another is called the *Ters of Trade*.

Whether or not countries A and B enter into trade depends on the Terms of Trade. Indeed whether or not they or any two countries trade between each other – in the absence of controls like customs barriers – depends on their mutual advantage from exchanging goods, each making decisions based on opportunity costs. Figure 16.4 makes clear the reasoning for these choices by both A and B. By specialising in cloth production country A gives up 10 units of wheat for each 8 units of cloth produced. That is: 10 units of wheat are sacrificed when one unit of scarce resources (a bundle of scarce factors) is devoted to making 8 units of cloth. The opportunity cost of each unit of cloth produced is 1·25 (10 ÷ 8) units of wheat. So if A is to specialise in cloth production, it must receive at least 1·25 units of wheat for each unit of cloth it produces.

Any exchange with a rate lower than this makes trading with B not worthwhile. If the exchange were only 1 to 1, country A would be at a disadvantage. It would have sacrificed the production of 1·25 units of wheat, to produce a unit of cloth which can be exchanged for only one unit of wheat. On the other hand at any exchange rate above 1 unit of cloth to 1·25 units of wheat, A would gain from this trade.

To summarise: for trade to be beneficial to A, the Terms of Trade must be greater than the amount of wheat it could obtain domestically with the resources used to produce a unit of cloth. So the opportunity cost sets a limit below which trade between countries is of no benefit.

For country B as well, opportunity costs set the limit on the Terms of Trade through which *it* might benefit. Look again at Figure 16.4. By similar calculations to those for country A, the least amount of cloth may be calculated that country B can

Trade between two wheat-and-cloth economies, Countries A and B

Country B's opportunity cost –
  B may produce from one unit of resource:
    either 10 units of cloth
      or 15 units of wheat

In deciding to make 15 units of wheat B gives up 10 units of cloth.

The opportunity cost of a unit of wheat is therefore
  $\frac{10}{15}$ units of cloth.

For trade to be worthwhile to country B, it must get more than 10 units of cloth from A for every 15 units of wheat.

That is at least $\frac{2}{3}$ of a unit of cloth for each unit of wheat. In other words: B is willing to *pay* at most 1 unit of wheat for each $\frac{2}{3}$ units of cloth, or 1·5 units of wheat for 1 unit of cloth.

By trading with A at 1·4 units of wheat for each unit of cloth (see text), B gets 10·714 units of cloth for each 15 units of wheat. That is: 15 units of wheat 'buy' $\frac{15}{1\cdot4}$ units of cloth, equal to 10·714 units.

On trading 1010 units of cloth for 1414 units of wheat the countries gain through this specialisation *and* trade –

	Before specialisation (see Figure 16.2)		Before trade		After trade	
	cloth units (1)	wheat units (2)	cloth units (3)	wheat units (4)	cloth units (5)	wheat units (6)
Country A	480	1400	1600	—	590	1414
Country B	1000	3000	—	4500	1010	3086
	1480	4400	1600	4500	more of each than in cols (1) and (2)	

Both countries have more of each good than they had before specialisation and trading.

Figure 16.4   Trading between two simple economies.

beneficially exchange for wheat. There must be 10 units of cloth for every 15 units of wheat, or $\frac{2}{3}$ of a unit of cloth for each unit of wheat. That is: the *most* it will pay for each unit of cloth is 1·5 units of wheat.

Again we can see the measure of output sacrificed: here, 10 units of cloth, for every 15 units of wheat country B makes at home.

Gains from trade

Mutually beneficial trade can occur between any two countries when the Terms of Trade lie between the limits set by each country's opportunity costs. Repeating our example, therefore, country A must receive 1·25 units of wheat or more for each unit of cloth. While country B must receive at least $\frac{2}{3}$ of a unit of cloth for each unit of wheat, that is the same as paying no more than 1·5 units of wheat for each unit of cloth. If B gives more than this rate of wheat for cloth, the country loses out for it would have been better to make the cloth domestically.

When the Terms of Trade lie between the limits of 1 unit of cloth at least equal to 1·25 units of wheat and at most 1·5 units, then the cloth–wheat trade between countries A and B will benefit both of them. We can calculate the effect on both countries when one unit of cloth is exchanged for 1·40 units of wheat (see Figure 16.4). For every 8 units of cloth exchanged, country A gives 11·20 units of wheat (8 × 1·40); this is 1·20 units more wheat than A might have produced at home. Country B benefits from the exchange at this rate, with 0·714 more units of cloth than might have been made by sacrificing wheat production. For country B gives up 15 units of wheat for 10 units of cloth made at home, but exchanges 15 units of wheat for 10·714 units of cloth (15 ÷ 1·40).

World trade
The exact Terms of Trade within the opportunity cost limits set by the differing *factor costs* of production in two countries depend on several influences. Among these are the demand and supply conditions and elasticities for the goods in both countries.

Figures 16.2 and 16.3 show the position before and after specialisation by the two countries A and B in our example, but *before* they traded. Figure 16.4 shows what happens when they have traded. Note that both countries end up with more wheat and cloth than they each had before specialisation and trading.

The principles illustrated for our two country and two commodity 'world' apply in real life, but are complicated by the number of countries importing and exporting and the variety of goods and services involved. In practice, therefore, the Terms of Trade are measured by the relationship between the price for imports and exports. This relationship can be expressed as an index number allowing subsequent comparisons, much in the way retail price indices were used on page 180.

The Terms of Trade may then be calculated as an index number:

$$\text{Index number for Terms of Trade} = \frac{\text{Index of export prices}}{\text{Index of import prices}} \times 100$$

	Export Price Index	Import Price Index	Terms of Trade
	(1)	(2)	$\frac{(1)}{(2)} \times 100$
1963	76·1	78·8	96·6
1964	77·3	81·2	95·2
1965	79·3	81·3	97·6
1966	82·2	82·6	99·6
1967	83·4	82·8	100·8
1968	90·0	92·7	97·1
1969	93·0	95·6	97·3
1970	100·0	100·0	100·0
1971	105·6	104·7	100·8
1972	111·1	109·7	101·3
1973	126·0	139·7	90·2
1974	162·7	217·3	74·9

Source: *Economic Trends Annual Supplement 1975* (HMSO).

Figure 16.5   UK Terms of Trade 1963–74.

This gave the series of index numbers in Figure 16.5 for UK Terms of Trade for the years 1963 to 1974.

An increase in the index number – an improvement in the Terms of Trade – shows that export prices have increased relative to import prices. In this situation the country will have to give fewer goods in exchange for a given quantity of imports.

A decrease in the index number – a deterioration in the Terms of Trade – shows that exported goods have become cheaper in relation to imported ones. More goods must be exported, therefore, in exchange for a given quantity of imports.

Interpretations of Terms of Trade

Comparisons of the index figures for Terms of Trade in one period with another, and between countries must be made with caution. For these indices represent measures of the relationship between export and import prices. When examining the effects of changes in the Terms of Trade, we must remember that the changes in *quantities* of imports and exports depends on how quantities respond to price changes – the elasticities of demand for imports and exports.

A favourable movement in the Terms of Trade when export prices have increased while import prices remain steady can lead to lower quantities of goods being exported, since overseas buyers may buy fewer goods at the higher prices. More precisely: if the demand for our exports is elastic, earnings of foreign currency will decrease on the favourable movement in the Terms of Trade. For example a 10% increase in our export prices results in foreigners' demand and therefore our foreign currency earnings decreasing by more than 10%.

There are other repercussions from changes in the Terms of Trade. If these move in Britain's favour, for example, when the price of imports falls with no change in export prices, the terms will have moved unfavourably for some exporting countries. So in paying less per tonne for imported sugar while still getting the same price for exported motor-cars, the British economy tends to benefit at the expense of the sugar producer. Many producers of goods imported into Britain live in the developing countries of the Third World, and their incomes fall when the Terms of Trade move in Britain's favour. Yet the British and western world demand is inelastic for many Third World commodities such as sugar, copper, and so on. There is only a limited amount which the western countries will buy regardless of the low prices.

The effect of the inelastic demand for many primary products exported by developing countries leads to a fall in their incomes when these goods' prices fall. (Look again at Figure 10.5, page 141.) They then have less money as individuals, and as states, to buy their imports of the developed world's machinery and other manufactured goods, including those that are exported from Britain.

Assignments

16.1 Devise a hypothetical example of a two-country and two-goods 'world'. Show that in cases where the first country is better than the second at producing both goods, the output is maximised if production is arranged according to the Principle of Comparative Cost, and show that both countries then can gain from trade.

16.2 What are the important differences between international trade and trade within a single country? (L 1971)

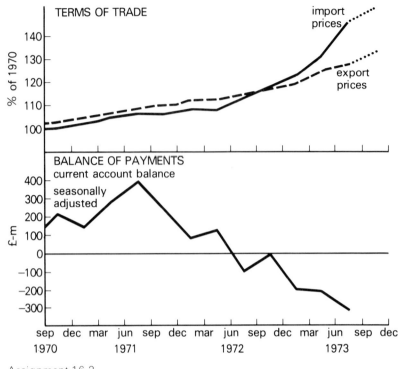

Assignment 16.3

16.3 Study the diagrams and answer the following questions:
- (a) (i) Explain how Terms of Trade are calculated. What approximately were the Terms of Trade in December 1971 and September 1972?
  - (ii) When were the Terms of Trade unfavourable between September 1970 and September 1973?
  - (iii) What factors could cause an unfavourable movement in the Terms of Trade?
- (b) Describe the main trends which took place in the United Kingdom's balance of payments on current account since September 1970 and give possible reasons to explain the changes which took place.
- (c) If the Terms of Trade are favourable, does it necessarily mean that the balance of payments on current account will be in surplus? (JMB 1975)

Barriers to trade

Free trade

We have seen that by specialising and following the Principles of Comparative Cost, there can be an increase in the total world output. If each country specialises in the production of those goods and services it is best suited to make or grow according to the Principle of Comparative Cost, then maximum output would be achieved from the world's limited resources.

Yet this does not happen in practice for countries and regions create barriers to trade and distort the pattern of production suggested by the Principle of Comparative Cost, despite the potential advantages.

Such distortions lead to costs being incurred, as we can see by looking again at our example in Figure 16.4. For if countries A and B or any other countries do not take

Figure 16.6   Trade barriers.

advantage of specialisation through trade, then they must pay a price in missed opportunities for 'more output from given resources'.

The reasons for barriers

Barriers to trade between countries and the discouragement of international specialisation are erected for social and political as well as economic purposes (see Figure 16.6). These arise for four reasons:

1. Strategic arguments – should a country lose its capacity to make goods needed in war, then it is open to an aggressor. You could not expect one of the super powers to specialise in food production while another specialised in armaments, however great the comparative benefits in terms of increased output from specialisation and trade.

2. Infant industries – a country reasons that certain domestic industries are just starting up and at least for a period need protection from foreign competition. This protection will allow them to develop to a stage where they can compete in world markets. However all too often it seems these industries rarely admit after any period to being ready for world competition, so the barriers may stay.

3. Protection against 'dumping' when a country sells goods to another at less than the cost of making them it is said to be 'dumping' them – hoping perhaps to undermine the importer's domestic industry. Then the dumper may attain a monopoly position and in future charge monopoly prices. There are examples quoted in the press from time to time of radios from Japan and suits from East Germany, coming into Britain at prices believed to be below the cost of their production in the exporting country. But how far a specific good's low price is a result of comparative cost advantage, and economies of scale, and how far it is due to 'dumping', may be hard to determine. This is especially difficult when comparative standards of living are lower in the exporting country than in the importing country.

4. Protecting domestic employment – countries often put forward the argument, with sound social reasoning, that imports should be restricted to protect jobs, for comparatively cheap imports may drive producers out of business with consequent unemployment. Fostering this idea, however, leads to a distortion of the pattern of world specialisation from that suggested by the Principle of Comparative Cost with a consequent decrease in world output. If the factors of production – including labour and machinery – are mobile, then they will be drawn into the production of those goods which have comparative cost advantage over foreign producers. This reasoning would mean that the Lancashire cotton industry's workers might move to other industries where they have a comparative cost advantage. Such changes involving the mobility of factors (chapter 3) tend to take time, even if resources are devoted to making the factors mobile rather than protecting an industry which no longer has comparative cost advantage. Nevertheless barriers are useful to protect the workers in a declining industry while phasing out its production and phasing resources into production which now has comparative cost advantage.

Forms of barrier

There are three main methods by which countries restrict international trade – tariffs, import quotas and subsidies.

Tariffs are a surcharge or 'tax' on imports, raising their price compared with home-produced goods. Purchase of these taxed imports is then hopefully reduced and more of the now similarly priced or cheaper home-produced goods are sold. However, the consumers pay higher prices than they would otherwise and the effectiveness of tariffs in reducing consumption of imported goods depends on their elasticity of demand.

Import quotas are a physical limit to the quantities of imports. A quota on the import of portable black-and-white TVs from Taiwan into the UK was set at 70 000 for 15 months from 1 October 1976. In the same year the USA imposed quotas on special steels imported from Europe (including Sweden) and Japan.

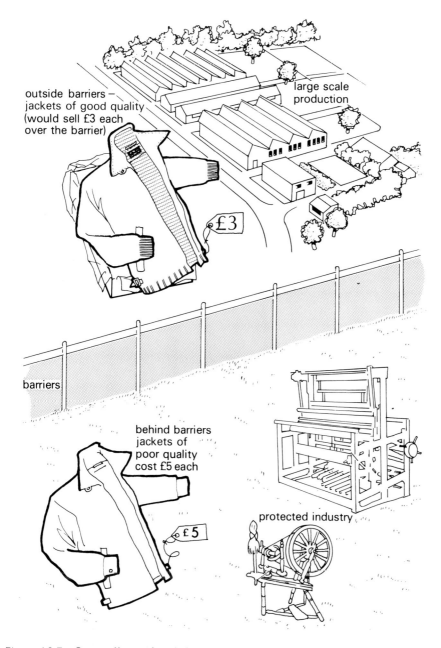

Figure 16.7   Some effects of trade barriers.

The third method involves paying a subsidy to home producers to decrease their costs and make domestically produced goods as cheap or cheaper than foreign goods. Again this hopefully encourages the consumer to buy home-produced goods. However, since the subsidies are paid out of taxes, taxpayers are subsidising those who consume these goods.

Such import restrictions are sometimes applied for short periods to help balance the payments for imports against those received from exports, as we will see later in this chapter. But such restrictions cannot last overlong without dealing with the fundamental problems causing the imbalance. In recent years in the UK one of these fundamental problems has been the difference in the rate of UK inflation from that of its trading partners (see chapter 17). Also such measures can be self-defeating, because importing less means that others can buy less of the country's exports.

Various attempts have been made to achieve the gains of trade between countries without losing some of the protection from foreign competition. In the 1950s the European Free Trade Area (EFTA) was formed to eliminate trade barriers between member countries. There have also been several groups of countries in 'customs unions'. These eliminate trade barriers between countries in the group but keep tariffs on imports from non-member countries. Examples are the European Economic Community (EEC), and an equivalent East European organisation, COMECON.

Summary
All restrictions distort the world pattern of specialisation (see Figure 16.7). This results in a lower world output of goods and services, as some countries continue to produce goods for which they do not have – or no longer have – a comparative advantage. The loss of possible benefits is the economic price paid for some political and social benefits.

Balance of Payments
Figures 16.8 to 16.13 set out the salient features of the balance of payments for the United Kingdom in 1973. This year was the most typical of recent years – 1974 figures were unusual because of the drastic change in oil prices. Assignment 16.7 below suggests ways of updating the 1973 figures.

About 20% of the goods and services bought in Britain in 1973 came from abroad. To pay for these Britain needed foreign currencies earned by selling exports. A balance of payments account is drawn up periodically to see how well the economy is doing in its dealings with the rest of the world. The 'current' part of this account is divided into *visible* trade – tangible goods bought and sold by Britons – and the *invisibles* – services which 'cannot be seen'. The types of item in each group are shown in Figure 16.8.

Trade gap
There is little difficulty in remembering the various types of goods which form the visible trade. The difference between receipts due from and payments due for visibles is known as the *balance of trade*. If visible exports exceed visible imports the balance is favourable; but should imports of visibles exceed visible exports, the balance is unfavourable. Note in Figure 16.8 that this unfavourable balance is known as the *trade gap*.

Invisibles
The invisible receipts listed in Figure 16.8 include some items which you might not realise were earnings from exports: money received from tourists and businessmen visiting Britain from abroad; charges for services in banking and other advice from institutions in the City of London and the sale of *know-how* and *intellectual capital* –

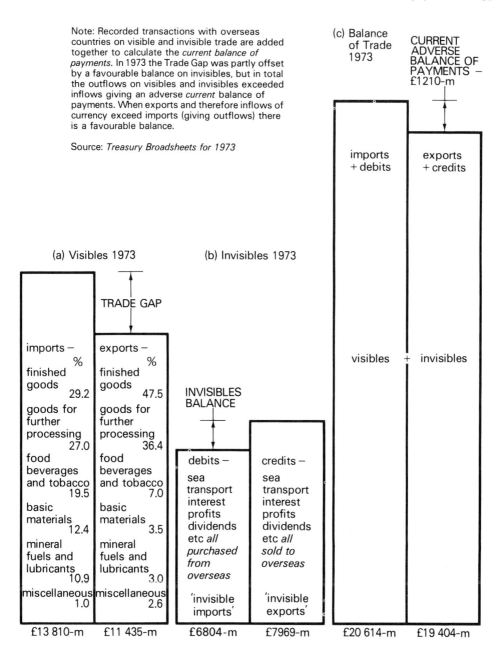

Note: Recorded transactions with overseas countries on visible and invisible trade are added together to calculate the *current balance of payments*. In 1973 the Trade Gap was partly offset by a favourable balance on invisibles, but in total the outflows on visibles and invisibles exceeded inflows giving an adverse *current* balance of payments. When exports and therefore inflows of currency exceed imports (giving outflows) there is a favourable balance.

Source: *Treasury Broadsheets for 1973*

(c) Balance of Trade 1973 — CURRENT ADVERSE BALANCE OF PAYMENTS − £1210-m

imports + debits | exports + credits

visibles + invisibles

(a) Visibles 1973

TRADE GAP

imports − % | exports − %
finished goods 29.2 | finished goods 47.5
goods for further processing 27.0 | goods for further processing 36.4
food beverages and tobacco 19.5 | food beverages and tobacco 7.0
basic materials 12.4 | basic materials 3.5
mineral fuels and lubricants 10.9 | mineral fuels and lubricants 3.0
miscellaneous 1.0 | miscellaneous 2.6

(b) Invisibles 1973

INVISIBLES BALANCE

debits − sea transport interest profits dividends etc *all purchased from overseas* | credits − sea transport interest profits dividends etc *all sold to overseas*

'invisible imports' | 'invisible exports'

£13 810-m | £11 435-m | £6804-m | £7969-m | £20 614-m | £19 404-m

Figure 16.8 Balance of payments for the UK in 1973.

technical knowledge, expertise and ideas. The 'private sector' items here include the receipts from public corporations, but not other government receipts.

The Government receives a small amount of invisibles, but as we will see in Figure 16.9 they pay out considerably more, for the Government must pay for embassies abroad, for stationing British troops abroad, and for contributing to com-

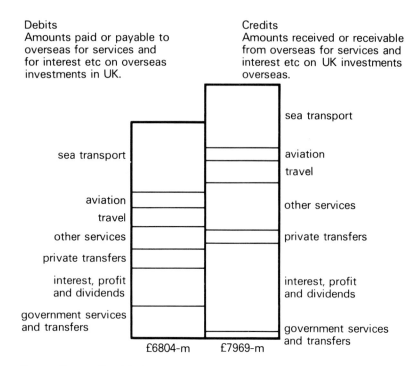

Source: *Treasury Broadsheets*

Figure 16.9   UK invisibles account – transactions 1973.

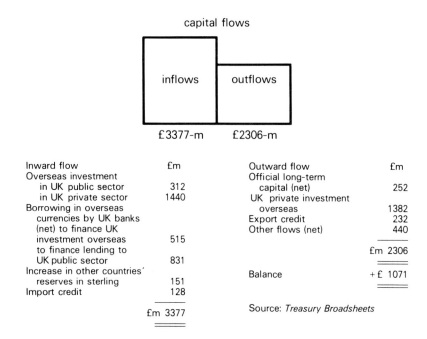

Inward flow	£m	Outward flow	£m
Overseas investment		Official long-term	
in UK public sector	312	capital (net)	252
in UK private sector	1440	UK private investment	
Borrowing in overseas		overseas	1382
currencies by UK banks		Export credit	232
(net) to finance UK		Other flows (net)	440
investment overseas	515		
to finance lending to			£m 2306
UK public sector	831		
Increase in other countries'		Balance	+£ 1071
reserves in sterling	151		
Import credit	128		
	£m 3377	Source: *Treasury Broadsheets*	

Figure 16.10   UK capital inflows and outflows 1973.

Recorded transactions and net currency flow 1973

Recorded transactions —

	£m
Current account balance, net outflow	−1210
Capital account, net inflow	+1071
Capital transfers, special 1973 item paid to certain overseas holders of sterling, under guarantees	− 59
Net outflow on recorded transactions	− 198
Adjustment for differences on estimates used in recording transactions, time lags between recording some items and currency movements, etc — *balancing item*	+ 408
Net currency inflow for 1973	+ 210

The net inflow of £210-million for 1973 was added to official reserves of gold and foreign currency.

Source: *Treasury Broadsheets.*

Figure 16.11   Balancing the accounts.

mon defence policies. There are also transfer payments to British old-age pensioners and others entitled to British government allowances although living abroad.

The feature of public and of private *transfer receipts* and payments is the fact that there is no service given or received in exchange for them. The birthday present of $25 from Aunty Lou in Kansas is a transfer receipt in these figures.

British invisible exports invariably exceeded invisible imports, but how large this invisibles' surplus remains in future years depends on several conditions. Any increase in overseas companies' investment in the UK leads to higher exports of profits and dividends, perhaps not matched by incoming profits from increased British investment overseas. Any fall in the British share of world shipping will lead to a fall in invisibles through less freight income from foreign customers. If those with know-how and abilities in demand abroad move away from Britain then the invisible receipts they earn will go elsewhere. And so on (see Assignment 16.9 below).

Capital account

The position on exports and imports as the current account balance of payments are only part of the whole picture describing the total receipts and payments of foreign currencies. For in addition to receipts and payments on current account, there are investments made between countries. In the UK money may be borrowed from overseas companies or invested by them in their manufacturing organisations within the UK.

The British Government may borrow from overseas. On the other hand there are capital outflows such as investments made by British companies in overseas factories and loans by the British Government to other governments and to finance British exports.

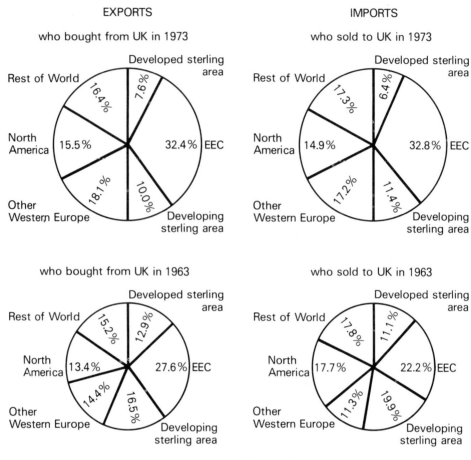

EXPORTS
who bought from UK in 1973

IMPORTS
who sold to UK in 1973

who bought from UK in 1963

who sold to UK in 1963

Notes: EEC members in 1973 for all EEC percentages; developed sterling area – Australia, New Zealand and South Africa; North America – USA and Canada; Rest of World includes Latin America and Soviet bloc; developing sterling area – covers some Commonwealth countries.

Source: *Treasury Broadsheet*

Figure 16.12   Changing patterns of UK international trade.

Most capital transactions have matching future interest or profit receipts and payments (appearing as invisibles – received or paid – on current account). (See Figure 16.10.)

Balancing the accounts

When the current transactions are added to capital flows (Figure 16.11) the net difference in (+) or out (−) represents the net inflow or outflow of all currencies. That is: the total currency flow. If the flow is a net influx of funds then there is an addition to reserves. A net outflow depletes them. But either flow may be subject to adjustment for special transactions with the International Monetary Fund (IMF) described below. In 1973 the inflow of £210 million shown in Figure 16.11 was added to the reserves.

Amounts received by UK or allocated to UK from EEC in years 1973 and 1974

	£
Loans	
European Investment Bank provided finance for Regional Development and to assist firms modernise to face competition on removal of trade barriers (includes allocation of loans at low interest rates)	200 600 000
Grants and subsidies	
European Coal and Steel Community (ECSC) Fund for resettlement and retraining former minders and former steel workers on reorganisation of their industries	19 988 000
European Social Fund for resettlement and retraining workers not covered by ECSC above	56 641 000
Agricultural Guidance and Guarantee Fund under the Common Agricultural Programme (CAP) described in chapter 17	186 983 000
Disaster Aid	31 000
Miscellaneous research	654 000
Total receipts	£464 897 000

Amounts paid by UK into EEC funds

	£
Contributions to budget:	
1973	169 000 000
1974	216 000 000
Paid into lending institutions' resources	63 000 000
	£448 000 000

The above statements do not include amounts for the Community Loan Fund (set up in October 1974 to help member countries with balance of payments difficulties) nor the Regional Fund operating in 1975 in the way described in chapter 17.

Figure 16.13   EEC contributions.

The reserves are the gold and foreign currencies held by the Bank of England. They may be supplemented under international agreement from time to time by drawing on funds held by the International Monetary Fund. This was set up 'after the spirit of cooperation between Britain and its Allies during the Second World War transformed the outlook for concerted international control of the world's monetary system'. (*International Monetary Co-operation*, CIO London.) The experience between the wars had shown the need for such action, and the IMF is one example of the determination of post-war governments in many countries to attempt concerted action on the world's monetary system.

Some facets of UK balance of payments
A detailed review of the history of the UK balance of payments is beyond this book's level of study. But some important features of the British economy are connected with this balance. We have seen in Figures 16.8 to 16.13 the main features of the transactions affecting it, and reference has also been made (page 232) to the use of trade barriers to 'help' the balance of payments. Looking back from 1976, however, the UK's dealings with other countries has resulted in a Trade Gap year by year (only a few years – 1956, 1958 and 1971 – showing a favourable balance of trade since 1919). Visible imports exceed exports mainly because the UK buys a high proportion of its raw materials from abroad. Therefore, large Trade Gaps have tended to occur in periods when the domestic economy was expanding. The sharp rise in imported oil prices has accentuated the gap in the mid-1970s but by 1980 North Sea oil is likely to swing this balance the other way.

Until the fairly recent past, the Trade Gap has generally been more than covered by the favourable balance on invisibles. These, however, have declined in recent years because, in simple terms, there has been a decrease in profits and dividends coming in from abroad and there has been an increased level of government spending abroad. The fall in dividends and profits came about mainly because the British sold many overseas investments during the two world wars, while the increase in government expenditure came about through increased spending on stationing British troops abroad and maintaining embassies and diplomats. In 1919 the net inflow from invisibles covered 25% of the outflow required to pay for visible imports, yet by 1970 invisibles covered only 8% of this outflow.

How much foreign trade is done by the UK?
Figure 16.12 shows what the British bought and sold in trade with the rest of the world in 1973. There is an interesting shift in the pattern of this trade since 1963: less food but more manufactured goods were being imported by 1973. This arose in part from the need for capital goods to increase British production, and in part from an increased home demand for consumer goods.

The changing pattern of goods reflects in part a change in the countries with which Britain traded. In 1963 the trade was 19.9% with developing countries in the Commonwealth or associated with the UK because they held their reserves in sterling. (This was the 'sterling area'.) By 1973 a great deal of the trade had shifted, with an increase in transactions with member countries in the EEC (see Figure 16.12).

The European Common Market
In addition to trade with the EEC there are payments of contributions to the Community Budget offset by receipts under various Market agreements (see Figure 16.13). The major portion of receipts is from the Agricultural Guidance and Guarantee Fund described in chapter 17.

Assignments

16.4 Describe the pattern of foreign trade of the UK at the present time with regard to the main types of exports and imports, and their geographical distribution. (AEB 1974)

16.5 What are the main imports and exports of the United Kingdom? Indicate the advantages of international trade to the United Kingdom. (L 1971)

16.6 Discuss the likely effects on Britain's balance of payments of:
  (*a*) a decision to equip the Royal Armoured Corps with American-armoured vehicles;
  (*b*) a very successful tourist promotion campaign in America, entitled 'Visit Britain Now!';
  (*c*) a complete stoppage for two months by French dockers;
  (*d*) a refusal by Middle East states to allow British banks to continue operations in their territories. (AEB 1972)

16.7 Update details in Figures 16.5 and 16.8 to 16.13 from up-to-date copies of the various sources quoted with these diagrams.

16.8* Group research: playing Monopoly can provide many examples of the element of chance in some financial matters. Using two boards with each player having a counter-symbol on each, halve all values and penalties on the second board. A player may then use his or her money to buy property on either board. Note the effect over a game or series of games, on the flow of funds between the 'low-values second board' and the normal-value first board. What are the implications for two such trading economies?

16.9* What are the effects on the UK balance of payments of a brain and fame – the famous artist or pop-singer – drain?

16.10* Discuss: 'Any distortion of world specialisation away from the pattern suggested by the principle of comparative cost inevitably leads to a lowering of world standards of living.'

Suggested further reading

Donaldson, Chapters 3 and 12
Harvey, Chapter 14
Powicke, Chapters 13, 14 and 15
Stanlake, Chapters 26 and 27

Chapter 17
Current issues

We can now begin to consider current economic issues of our time. As a guide to the way this may be done we have included three issues of 1976, although at the time of your studies you may find different issues need analysis as topics of current importance and likely subjects for examination questions.

We began our study with a definition of economics as a science that studies human behaviour as a relationship between ends and scarce means that have alternative uses. We conclude with examples in this chapter considering the effects of the issues discussed, on individuals as well as on communities. For no matter what figures are discussed or economic principles argued, their effect on people must never be forgotten. Nor should we overlook what is happening or has happened on the ground, the physical events underlying figures and other data – the goods delivered to a buyer accepting a trade bill, the events that cause a condition of momentary supply, the time needed to build power stations that make the 'short period' or 'short run' a matter of years in the electricity supply industry.

Unemployment

Unemployed factors of production
While most of us think of unemployment as people wanting work but unable to find jobs, any factor of production may be unemployed. Land may be left fallow, and machines can lie idle. When any factor is not fully employed – look back at Figure 1.2, page 14 – production/output falls inside the Production Possibility Curve. The maximum output is not being achieved from the scarce resources.

Some factors *may* not deteriorate when not employed for a time. Many types of machine can be put in wraps, although they may become obsolete while out of use. Land will not entirely change its nature although perhaps it will become overgrown with scrub and weeds. However men and women out of work deteriorate mentally and physically. This in itself is a high social cost and there are others, despite relief benefits as old as the Poor Laws of Elizabeth I, if not earlier.

Despite unemployment benefits the unemployed lose income, and have less purchasing power than they had when they were in jobs. Curing the social evil of unemployment was and is a primary objective of government economic policy as we saw in chapter 15. However there is no known way of reducing it to zero, for at any moment in time there will be people (and other factors) changing occupations. Therefore since the Beveridge Report, *Full employment in a free society* (1944), successive governments have aimed at maintaining a high and stable level of employment.

Types of unemployment

If you are out of work the niceties of reasons or causes do not help much, but in studying possible lines of action to curb if not cure unemployment, we must identify its various components and their causes. Its types can be considered under four headings, classified in the Beveridge Report as *frictional, structural, seasonal* and *cyclical* unemployment.

Frictional unemployment, Beveridge said, is 'caused by individuals . . . not being completely interchangeable and mobile . . . then [although] there is an unsatisfied demand for labour, the unemployed workers are not of the right sort or in the right place to meet the demand.'

Frictional unemployment occurs because of the geographical and occupational immobility of labour. As the pattern of *demand for labour* changes in response to changes in the pattern of demand for goods and services (something that is constantly happening) difficulties arise. This friction occurs as we saw in chapter 3, inhibiting or slowing down many individuals from changing their jobs. They may live in an area of declining industry but are not prepared to move to a locality where there is a demand for their labour in a new or expanding industry.

Structural unemployment arises when there is a substantial decrease in the demand for one product, particularly when this product comes from an industry concentrated in a few areas. The resulting decline probably takes place over a fairly long period as the structure of demand in an economy changes. The distinction between structural and frictional unemployment is more a question of degree rather than type. Frictional unemployment arises as workers take time to move to expanding industries but are nevertheless between jobs. With structural unemployment, few if any new jobs are created – there are no opportunities for alternative work – as occurred in the Lancashire cotton industry, in coal mining before oil prices rose, and in shipbuilding. All of these are UK industries where the structure of demand has been changed largely due to overseas producers now satisfying their own and other market demands. Changes in the structure of demand and production methods often involve the introduction of labour-saving machinery, giving rise to *Technological Unemployment*, a form of *Structural Unemployment*.

Seasonal unemployment results from the seasonal fluctuations in demand for some products, resulting in fewer jobs connected with their production from time to time over the year. Fewer ice-cream sellers are employed in the winter than in the summer. The number of jobs in summer holiday resorts falls substantially in the winter. Yet in the summer there are no jobs for Father Christmases who have a short winter season of employment.

In the motor industry the demand for cars is seasonal, as fewer cars are bought in the winter than in the spring and summer. The building trade employs fewer men in winter than in summer when settled weather and long hours of daylight make outside work possible. Similarly many jobs connected with farming and market gardening are seasonal in character.

Cyclical unemployment arises from the ups and downs in the economy, the booms and slumps over a trade cycle. (The name describes periodic fluctuations in the level of economic activity.) An important feature of such fluctuations in activity and unemployment is that they are usually felt most markedly in the capital goods industries and those dependent on exports. In the years between the world wars, cyclical unemployment was severe. It was superimposed on pronounced structural unemployment particularly affecting the industries at that time susceptible to cyclical unemployment – iron and steel, shipbuilding, heavy engineering and coal-mining, among them.

Regional patterns of unemployment

In analysing any problem you need to collect the facts, to learn of existing conditions and the background of a situation. We saw the uneven geographical spread of unemployment in the UK (chapter 6), that has come about in areas where industries which once enjoyed comparative advantage are concentrated and now declining. Labour does not want to move to new areas, nor are new industries attracted to these older industrial regions because often the transport costs, among other things, discourage entrepreneurs from moving into the area. In other words: the areas do not offer comparative advantage to new industries. The Government regional policies, as described in chapter 6, are designed to offset these disadvantages and encourage new industries to set up where there is high unemployment. However the effect of tax allowances under these policies has tended to attract capital-intensive production plants with large investments in machinery, rather than entrepreneurs with job-intensive industries which would substantially reduce unemployment.

The history

The uneven spread of unemployment has been felt by these regions for several decades. With the decline in shipbuilding, coal-mining (as a once highly labour-intensive industry), and similar heavy industries, the regions of high unemployment have been in a worse situation than the rest of the country in good times as well as bad. They suffered especially acutely in the 1930s when, for example, in 1932 the rate of unemployment in the country as a whole was 22·1%, one in five of the workers in the National Insurance scheme of that period. A far worse position arose in these older industries (see Figure 17.1). This was also reflected in disparities between regions – 22·3% unemployed in Wales in 1937 when the London level was 6·3%.

The slump in trade leading to this heavy unemployment came between 1921 and 1939 when on average 14% of insured workers were unemployed. On the mobilisation of resources for World War II, the unemployment figures fell – a cure more destructive than even the evil of unemployment. From 1948 until 1970 unemployment was generally between $1\frac{1}{2}$% and 3%; the average rate was equal to 1·9% of the *work force* being unemployed (see Figure 17.2). Since 1967, however, there has been an upward trend, and although this had not reached the inter-war levels there is still regional imbalance. When the national rate was 4·2% in 1975 with over 1 000 000 unemployed, there were only 3% out of work in the southeast but 7·9% in Northern Ireland.

What are the cures?

In looking at any problem of this nature one may find that the experiences of other countries have *some* useful lessons. In the USA and Italy among other countries there are similar problems of regional imbalance in employment, but their governments' solutions may not always be wholly relevant to a British problem or vice versa. (See Assignment 17.5 below.)

If unemployment is due to the lack of geographic or occupational mobility –

Unemployment examples in 1930s

	% of insured workers	Unemployment by regions 3rd quarter average 1975	%
1932		1975	
UK total	22·1	UK total	4·3
Examples for industries –		North	6·0
iron smelting etc	47·8	Yorks & Humberside	4·1
pig iron manf	43·8	East Midlands	3·8
laundry & dry cleaning	9·4	East Anglia	3·7
tram & bus services	5·9	South East	3·0
1937		South West	4·9
Examples by regions –		West Midlands	4·4
Wales	22·3	North West	5·4
London	6·3	Wales	5·8
Examples for industries –		Scotland	5·3
shipbuilding	23·8	Northern Ireland	7·9
jute	26·8		
scientific instruments	2·8	Source: *Beveridge Report* and *Economic Trends*	

Figure 17.1   Examples of unemployment as proportion of insured workers during 1930s, and unemployment by regions in 1975 as percentage of total employees (employed and unemployed).

% of UK total 'employees' unemployed

Year	%	Year	%	Year	%
1948	1.8	1958	2.2	1968	2.5
1949	1.6	1959	2.3	1969	2.5
1950	1.5	1960	1.7	1970	2.7
1951	1.2	1961	1.6	1971	3.4
1952	2.1	1962	2.1	1972	3.7
1953	1.8	1963	2.6	1973	2.6
1954	1.5	1964	1.7	1974	2.7
1955	1.2	1965	1.5	1975	4.2
1956	1.3	1966	1.6		
1957	1.6	1967	2.5		

Source: *Economic Trends Annual Supplement 1975* (HMSO)
The British Economy Key Statistics 1900-1970
(London and Cambridge Economic Service)

Figure 17.2   Unemployment in the UK 1948 to 1975.

frictional or maybe structural to a degree – the efforts of governments to improve mobility will help. Bringing work to the workers or helping workers to become more mobile are possible policies. In the latter, British governments have taken a number of steps: establishing retraining centres and paying grants while retraining; grants towards the costs of moving homes; and setting up 'occupation shops' advertising jobs to improve the unemployeds' knowledge of work available in more than just his or her locality.

In a period of cyclical – sometimes called demand deficient – unemployment, the Government may take steps to increase the demand for goods and services. This reflation of the economy by fiscal and/or monetary policies means decreasing taxes and possibly increasing government expenditure or both, among other measures. Consumers, for example, then have more to spend and so may increase demand with consequently greater employment. But chapter 15 showed how governments must make trade offs in pursuing several desirable objectives. They are therefore limited in the actions they can take, especially in matters of reflation with dangers of rising prices – inflation.

Assignments

17.1 Describe the economic policies with which the government attempts to control unemployment in the United Kingdom. (JMB 1975)

17.2 Outline the main features of the unemployment problem in the UK at the time of your studies.

17.3 Would an increase in the general level of demand solve the problem of British regional unemployment? (ICSA 1973)

17.4* Discuss: 'Can unemployment ever be reduced to zero?'

17.5* Group research: look up the rates of unemployment in two EEC and two other countries and compare these with the rate in the UK over the last five years recorded. How can you account for the differences?

Inflation

What is inflation?
Inflation is a rise in the *general* level of prices over a period. This, as set out in chapter 14, is equivalent to a period of falling value for money. The fact that price levels are rising is not of itself as important as the extent and speed of their increase. They may rise gently at 2% to 4% a year, as they did in the UK and in most other industrial countries from 1952 to 1965. This is sometimes called 'creeping inflation'.

On other occasions the general price level may rise quickly as it did in the UK between the last quarters of 1974 and 1975 with a rise of 21%. Figure 17.3 shows how the level of UK retail prices (measured by the Retail Price Index) changed for the years 1948 to 1975 based on the figures in Figure 14.7, page 185. The extent of inflation is shown by the slope of this graph indicating how much prices increased from one year to the next.

Although the mid-1970s UK rate was disastrous enough, as we will see in a moment, even greater rates have been experienced in some countries – in mid-1946

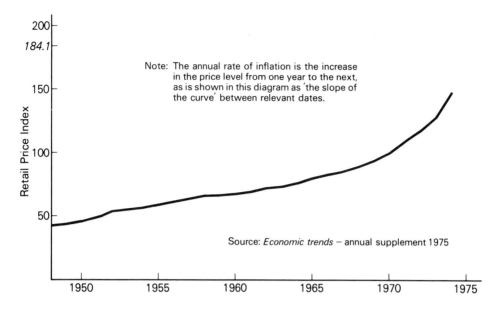

Figure 17.3   Inflation in the UK (using Retail Price Index of Figure 14.7 on page 185).

the annual rate in Hungary was $13 \times 10^{54}\%$ ($10^6 = 1\ 000\ 000$). Such rapid inflation is called *hyper-inflation* and can destroy people's confidence in a currency, so that it is no longer willingly accepted – the essential feature of money – in payment for goods and services nor in settlement of debts. Some other good is then likely to replace the currency as an acceptable form of money – the cigarette became the media of exchange in 1945 in Germany.

The actions of governments in these situations are directed at restoring confidence in the currency. They usually have no alternative but the introduction of a new form of currency. In the German hyper-inflation of the 1920s, the Reichsmark replaced the Mark in 1924. Then the government hopes, perhaps by other actions taken at the same time, to restore confidence with the new currency. This may be helped by tying this new currency to gold or silver, or basing it on some other factor (e.g. land), as promises to pay so much gold or whatever for various denominations of note.

Why bother about inflation?
People may be discouraged from saving during inflation because money's value is falling. The car you want may rise in price so you buy it sooner than later. You and others may not want to use the inflating currency as a store of wealth, preferring to buy things expected to hold their value – a Picasso painting, perhaps, precious metals, land, or even consumer durables.

Those who save money, or creditors owed it, find when they later come to spend the money, its value in real terms has fallen. This discourages people from forgoing current consumption in order to accumulate resources for investment, with a sacrifice of potential growth in future output. On the other hand, those owing money will find the cost of repayment when due is less in real terms. For example the family who bought a house with a mortgage in 1950 has found that the real cost of repayments have decreased. The money amounts repaid each month have become a smaller proportion of their inflating money incomes.

Less fortunate in these times are those on fixed incomes; pensioners and others see inflation erode the real value of pensions and allowances. This, together with the effect on savers and creditors, results in an arbitrary redistribution of real incomes. Those whose income keeps up with inflation gain at the expense of those on fixed incomes, and the debtor gains at the expense of the creditor.

When and if incomes rise as inflation continues, more wage and salary earners are dragged into the net of taxation. This fiscal drag has the effect of increasing taxes on the rising incomes, particularly of the low paid. Tax allowances seldom maintain their real value during inflation.

Finally there is the effect of inflation on the overseas trade of countries (see chapter 16). If the inflation rate in a country exceeds that of many of its trading partners, as was the case in the UK in the summer of 1976, the balance of payment tends towards a deficit. This happens for two reasons. As the prices of our exports rise more quickly than those of our competitors, the demand for our exports tends to decrease. The amount of the decrease is determined by the elasticity of demand for these exports. Consumers in the UK also find prices of home-produced goods are rising more sharply than imports and so tend to buy the latter. Falling exports and rising imports both worsen the balance of payments.

Causes of inflation?
Economists differ in their views of the exact causes of inflation. But as with any problem, causes can differ between periods of time and different places. Two main explanations or groups of explanations are generally given for inflation – cost push and demand pull – though these are not always mutually exclusive. One does not necessarily preclude the other.

The two types of explanation correspond to the demand and supply sides of markets for goods and services – the relationship between the total demand for goods and services, and the total supply or amount available.

Cost Push forces arise from the supply side of the market. This can happen because the price of raw materials rise, imported oil is an example. Factor costs can increase: wage costs may rise because increased payments to labour are not matched by increased productivity – output per man hour. Under these circumstances, prices tend to rise even though firms may in part offset increased costs against their profits. The push, however, can sometimes arise from increased profit margins. Then in much the same way as the price of a good rises when there is a decrease in the conditions of supply (chapter 9), the general price level rises with a shift to the left in the supply curve for total output of goods and services.

Demand pull forces operate when people plan to consume and invest more than the total output currently available. The resulting excess of demand at current prices tends to raise prices, much in the way an increase in the conditions of demand raises the price of a commodity as you saw in chapter 9. Demand pull can also occur through a decrease in taxes or excess government spending. Many economists argue that this increased demand, the increase in the aggregate demand conditions, occurs when the Government 'prints too much money'. That is: too much paper and credit-money is chasing too few goods.

Disentangling causes and effects

As with many of the problems we study in economics there are no simple solutions of cause and effect in this subject of inflation. With cost push inflation stemming from rising costs, and demand pull inflation stemming from an excess demand for goods and services, the two types of inflation are not always easily disentangled. For once they get rolling the *inflationary spiral* tends to operate with rising prices chased by rising wages, or it may be that rising wages are chased by prices, whatever the mechanism involved. The spiral may continue to swirl upwards, for example, when wages are negotiated according to the cost of living or for other reasons, contributing to further price rises and subsequent wage increases.

Those economists who consider cost push to be the principal cause of UK inflation in the mid-1970s argue that cost increases, especially for wage costs, cause rising prices, and that trade unions among others push up labour costs, independent of the demand for their members' services. Those arguing from the demand pull standpoint consider that inflationary pressures affect wages – the price of labour – only *after* inflation has raised prices in the market. Their argument is that an increased demand for goods and services leads producers to increase their demand for labour (a *derived demand*) with consequently higher wages offered (bid up) to attract the scarce labour required to increase output. Or maybe workers – in a union or not – respond to the increased demand for their labour by seeking increased wages.

This chicken-and-egg situation is the problem. Which occurred first? Did the inflationary push from increasing costs trigger the spiral or was it triggered by the inflationary pull of increased demand? Put another way: did increasing wages and other costs push up prices, or did excess demand first pull them upwards?

Controlling inflation

A government believing demand pull is the cause of inflation will cut demand for goods and services – a *deflation*. The Government can bring this about by cutting its own demand for goods and services, and the demands of consumers and producers. By budgeting for a surplus, taking in more taxes than the Government spend, demand is damped down. Monetary measures may also be taken. Credit can be made harder and more expensive for individuals and firms to get. The supply of money – notes-and-coin and credit-money – can be cut, a solution favoured by the *monetarists*.

When inflation is thought to result from cost push causes, UK and other governments can adopt an incomes policy. But there is little a government can do to reduce the costs of imported raw materials. However since wages and salaries account for about 60% of all costs, any form of control over them goes some way towards holding back the push of cost increases. Likewise control of profits, dividends, interest and rents, although these generally form a smaller proportion of 'costs', can help to make all suppliers of factors share in the restraint. An incomes policy is usually accompanied by control of prices. Price control keeps to a minimum the increases which are passed on in higher prices. This should reduce the erosion of real wages by inflation and therefore reduce the money wage increases required to maintain the level of real wages in an attempt to dampen or slow down the wage spiral.

The following Assignments bring out the type of information you need to note on this topic at the time of your study.

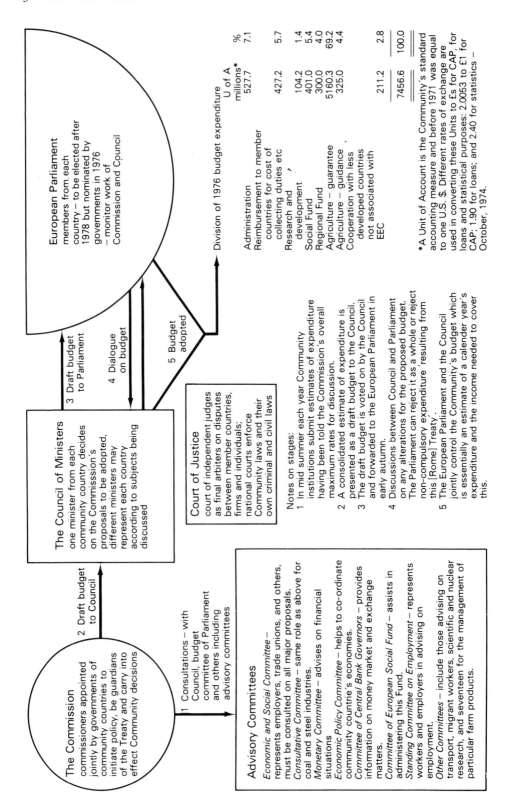

Figure 17.4 EEC organisation.

Assignments

17.6 What is meant by inflation? Which sections of the community are likely to (*a*) benefit, and (*b*) suffer during a period of inflation? (AEB 1974)

17.7 Explain the difference between *real wages* and *money wages*. Why are these differences more apparent during an inflationary period? (L 1972)

17.8 What is inflation? Discuss its possible effects. (JMB 1975)

17.9 Discuss: how might the following groups be 'protected' during inflation – (*a*) old age pensioners; (*b*) savers; and (*c*) taxpayers.

The European Economic Community

History

The third issue to be considered is the Common Market. Something of the Community's activities were noted in chapters 6 and 16 and Figure 17.4. In this chapter are some facts about its history and a summary of the pros and cons from a UK point of view.

One main aim of the Community is peace in Europe, forging closer political links between Europeans. While this is more than an economic aim, in the context of European history the intertwining of economic pressures and war suggests peace can be as much dependent on economic concord as on other harmonies. The founders of the Community brought together France, Germany, Italy and the Benelux countries (Belgium, Holland and Luxembourg) in the signing of the Treaty of Rome in 1957. This Treaty 'specified that the Common Market had to harmonise national economic policies and apply common policies for the whole community, particularly in the spheres of agriculture, transport and trade with the rest of the world' (*Unity in Europe*, an EEC Commission booklet). The Treaty built on the experience of the six founder members in operating the European Coal and Steel Community since 1951. That year these countries had created a European coal and steel industry from their separate national industries.

The United Kingdom joined the Community in 1973, and after some renegotiation of the terms of entry voted in a referendum to remain in the Community in 1975.

The EEC also has special arrangements with some territories overseas (see Figure 17.5). There are also countries with aspirations to join as full members such as Greece, Portugal and Spain in 1976. Formal negotiations were begun in July 1976 for the full membership of Greece.

Trade

The EEC is essentially a customs union without tariffs or other barriers on mutual trade, although provisions of the Treaty permit temporary barriers for members in trading difficulties. The Community has barriers against non-Market countries' imports, protecting its own producers from competition of the 'outside world'.

The advantage of the large market with a population in 1974 of 253 million enables Europeans to benefit from increased specialisation and economies of scale. These give potential for economic growth not possible within their own territories. There is also no restriction on the movements of factors of production within the

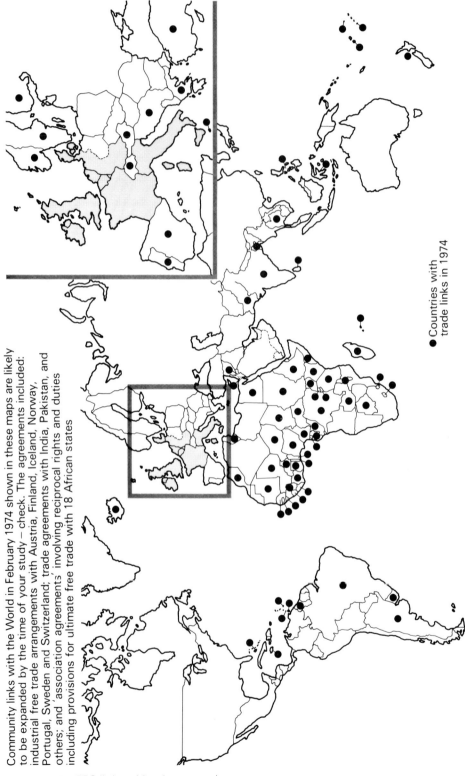

Community links with the World in February 1974 shown in these maps are likely to be expanded by the time of your study – check. The agreements included: industrial free trade arrangements with Austria, Finland, Iceland, Norway, Portugal, Sweden and Switzerland; trade agreements with India, Pakistan, and others; and 'association agreements' involving reciprocal rights and duties including provisions for ultimate free trade with 18 African states

● Countries with trade links in 1974

Figure 17.5   EEC links with other countries.

Community, as well as the unrestricted movement of goods and services – making this a common market. So any worker may move freely to a job anywhere in the Community, and under other provisions of the Treaty may draw up to six months' unemployment benefit wherever he or she has worked.

Harmonisation

A major difficulty in 1976 in merging the economies of member countries has been reconciling the various social and economic policies each country had followed. Each had developed its own policy on such problems as regional unemployment, curbs on monopoly, methods of taxation, encouragement of agriculture and similar policies.

Members have, therefore, spent some years harmonising these policies. Tariff concessions, for example, given to Commonwealth countries by the UK are being phased out, while all UK barriers to trade with other members were removed in 1977, after being reduced in stages.

Common agricultural and other policies

The pattern of agriculture in Europe has developed over the centuries in part for reasons of natural advantage and in part from institutional influences. The French laws on inheritance tended to break up farms as each son took a part; the English gave the eldest son the right to inherit the whole of his father's farm. The size of farms in France are therefore usually smaller than the average English holding. In Germany many farmers work only part-time on their holding and have a second job often in industry.

The Community's agricultural policy in harmonising these patterns of agriculture aims at making Europe more self-sufficient in food supplies, and has established the intervention scheme for agriculture. The intervention price maintains farmers' incomes by buying up farm produce when the prices for it falls below the intervention price. On entering the market for beef, butter, milk, wheat, wine, apples and many other commodities, the Community's commission acquires the large accumulations of surplus production such as butter mountains and wine lakes in the mid-1970s. These were sold off outside the Community, artificially keeping the price to Community consumers high. However some surpluses have been sold to pensioners at special prices on occasions.

Many consumers resent these artificially high prices, preferring the system of agricultural support used for some years in Britain. This is being discussed with a view to harmonising it with other policies. Under this system farmers sell their produce at the prevailing market prices, and are subsidised when these prices might give them an inadequate income or discourage production of food. All consumers enjoyed cheap food under this system but taxpayers paid the bill for subsidies.

Other policies include the use of Value Added Tax, which is intended eventually to form a single indirect tax with possibly one set of rates applied throughout the Community. In harmonising the other forms of similar taxes – the British had Purchase Tax on the price of many goods – to a Value Added Tax, a portion of each country's VAT collections are intended to form part of the Community's own resources. These will be revenues for the Community and independent of member countries, being raised from customs duties on imports into the Community, agricultural levies, and a percentage of each country's collection of VAT. In 1976 there were transitional arrangements to provide funds for Community activities by contributions from member governments.

Some sources of aid for member countries are shown in Figure 16.13, page 241. The Regional Development Fund was set up in 1975 by an initial transfer of £650 million of Community resources, to further the coordination of national regional policies and give these common objectives. This initial £650 million was to be spent during 1975–77 on regions of declining industry, those undergoing industrial change, and those with structural under-employment. The Fund was – and is – also to be used to aid agricultural regions faced by special problems of terrain and climate as in mountain areas.

Aid from the Regional Development Fund is given to create new jobs, to maintain threatened jobs, and to stimulate a flow of capital. The funds for projects aided are expected to have a multiplier effect, that is: each £1 of aid eventually creating a greater amount of income. The regions benefiting from this scheme are those designated by member governments and include Areas for Expansion in the UK. Aid from the Regional Fund is meant to increase the total resources available for a region's development and is *not* a substitute for national aid to the area. For the intention is to use Community funds to enlarge the number of projects, creating more new jobs than member countries can achieve individually.

There is also an intention to fix exchange rates within limits, between member countries, with the aim of eventually having a common currency or at least each country's currency being interchangeable in payments for goods and services and settlement of debts within the Community.

Summary

These various policies and Treaty commitments can be summarised from the British point of view as follows:

Pros – 1 Political differences are settled by conference in preference to conflict.
2 Opportunities for benefits of specialisation in larger markets and for economies of scale are increased.
3 Efficiency is increased as factors of production tend to move according to comparative cost advantage within the Community, and inefficiency is not protected by barriers to competition.
4 Some believe that the agricultural policy will ensure supplies of food.

Cons – 1 The United Kingdom lost some sources of cheap food.
2 Contributions to Community funds are high because of the 'intervention price policy' and its administration under the agricultural arrangements.
3 There is some loss of sovereignty for individual member countries.
4 Common external tariffs possibly protect inefficient producers within the Community, distorting world production from the pattern set by comparative cost advantage.
5 The agricultural policy, through high prices, encourages supply yet discourages demand.

The future

In this chapter we have seen three economic problems and the issues involved in the mid-1970s. By the time of your studies, these problems – like others – may be of a different character. But the economic tools you have learned to use will be as effective in your analysis of issues and problems of your time, as they are in this study.

Assignments

17.10 'The concept of *a* common market is an attempt to obtain the gains of international trade while enjoying the protection of trade barriers.' Explain this statement with reference to the EEC.

17.11 List the members of the EEC and the date they joined, and in a separate list include any prospective new members at the time of your study.

17.12* Group research: update Figure 17.4 summarising the main changes at the time of your study on this and on Figure 16.13 updated in an earlier Assignment.

17.13* Discuss the changes noted in the Assignment above.

17.14 You have seen economics as the science studying the relationship between scarce resources and unlimited wants, as an approach by analysis and a way of thought rather than a collection of facts and value judgements. Discuss these statements in relation to one current matter of public concern.

Suggested further reading

Donaldson, Chapters 9 and 11
Harvey, Chapters 15, 23 and 26
Stanlake, Chapters 25 and 32
P Donaldson, *Economics of the Real World* (Penguin, 1973), Chapter 6

Chapter 18
Multiple choice questions

Select the correct answer to the following questions from the lettered choices. For solutions see page 280.

Chapter 1

1   Economics is concerned with choice. Is this because . . .

A there are unlimited resources
B goods are not free
C resources are scarce relative to people's wants
D it is difficult for people to decide what they want
E there are limited wants

2   In the Production Possibility Curve shown in Figure 18.1 the community is producing at point S. Why is it producing there? Is it because . . .

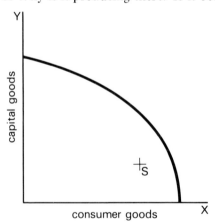

Figure 18.1

A it is not using all of its resources fully and efficiently
B it is experiencing diminishing returns
C it has scarce resources by comparison with other countries
D it has unlimited wants
E it is experiencing inflation

3   What is the opportunity cost of a good? Is it . . .

A the cost of buying it in a competitive market
B the cost of replacing it when worn out
C its worth to its consumer
D the most desirable alternative which has to be sacrificed in order to obtain it
E its original price

4   In a *command* economy the problem of 'what to produce' is solved by one of the following. Which one?

A the price mechanism
B the State
C individual producers
D consumers' spending habits
E market forces

5   What kind of economy is the United Kingdom? Is it . . .

A a laissez-faire system
B a collectivist system
C a mixed system
D a command economy
E a free-market system

Chapter 2

6   What is the main problem with the World's population in the 20th century? Is the main problem . . .

A too few male births
B increasing migration of people in the West
C its growth in relation to available resources
D increase in the death rate
E too few female births

7   In the UK a census of population is carried out regularly. What is the reason for the regular census? Is it to . . .

A assess people for tax purposes
B compile electoral registers
C calculate the cost of living
D measure the size and structure of the population
E measure people's spending habits

8   Which of the following is/are included in the 'total working population'?

1 the unemployed
2 the self employed
3 school students over 16

Choose your answer, using the code below.

Code   Choose **A** if 1 2 3 are all included
              B if 1 2   only are included
              C if   2 3 only are included
              D if 1   only is included
              E if   3 only is included

9   A decline in the UK birth rate is likely to lead to which of the following? Choose your answer letter using the code below.

1 an increased life expectancy
2 decreased demand for teachers
3 a fall in pram sales

Code   Choose **A** if 1 2 3 are all likely
              B if 1 2   only are likely
              C if   2 3 only are likely
              D if 1   only is likely
              E if   3 only is likely

Chapter 3

10   Four of the following are factors of production? Which one is not?

A skilled workers
B electric drills
C factory buildings
D money in a firm's safe
E components

11   Which of the following factors of production would an economist call *land*?

A plant
B factory buildings
C coal
D agricultural labour
E agricultural machinery

12 Which of the following statements about factor payments is/are true?

1 the factor payment to land is profit
2 the factor payment to labour is wages
3 the factor payment to capital is interest

Choose your answer using the code below.

Code Choose A if 1 2 3 are all true
B if 1 2   only are true
C if   2 3 only are true
D if 1   only is true
E if   3 only is true

13 Which of the following statements about *mobility of labour* is/are true? Mobility of labour is the . . .

1 number of cars per head of population
2 ease of movement between areas
3 ease of movement between occupations

Choose your answer using the code below.

Code Choose A if 1 2 3 are all true
B if 1 2   only are true
C if   2 3 only are true
D if 1   only is true
E if   3 only is true

14 Which of the following measures would improve the mobility of labour? Choose your answer letter using the code below.

1 more retraining schemes
2 payment of removal expenses
3 more information on job opportunities

Code Choose A if 1 2 3 would all help
B if 1 2   only would help
C if   2 3 only would help
D if 1   only would help
E if   3 only would help

Chapter 4

15 Four of the following statements about division of labour are true. Which one is *not* true?

A division of labour is limited by the size of the product
B division of labour may lead to monotonous repetition with a lack of job satisfaction
C division of labour allows the use of specialised machinery
D division of labour is limited by the size of the market
E division of labour can take advantage of people's particular abilities

16 What are fixed factors of production? Are they factors that ...

A cannot be moved
B do not vary with output in the short term
C are bought by producers at a fixed price
D have only one use
E vary with output in the short term

17 What is the marginal product of a factor of production? Is it ...

A the total amount it can produce
B the cost of employing an extra unit of the factor
C the amount total output changes when one extra unit of the factor is employed
D the cost of producing one more unit of output
E its price

18 What is the Law of Diminishing Returns? Does it state that ...

A division of labour should be organised according to the principle of comparative advantage
B when all factors of production are varied output alters correspondingly
C prices inevitably rise
D the application of additional variable factors to a fixed one leads eventually to decreasing marginal product
E there are decreasing returns to scale

19   Which of the following statements about *average fixed costs* is true?

   A they are constant
   B they increase with output
   C they include the cost of raw material
   D they decrease with output
   E they are zero

Chapter 5

20   What do economists mean by *returns to scale*? Are they referring to the way output changes as . . .

   A new products are produced
   B the Law of Diminishing Returns operates
   C all inputs are increased in the same proportion
   D labour saving machinery is employed
   E shift working is introduced

21   Which of the following do economists call an internal economy of scale?

   1 cheaper raw materials through bulk purchasing
   2 the use of a greater degree of division of labour
   3 the growth of associated industries and services

   Choose your answer using the code below.

   Code   Choose A if 1 2 3 are all internal economies of scale
                     B if 1 2   only are internal economies of scale
                     C if   2 3 only are internal economies of scale
                     D if 1   only is an internal economy of scale
                     E if   3 only is an internal economy of scale

22 What is horizontal integration? Is it . . .

   A taking on more workers
   B branching out into a new type of production
   C setting up production in a different location
   D acquiring businesses producing similar products
   E acquiring businesses producing your components

23   Which of the following would be an external diseconomy of scale?

A increased pollution and traffic congestion
B excessive 'red tape'
C loss of goodwill from employees and customers
D slowness in responding to changes in demand
E the monotony of repetitive work

24   Which of the following is/are not true?

1 Many small firms are one man businesses
2 Small firms are common in the motor car manufacturing industry
3 Small firms are rare in the United Kingdom

Choose your answer using the code below.

Code   Choose A if 1 2 3 are all untrue
                B if 1 2   only are untrue
                C if   2 3 only are untrue
                D if 1   only is untrue
                E if   3 only is untrue

Chapter 6

25   Which of the following statements about bulk reducing industries will be true in general?

A they produce near to their market
B they produce near a railway line
C they produce near their raw material sources
D they produce near to the coast
E they produce mid-way between their markets and raw material sources

26   Which of the following industries is likely to be located away from its market?

A dry cleaning
B retailing
C baking
D steel manufacturing
E cinemas

27 Which of the following is/are an acquired advantage of a particular location?

1 nearness to raw materials
2 availability of a skilled labour force
3 its reputation

Code Choose **A** if 1 2 3 are all acquired advantages
                B if 1 2   only are acquired advantages
                C if   2 3 only are acquired advantages
                D if 1   only is an acquired advantage
                E if   3 only is an acquired advantage

28 Which of the following represent likely disadvantages of concentration of industries in particular areas?

1 increased cost of raw materials
2 diminishing returns
3 risk of heavy unemployment should the industry decline

Choose your answer using the code below.

Code Choose **A** if 1 2 3 are all likely disadvantages
                B if 1 2   only are likely disadvantages
                C if   2 3 only are likely disadvantages
                D if 1   only is a likely disadvantage
                E if   3 only is a likely disadvantage

Chapter 7

29 Which of the following must be repaid *first* should a firm go into liquidation?

A preference shares
B debentures
C equity
D cumulative preference shares
E participating preference shares

30 Which of the following could best be regarded as an entrepreneur?

A the managing director of a public limited company
B a preference shareholder
C a shop steward
D a self employed window cleaner
E an automobile assembly worker

31   Which of the following is not a Nationalised industry?

   A British North Sea Oil Corporation
   B British Rail
   C Central Electricity Generating Board
   D British Airways
   E British Shoe Corporation

Chapter 8

32   What is the yield on a share? Is it . . .

   A its purchase price
   B its dividend
   C its dividend as a percentage of its face (or nominal) value
   D its dividend as a percentage of its market price
   E the amount it can be sold for

33   Which of the following statements about the Stock Exchange is not true?

   A it is a market for existing securities
   B it publishes share prices daily
   C its 'floor' is not open to members of the public
   D it is nationalised
   E it has its main trading floor in London

34   What is a person who sells shares believing their prices will fall known as? Is he known as a . . .

   A bull
   B jobber
   C bear
   D broker
   E banker

35   What is the yield on a share of £1 nominal value paying a dividend of 5%, purchased on the Stock Exchange for 50p? Is it . . .

   A 20%
   B 10%
   C 5%
   D 1%
   E none of these

Chapter 9

36 In economics, how is a market defined? Is it defined as . . .

A the commercial centre of a city
B a place where buyers meet
C an area over which buyers and sellers negotiate the exchange of a commodity
D a place where goods and services are produced
E the shopping centre of a city

37 On what assumption is the demand curve for a commodity drawn? Is it on the assumption that . . .

A the conditions of demand remain unchanged
B people buy more of a good when its price rises
C the quantity supplied does not change
D the commodity's price does not change
E producers maximise their profits

38 In Figure 18.2 a shift in the demand curve from D to D_1 could be due to one of the following. Which one?

A an increase in the good's price
B a decrease in the conditions of demand
C a rise in the price of a close substitute
D a rise in the price of a complement
E an increase in the quantity supplied

Figure 18.2

39   Consider two goods X and Y. If a rise in the price of X leads to a decrease in
      the quantity of Y demanded, then X and Y are said to be related. Are they . . .

      A superior goods
      B substitutes for each other
      C complements for each other
      D in joint supply
      E in inelastic demand

40   On what assumption is the supply curve for a commodity drawn? Is it on the
      assumption that . . .

      A consumers demand more at lower prices
      B the commodity's price does not change
      C incomes remain unchanged
      D all influences on supply other than price are held constant
      E consumers' tastes do not change

41   In Figure 18.3 a shift in the supply curve from S to S₁ is most likely to result
      from one of the following. Which one?

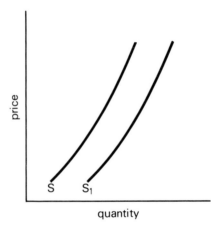

Figure 18.3

      A imposition of tax on this good
      B an increase in the wages of workers producing this good
      C payment of a subsidy to producers of the good
      D a change in consumers' tastes
      E an increase in this good's price

42 Figure 18.4 shows the original demand and supply curves for hi-fi sets (D and S). Which of the following statements is/are true, other things being equal?

1 S_1 illustrates a decrease in the price of components used in the manufacture of hi-fi sets

2 S_2 illustrates an increase in the wages of workers making hi-fi sets

3 D_2 illustrates a rise in consumers' incomes

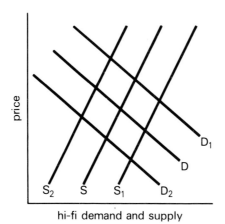

Figure 18.4

Choose your answer using the code below

Code   Choose **A** if 1 2 3 are all true

               B if 1 2   only are true

               C if   2 3 only are true

               D if 1   only is true

               E if   3 only is true

Chapter 10

43 What is the equilibrium price in a market? Is it the price at which . . .

A the number of buyers equals the number of sellers

B consumers do not wish to buy any more of the good

C the quantity buyers want to buy is the same as the amount sellers wish to sell

D there is an excess of supply over demand

E demand exceeds supply

44   To which of the following will a decrease in the conditions of demand, other
things being equal, lead? Will it lead to . . .

1 an increase in the quantity exchanged
2 a decrease in price
3 a decrease in the quantity exchanged

Choose your answers using the code below.

Code   Choose A if it will lead to 1 2 3
              B if it will lead to 1 2   only
              C if it will lead to   2 3 only
              D if it will lead to 1   only
              E if it will lead to   3 only

45   Figure 18.5 shows the effect of an increase in the conditions of demand for a
certain good.
Which of the following statements are correct?

1 the new equilibrium quantity is Q
2 the momentary supply curve is QS'
3 the new equilibrium price is P_I

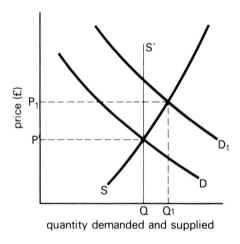

Figure 18.5

Choose your answers using the code below.

Code   Choose A if it will lead to 1 2 3
              B if 1 2   only are correct
              C if   2 3 only are correct
              D if 1   only is correct
              E if   3 only is correct

46   What does price elasticity of demand measure? Does it measure the responsiveness of . . .

A the conditions of demand to price
B demand to supply
C price to consumers' incomes
D quantity demanded to changes in price
E output to price

47   For a particular good the elasticity of demand is 0·9. What does this indicate? Does it indicate that . . .

A price is constant
B demand is elastic
C quantity demanded is constant
D demand is inelastic
E demand is perfectly inelastic

48   Which of the following statements about Figure 18.6 are true?

1 curve x illustrates unitary elasticity of demand
2 curve y illustrates varying elasticity of demand
3 curve z illustrates perfectly elastic demand

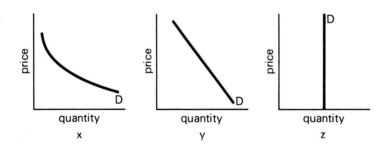

Figure 18.6

Choose your answer using the code below.

Code   Choose A if 1 2 3 are all true
               B if 1 2   only are true
               C if   2 3 only are true
               D if 1   only is true
               E if   3 only is true

49   Which of the following goods is likely to have the most inelastic demand?

A salt
B luncheon meat
C mink coats
D orange juice
E tinned peas

Chapter 11

50   What is the single seller of a product? Is he a . . .

A monopsonist
B one man business
C monopolist
D perfect competitor
E duopolist

51   Which of the following is a monopolist able to do? Can he . . .

A spread his overheads by reducing his output
B fix both his price and his quantity supplied at whatever levels he wishes
C increase his price without losing any buyers
D fix either his price or quantity supplied
E avoid diminishing returns

52   Which of the following are aspects of a producer's monopoly power?

1 the immobility of factors of production
2 the elasticity of demand for his product
3 ability to erect barriers to entry

Choose your answer using the code below.

Code   Choose A if 1 2 3 are all aspects
                B if 1 2   only are aspects
                C   2 3 only are aspects
                D if 1   only is an aspect
                E if   3 only is an aspect

53   Which of the following examples is most likely to be a scale monopoly?

  A a local shop
  B a railway system
  C a wheat farmer
  D a drug manufacturer holding a patent
  E a hairdresser

Chapter 12

54   Why are Premium Bond prizes not included as income for National Income purposes? Is it because . . .

  A they are won by luck
  B they are not taxable
  C they do not correspond to any current production
  D they are a form of economic rent
  E they are a form of interest

55   Which of the following types of incomes are excluded when calculating National Income?

  A sickness benefit
  B productivity bonuses
  C rents
  D incomes of the self employed
  E profits

56   Which of the following statements about the calculation of National Income is/are true?

  1 Gross Domestic Product of Market Prices + subsidies − taxes on expenditure = GDP at factor cost
  2 National Income = GNP at factor cost − capital consumption
  3 GNP at factor cost = GDP at factor cost + the trade gap

Choose your answer using the code below.

Code   Choose A if 1 2 3 are all true
                B if 1 2   only are true
                C if   2 3 only are true
                D if 1   only is true
                E if   3 only is true

57   In calculating National Income by the expenditure method, which of the following is excluded?

A expenditure on investment
B government expenditure on goods and services
C taxes on expenditure
D expenditure on services
E local authority expenditure on salaries

Chapter 13

58   Which of the following is the most suitable measure of living standards?

A money National Income
B real National Income per head of employed population
C the retail price index
D real National Income per head of the population
E Gross Domestic Product at Market Prices

Look at the following information on a hypothetical economy. Use it and the answer code below to answer questions 59–61.

	1930 £m	1980 £m
National Income	100	400
Index of Prices	50	100
Population (millions)	15	30
Employed Population (millions)	10	16

A remained constant
B doubled
C increased by 25%
D increased four times
E halved

Select the letter which completes the following statements.

59   Between 1930 and 1980 real National Income _____

60   Between 1930 and 1980 real NI per head of the population _____

61   Between 1930 and 1980 real NI per head of the employed population _____

Chapter 14

62 One of the following is *not* a function of money. Which one?

A unit of account
B medium of exchange
C limited liability
D standard of deferred payment
E store of wealth

63 If a Discount House discounts a Bill of Exchange worth £200 (in two months time) for £194, what would be the discount rate? Would it be . . .

A 18%
B 12%
C 6%
D 24%
E 3%

64 What does a doubling in the general level of prices mean to the value of money? Does it mean that the value of money is . . .

A doubled
B unchanged
C rising
D halved
E trebled

65 The information given in the table below refers to a simplified 'basket of goods' consisting of meat and vegetables:

Item	Weighting	Price per kilo (£) Year 1	Year 2
Meat	60	1·50	2·0
Vegetables	40	0·25	0·50

Taking year 1 as base year (index = 100), what is the price index of this basket in year 2? Is it . . .

A 85
B 200
C 133
D 110
E 140

66   Which of the following assets of a commercial bank is most liquid?

A special deposits
B money at call and short notice
C cash in hand
D discounted bills
E personal loans to customers

67   Through which of the following do banks settle their indebtedness to each other?

A Issuing Houses
B Merchant Banks
C Discount Houses
D Acceptance Houses
E Clearing Houses

68   Four of the following are functions of the Bank of England. Which one is *not*?

A lender of last resort
B collection of taxes
C bankers to the government
D management of National Debt
E commercial banks' banker

69   Which of the following policies would be inappropriate if the Bank of England was aiming to reduce the supply of credit-money?

A increase in minimum lending rate
B sale of securities through open market operations
C reduction of special deposits
D increase of special deposits
E issue directives

Chapter 15

70   If the government wished to decrease consumption through altering VAT, what would it do? Would it . . .

A increase the rate on goods and services in inelastic demand
B remove the tax from luxury goods
C increase the rate on goods and services in elastic demand
D decrease the rate on all goods and services
E increase the rate on goods with unitary elasticity

71   Which of the following statements about Figure 18.7 is/are true?

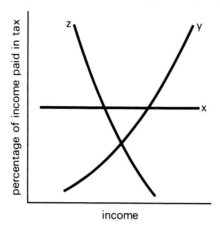

Figure 18.7

1 Curve x illustrates a proportional tax
2 curve y illustrates a progressive tax
3 curve z illustrates a regressive tax

Choose your answer using the code below.

Code   Choose **A** if 1 2 3 are all true
            B if 1 2   only are true
            C if   2 3 only are true
            D if 1   only is true
            E if   3 only is true

72   Which of the following is a progressive tax?

A Local Authority Rates
B VAT
C Income Tax
D motor vehicle licence duty
E excise duties

73   The imposition of a sales tax on a good or service can be illustrated on a supply and demand diagram by one of the following. Which one?

A a movement down the supply curve
B a leftward shift in the demand curve
C a movement up the supply curve
D a leftward shift in the supply curve
E a rightward shift in the supply curve

74   If a government was budgeting for a surplus which of the following measures would it be likely to implement?

1   an increase in government spending
2   a decrease in government spending
3   an increase in taxation

Choose your answer using the code below.

Code   Choose **A** if it would choose 1 2 3
              B if it would choose 1 2   only
              C if it would choose   2 3 only
              D if it would choose 1   only
              E if it would choose   3 only

Chapter 16

75   What is an excess of imports of visibles over exports of visibles known as? Is it . . .

A a favourable Balance of Trade
B a Trade Gap
C a deficit on current account
D the total currency flow
E Net Property Income from Abroad

76   In order to obtain the maximum output, world production should be organised according to what principle?

A returns to scale
B common markets
C Balance of Payments stability
D Principle of Comparative Cost
E diminishing returns

77   What are the '*terms of trade*'? Is it the name given to . . .

A trade restrictions
B the relationship between the price of exports and imports
C the gains from trade
D trade agreements
E deficit on current account

78 Which of the following is *not* a 'trade barrier'?

1 subsidies
2 quotas
3 dumping

Choose your answer using the code below.

Code Choose A if 1 2 3 are not trade barriers
               B if 1 2   only are not trade barriers
               C if   2 3 only are not trade barriers
               D if 1   only is not a trade barrier
               E if   3 only is not a trade barrier.

Chapter 17

79 Which of the following is *not* a type of unemployment?

A seasonal
B frictional
C structural
D cyclical
E functional

80 What is a period of rising prices known as?

A inflation
B reflation
C a boom
D deflation
E revaluation

81 Under which of the following was the EEC formed?

A GATT
B IMF
C Treaty of Rome
D Bretton Woods agreement
E Treaty of Versailles

Answers to Multiple Choice Questions

Question		Question		Question	
1	C	28	E	55	A
2	A	29	B	56	B
3	D	30	D	57	C
4	B	31	E	58	D
5	C	32	D	59	B
6	C	33	D	60	A
7	D	34	C	61	C
8	B	35	B	62	C
9	C	36	C	63	A
10	D	37	A	64	D
11	C	38	C	65	E
12	C	39	C	66	C
13	C	40	D	67	E
14	A	41	C	68	B
15	A	42	B	69	C
16	B	43	C	70	C
17	C	44	C	71	A
18	D	45	C	72	C
19	D	46	D	73	D
20	C	47	D	74	C
21	B	48	B	75	B
22	D	49	A	76	D
23	A	50	C	77	B
24	C	51	D	78	E
25	C	52	B	79	E
26	D	53	E	80	A
27	C	54	B	81	C

Appendix 1
Conversion Factors

Metric units have been used where possible throughout this book. But you may find while doing research for some of the Assignments that the data (in some government statistics, for example) is given in Imperial units. Below is a list of the conversion factors you are likely to need in economics.

Length

1 foot = 0·30 metres
1 yard = 0·91 metres
1 mile = 1·61 kilometres

Area

1 acre = 0·4 hectares
1 square mile = 2·59 square kilometres
1 hectare = 10 000 square metres

Volume

1 UK gallon = 4·55 litres

Mass

1 pound = 0·45 kilograms
1 UK ton = 1·02 tonnes

Appendix 2
Complete Reading List

C M Cipolla, *The Economic History of World Population* (6th edition, Penguin 1974)
P Donaldson, *Economics of the Real World* (Penguin 1973)
P Donaldson, *Guide to the British Economy* (4th edition, Penguin 1976)
H C Edey, Peacock and Cooper, *National Income and Social Accounting* (Hutchinson 1968)
R T Gill, *Economics: A text with included readings* (2nd edition, Prentice Hall 1974)
J Hanson, *A Textbook of Economics* (6th edition, MacDonald and Evans 1972)
J Harvey, *Elementary Economics* (4th edition, Macmillan 1976)
C D Harbury, *An Introduction to Economic Behaviour* (Fontana 1971)
J Harvey and M Johnson, *An Introduction to Macroeconomics* (Macmillan 1971)
D Lee, V Anthony and A Skuse, *Monopoly* (Heinemann 1968)
F W Paish and A J Culyer, *Benham's Economics* (9th edition, Pitman 1973)
J Powicke, D Iles and B Davies, *Applied Economics* (Edward Arnold 1972)
G Stanlake, *Introductory Economics* (3rd edition, Longmans 1976)
R Turvey, *Demand and Supply* (George Allen and Unwin 1971)
H Williamson, *The Trade Unions* (Heinemann 1970)

Index of definitions

Index

frictional unemployment, 245
FT index, 118
funds – see finance
furniture manufacture, 79, 81

gas and gas industry, 102, 103, 225
generalisations, dangers of, 170
Germany, 253, 255
gifts, 214–15
gilt edged and 'gilts', 212
Giro, 196–7
Glasgow, 30
goldsmiths, 175–7
goods as money, 174
government finance, 201–24, 250
government monopolies, 19, 149
Government of UK: 114, 190, 195,
197, 248; borrowing overseas, 239;
dated securities of, 208; expenditure of, 218–24; location of
industry and, 82–4; long-term
guide lines given by, 113; monetary policies of, 204–9; monopoly
and, 153–5; reports from, 218;
revenues of, 210–18; securities of,
115, 116, 206, 207, 210; Social
Survey by, 184; taxation and, 141
grants, 82, 220
Greater Nottingham Co-operative
Ltd, 100
Gross Domestic Product (GDP),
159, 160, 163
gross investment, 46, 47
growth of industries, etc., 69, 72, 114,
164, 222
guarantees, 105
Guernsey, 87

health services, 220
High Wycombe, 79
hire purchase, 107, 202, 203, 207
Holland, 168, 253
horizontal integration, 71, 72–3, 74
hospitals, 21
hours worked, 42–3
households – see also families, 184
housing grants, 220
hyper-inflation, 249
hypermarkets, 51, 88

Iceland, 254
immigrants and immigration, 25, 27
imports, 87, 184, 231, 234–6, 239,
240, 250
imputed interest, 199
income, national, 156–9, 165–71
incomes: 156, 168; demand and, 124;
policy, 251; taxation and, 213, 214;
total domestic, 157
Income Tax, 197, 213, 214
Index Numbers, 168, 180–3
Index Numbers for Terms of Trade,
230–1
Index weighting, 181–3, 184
India, 225, 256
indivisible factors, 67
Industrial and Commercial Finance
Corp. Ltd (ICFC), 113
Industrial and Regional Development
(1972), 84
industries: infant, 234; siting of, 79
Industry Acts, 83, 113, 114

industry – see production
inelastic demand, 138, 141, 146, 147,
231
inelastic supply, 142–3
inferior goods, 124
inflation: 235, 248–51; spiral of, 251
information, 51, 87
infra-structure, 69
inheritance, 214, 255
Inland Revenue, 213
inputs, 13, 35, 58–9
institutional forces, 41, 255
institutions, financial, 114, 186–202,
236
insurance – see also life insurance,
98, 111, 114, 178
integration, 71–4
intellectual capital, 236
interest: 69, 97, 105, 113, 114, 195,
199, 208, 213, 214; as price of
money, 203; flat rate, 108; true
rate, 109
Interim Index of Prices, 184
Intermediate Areas UK, 83, 84
internal economies of scale, 67–9
International Monetary Fund, 240,
242
international trade, 225–43, 250
intervention scheme, 255
investment and investors – see also
shares, etc.: 44, 94, 105, 111, 113,
115, 118–19, 201, 249; in industry,
114; overseas, 239
Investment Trusts, 111, 112
invisibles – invisible trade, 236, 237–9
I-owe-you (IOU) notes, 186
iron – see steel
Issued Capital, 95, 96
Issuing Houses, 110, 196
Italy, 253

Japan, 17, 234
Jarrow, 82
jobbers, Stock Exchange, 116, 117–
18
job opportunities, 50, 82
Joint-Stock Companies – see also
companies, 98, 190
joint ventures, 113

labour force participation rate, 42
labour – see also skilled, etc.: 35, 36,
38–42, 50–1, 61, 245; division of,
55
laissez-faire, 17
Lancashire, 79
land: 35, 36, 37, 82; factor rewards to,
39
large-scale production, 68–9, 75
lateral integration, 72–3
laws – see legislation
Layfield Committee, 218
lending, base for, 218
lender of last resort, 205
liabilities, 98
'life-boat' fund, 190
liquidation of companies, 96, 97
liquid assets, 178, 199
liquid reserves, 190
liquidity, 200, 206
liquidity ratio, 201, 206
living standards – see standards of

loan capital, 97–8
loans: 68, 97, 114; long-term, 105;
short-term, 105, 106–9
Local Authorities: 115, 215, 220–1;
rates and taxes, 217–18
Local Employment Act (1960), 83
Local Government – see Local
Authorities
location of industry, 78–84, 85
long-run – see long term
long-term periods, 59–60, 134
Luxembourg, 253

machinery specialisation, 56, 70
mail order, 89
Malthus, Rev T, theory of, 22–3
management, 95, 104, 114, 115
managerial economies of scale, 68
managing directors, 98
man-week, 60
marginal returns, 60, 61
marginal revenue, 145, 146
markets: 75, 89, 120, 133, 144–5, 150,
250; geographic, 120; perfectly
competitive, 120, 145; share prices
and, 115; wholesale, 86
maturity of bills, etc., 194, 207
marriage and the birth rate, 25, 26
mass production, 57, 75
Maxforus, 17, 18, 49, 226
measured-day-work, 41
medical services – see also hospitals,
27
Merchant Banks, 196
mergers, 71
Merseyside, 82
Middle East, 225
Midland Shire Farmers, 99, 101
migration, 25, 27, 82
milk, 78
minerals and mineral deposits, 35, 37,
225
Minimum Lending Rate, 195, 205,
207
minimum price, 68
Mint, the Royal, 205
mixed economy, 18
mobility of factors: 49–51, 55, 234,
245; geographic, 51, 82; occupational, 49
models as examples, 17
monetary supply, 134–5, 143
monetarists, 251
money: 175–209, 250, 251; definition
of, 179–80, 208; functions of, 176,
178–9; income, 166–70; market,
186–91, 195, 203; origins of, 175–
8; price of, 203; supply, 251; value
of, 167, 179–85, 248
money on call, 200
Money Shops, 197
Monopoly and Mergers (Enquiry and
Control Act) (1965), 154
monopoly and monopolists: 19, 120,
146–50, 155, 190, 224, 255; barriers by, 148–9; bilateral, 150; degree of, 147; factor markets and,
150; local, 149; power of, 147–8
Monopolies Commission, 152
monopsony, 120, 150
Monthly Digest of Statistics, 31, 185
mortgage debentures, 98